The American Open Road

THE AMERICAN OPEN ROAD

NARRATIVE AND POPULAR IMAGINATION

JEFFREY ALAN MELTON

THE UNIVERSITY OF ALABAMA PRESS
TUSCALOOSA

The University of Alabama Press
Tuscaloosa, Alabama 35487-0380
uapress.ua.edu

Typeface: Minion Pro

Cover image: vichie81 - stock.adobe.com
Cover design: Sandy Turner Jr.

Publication of *The American Open Road* is supported by the Clarence C. Mondale Endowment/American Studies Fund of the Department of American Studies, College of Arts & Sciences, The University of Alabama.

Cataloging-in-Publication data is available from the Library of Congress.
ISBN: 978-0-8173-2241-0 (cloth)
ISBN: 978-0-8173-6212-6 (paper)
E-ISBN: 978-0-8173-9569-8

For Kari

Contents

Illustrations

Acknowledgments

I COULD NOT have completed this project without the guidance and support of numerous people. In 2010, I first proposed the idea of a course on the American open road to Lynne Adrian, former chair of the Department of American Studies at the University of Alabama. She had the power to save me a lot of trouble right there by saying "no," but true to her nature, she was enthusiastic and fully supportive, and I was on my way. My experiences in that course and with the students who embraced it eventually encouraged me to write this book.

I am deeply indebted to George F. Thompson, who, as publisher in residence for the College of Arts and Sciences at the University of Alabama, was instrumental in helping me develop and shape the manuscript. His guidance was essential and derived from his extensive experience fortified by his interest in mobility. I am also indebted to the staff at University of Alabama Press who have worked to complete this project. Dan Waterman provided essential feedback and encouragement (and patience) as I worked to strengthen the manuscript and prepare it for publication. I am profoundly indebted to Jenna Portnoff, whose keen editorial eye greatly improved the manuscript. A small portion of the manuscript focused on motorcycles was published in significantly different form in my essay "'Immediate Consciousness' and the American Open Road: Robert Pirsig's *Zen and the Art of Motorcycle Maintenance*."

My daughters, Olivia and Rebecca, learned to drive as I worked on this book, and I am deeply thankful that they are comfortable behind the wheel. I am most indebted to my wife, Kari, for her continuing support. I would have never completed this book without her advice and encouragement. I am forever grateful for her faith in me.

Introduction

A View of the Road

Americans believe in the open road. The phrase conjures a mythical expression of freedom and exuberance that has captivated the popular imagination from the beginnings of the nation. As testament to its role as a reflection of American culture, the phrase itself—the American open road—is redundant, for the *road* in the United States, by overwhelming acclamation, is perpetually *open*. Yet the words are inextricable, together celebrating an exceptional ideology and confirming it as self-evident. Americans believe in the open road with such fervent passion that it serves as a secular faith built around audacious aspiration, undaunted optimism, and boundless imagination. This open-road faith is often inspiring and sometimes delusional but always compelling.

I believe in the American open road. Soon after I graduated with a BA from Clemson University in South Carolina, I drove to California in celebration and as a reenactment of the traditions of the open road. I carried with me a Rand McNally atlas and tracked my progress. In the summer before that journey, I read William Least Heat-Moon's runaway bestseller, *Blue Highways*, and was enthralled with the multifaceted experiences he recorded and the prospects it suggested. My trip was to be a great American adventure, though at the time I had no idea just how deeply my desire was tied to the history of mobility in the United States. That was in 1985. I should confess that the trip failed on many levels: a fan belt broke in Biloxi at the end of a very long first day, and so on. The car was a 1965 Mustang convertible, a wonderful automobile. It was twenty years old at the time, just a bit younger than I was, and perhaps neither of us was up to the challenge. The Mustang was prone to overheating, and I was an overgrown boy with a big idea but little fortitude to see it through. I must say, though, that I do not regret that trip—even the three days stuck in Williams, Arizona—and I have become more patient with that young man over the years.

This book is tied to that trip. I have remained intrigued by the idea of the American open road and its vibrant existence in the American consciousness. Like many Americans, I inherited a tireless fascination with mobility and have no intention of letting that go. I assume many others feel likewise. I hope this book in some way helps readers understand just how their own stories of the road are tied to a formidable narrative history. Like many Americans, my *auto*biography says much about me. As of the summer of 2016, I had owned the following cars: a 1966 Ford Mustang coupe, a 1965 Ford Mustang convertible, a 1983 Plymouth Horizon, a 1988 Pontiac Grand Am, a 1999 Toyota Camry, a 2002 Toyota Camry, a 2008 Toyota Prius, a 2009 Ford Ranger, and a 2011 Honda Odyssey. These vehicles are the story of my adult life, beginning as a seventeen-year-old junior in high school and continuing well into my fifties. There have been other cars since then, but they simply reaffirm the process completed with the purchase of the Odyssey minivan. All these vehicles reflect personal choices that were inextricably tied to social responsibilities, financial opportunities and limitations, and a remarkable breadth of options available to me as a middle-class American.

My parents gave me my first Mustang when I was a junior in high school. It was a 1966 coupe with a three-speed manual transmission. It cost $450 and was worth every penny. Even in 1978 dollars, that was an affordable, though still precious, gift for which I was deeply grateful. It carried me through college and dropped its drive shaft in the middle of the road only once. In sharp contrast, the Odyssey I bought new in 2011 had a sticker price over $34,000 and took five years to pay off. With its bold name, that minivan culminated the journey I began as a teenager toward mainstream respectability. The first car that I bought out of a clear sense of family obligation, and thus the first car of my authentic adulthood, was the 1999 Toyota Camry. I made this choice for dependability, not desire. With that first four-door sedan purchase, my wife and I made a public commitment to becoming responsible heads of a family, ready to embrace and love a dependable and safe family vehicle. We could be trusted to think in civic and social terms. I hasten to add that we still talk about that car with affection. Millions of others have made similar choices in the decades that have followed the end of World War II.

My car history situates me within a matrix of cultural values and practices and is likely more representative of my place in this time than any other facet of my life. Whereas I am not claiming that the stories underlying those cars have any provocative interest for posterity individually, I am certain that they provide a representative framework for examining the culture in which I have been living. The same goes for most Americans. If we want to learn something about those born in the second half of the twentieth century and the cultural dynamics that animated them, we should consider their cars. I suspect that anyone reading this could put together an interesting list of their own mobile history. What vehicles are on your list? What stories do they tell?

APPROACH AND SCOPE

In this study, I explore an ongoing and powerful cultural phenomenon. It is interdisciplinary in its methodology and brings under scrutiny various cultural documents supporting the centrality of the open road to American sensibilities. I have chosen to draw on as many texts as possible in exploring those stories, their themes, patterns, and values, while also being mindful of keeping the content and length of this book manageable. Consequently, many worthy roads are untraveled, and I make no claim of exhaustive coverage. Whereas I know well my limitations, I am equally certain that others will continue needed explorations and offer alternative ways to think about and, indeed, travel the roads that are all around us. This book complements those that have come before and after, and I hope it makes a useful contribution to the topic.

The pages that follow refer to several types of cultural texts—from poems and song lyrics to car advertisements and public-service documents—but the primary examination throughout focuses on the literary and cinematic narratives that have enjoyed the most profound impact on American culture and the most enduring public support. I therefore depend on literature (prose narratives, both fiction and nonfiction) and film (including television) as the primary sources for exploring the open road in the American imagination. I also refer, as needed, to other components of popular culture, especially automotive advertising, to establish and complement patterns that define road narratives during the automotive age. Americans have invoked the open road in evolving and often captivating ways, and with varying levels of success. There is much repetition and reliance on cultural assumptions in these expressions over the generations. Rather than be dismissive of such conventions or even clichés, I embrace them for their endurance and for what they reveal about national and personal aspirations. Although I have tried to cast a wide net for material that helps to illustrate such a broad subject, I favor narratives that have garnered the most attention from popular and critical audiences as the most influential and representative. Therefore, these pages will explore titles that most people will recognize in some way.

I should clarify my use of the phrase "road narrative." First, the choice is a matter of convenience and is a slightly more specific term than "travel narrative" in that the noun "road" grounds the narrative in travel along roadways—no rafts on the Mississippi, no steamships across the Atlantic, no railroads, no airplanes. Moreover, this text concerns itself with examinations of narrative responses to automotive travel, movement made possible by the internal combustion engine. Therefore, the intent throughout is to understand the experiences of people moving in vehicles along mostly paved roadways. Their stories captivate the ever-roiling American imagination.

I hope that the following pages tap into that restless energy and capture its expansiveness. Toward that goal, the book is divided into three sections. In part 1, I discuss the cultural context of the post–World War II boom that catapulted car culture to the forefront of American consciousness and solidified all facets of automobility in the American popular imagination. In part 2, I define major patterns and conventions of the road narrative as revealed in a wide range of works over time and medium, and I provide extended close readings of seminal narratives from the 1950s to the 1980s. In part 3, the three chapters take thematic approaches to explore persistent challenges to the open-road experience based on the tensions of race and gender. The goal throughout the study is for individual chapters to follow analytical frames illustrating a range of ways to read the road without being reductive or dogmatic. In this sense, the content that follows is like the numerous options suggested by any map and any full tank of gas. It is hoped that this structure allows for consideration of persistent characteristics of the American open road without being prescriptive or subservient to the grinding out of a convenient thesis.

The book makes no pretense of covering all worthy topics or, to use the obvious metaphor, driving all possible roads. Nonetheless, my intent is to demonstrate the enduring value of the open road in the United States and to celebrate the creators who have shared unforgettable road stories since the middle of the twentieth century and have thus shaped the nation's identity and popular imagination. The open road cuts a broad swath through American culture like the roadways that form an ever-changing matrix on the landscape itself. Every mile holds a narrative of some sort, and every car is tied to American dreams in one way or another. When happy, when lonely, when frustrated, when desperate, when inspired, when determined—we drive.

The American Open Road

Part I

The American Open Road and Popular Culture

1
Imagining the Road

Mobility and Narrative

THE MYTHOLOGY OF THE AMERICAN OPEN ROAD

The American open road as an idea reflects core assumptions within American culture. It is a unifying concept built on ever-present opportunities, challenges, and tensions between personal autonomy and social coherence. It reveals our highest aspirations as well as our most troublesome restlessness, and we see its grip on our popular imagination in many forms and varying circumstances. A core simplicity animates the American notion of the open road and thus places a wide range of cultural documents in service to its compelling promise. Though this book is primarily concerned with narratives of well-known works of literature and film, this opening chapter is framed by two essential poems: Walt Whitman's "Song of the Open Road," first published in 1856, and Robert Frost's "The Road Not Taken," first published in 1915, both preceding the chronology of this study. The rationale for this rhetorical approach should, I hope, become steadily clearer as the book progresses, but the choice is also obvious.

The logic is embedded in the titles of these famous poems. Both assume an implicit cultural resonance for the "road" as an idea. Walt Whitman's "Song of the Open Road" begins with the following:

> Afoot and light-hearted I take to the open road,
> Healthy, free, the world before me,
> The long brown path before me leading wherever I choose.

Henceforth I ask not good-fortune, I myself am
good-fortune,
Henceforth I whimper no more, postpone no more, need
nothing,
Done with indoor complaints, libraries, querulous
criticisms,
Strong and content I travel the open road.[1]

In these two stanzas, Whitman evokes the basic characteristics of the open road idea: an individual embarks on a journey, looking ahead with an attitude emboldened by confidence, each step girded by an audacious optimism. Whitman's traveler seeks a future unknown in its details but certain in its promise. "Song of the Open Road" captures the glorious and unapologetic energy so characteristic of Whitman's verse and so perfect for his subject matter. It remains engaging and useful in a variety of contexts.

A recent application of "Song of the Open Road" that appeared in the summer of 2016 provides a helpful illustration of Whitman's relevance. Several commercials for the Volvo S90 luxury sedan, all produced by Grey New York, employ a nonlinear narrative style that shows the triumph of an aspiring writer who finds his muse on the open road. At the core of every version is Whitman's poem, beginning with the lines noted above (with some editing) but also drawing on many other lines to serve as the ad copy.[2] The commercials tap into the same energy found in Whitman's original statement, enhanced with provocative images of the American western landscape. The narrative is beautiful. It is a successful, if a bit pretentious, artistic statement of open-road assumptions. Yes, that Whitman has been exploited to sell cars, especially a vehicle priced well above $50,000, is not without problems. But, more importantly, his words remain very much alive in American culture. How the concept of the American open road has been perpetuated in our popular imagination as fueled by the explosiveness of automotive culture after World War II is the overarching subject of this book.

The concept of the open road remains steadfast in its role as the most malleable yet stable expression of what Americans interpret as their birthright. It was implied from the beginning. The Declaration of Independence, while rhetorically establishing a rationale for rebellion, also sets in place the basic assumptions implied by the assertions of independence, the "unalienable Rights" that include "Life, Liberty and the pursuit of Happiness." It is the third item on the list—the inherent right to seek happiness—that is so intrinsically American. Its assertion has made possible the vast road mythology that evolved via its pervasive and continuing reaffirmation. Without the practical and symbolic freedom of mobility, "life" and "liberty" are wonderful but static statements of *being*. Pursuing happiness demands *doing*. For the ideals of the American open road, the "pursuit of happiness" quite simply means *going*.

That restless and tireless movement chasing ever-elusive happiness is revealed time and time again in our popular imagination. As Ronald Primeau notes in his *Romance of the Road*, "In hundreds of books, movies, poems, songs, and videos, the road journey is an epic quest, a pilgrimage, a romance, a ritual that helps explain where Americans have been and where they think they might be going."[3] Primeau goes on to acknowledge the ever-present potential within any road journey to alter the way we encounter every facet of our lives. I would make explicit the following assumption: that the road narrative provides a way not only to see the world but to see ourselves. Our pursuits, by practical necessity and symbolic desire, always forge an intertwining relationship between the road and the individual. In all cases, therefore, the melding of a complex road culture with the demands of narrative creates a powerful catalyst for both cultural and individual experiences. Audiences have seen the open road inexhaustibly revealed via myriad artistic expressions.

While the exigencies of the nation and the individual are always at play on the road, those encounters are multifaceted, sustaining assumptions and values while also challenging them. Any definition of the road trip in America, therefore, must embrace the contentious interplay of national and individual aspirations and failures. As Ann Brigham points out in *American Road Narratives*, "The road trip is not merely the means but the actual manifestation of an authentic American experience. Deemed a democratic undertaking, it both directs and projects an experience of Americanness."[4] Individual sojourners follow what can best be described as a cultural imperative. Americans are encouraged, even expected, to enact their own discoveries, to take to the road in some fashion and demonstrate development in how they see the nation and how they establish their places within its practical and cultural borders. Such acts embody a public and private performance of the pursuit of happiness.

The road as a metaphor for life is as old as written human expression, but it has found a particularly comfortable home in the American consciousness. John Brinckerhoff Jackson, a foundational figure in landscape study, provides an appealing overview of the "road as life" trope, writing, "It is only in the course of the journey that we discover our true destination."[5] No metaphor has been more persistent in human history. Sometimes it is stated directly, as when Sal Paradise proclaims, "The road is life" in Jack Kerouac's *On the Road*, but most often it is merely implied.[6] It is simple and clichéd, yet it nonetheless remains resonant. The key here is not the metaphor itself but how the road idea has been applied, adapted, and reworked in narrative forms and how the technologies associated with it—automobiles—influence mobile experiences.

The mythology of the American open road maintains a tight grip on our popular imagination, the ideal framework for our national narrative of perpetual optimism and forward-looking desires for the new. In *Open Road*, Phil Patton notes that change itself serves as American culture's "most unchanging premise," going on to state, "Movement is its most firmly fixed pattern, impermanence its most permanent condition, and the receding horizon its most steadfast goal. And America's restlessness is its most mercurial trope."[7] The basic assumption of any road narrative is that movement symbolizes change and thereby suggests implied personal expansion. Patton's use of the horizon extends the road/life metaphor by juxtaposing the geographical reality with the aspirational desire. In other words, movement toward a horizon serves as a recurring goal that captures both the power of the dream and its ongoing lure and inherent frustration.

Like the title character's signature song from the musical *Annie*, with lyrics by Martin Charnin, the road inspires a dream of "tomorrow" while also acknowledging the core fact that it perpetually remains out of reach, "always a day away." The horizon, the tomorrow of any road narrative, is the destination of happiness. Thus the ever-hopeful road goal must forever reside just beyond the horizon, always a day away, or always just around the next curve in the road—never *here*, but forever *there*. For those who obsess over the many mirages and roadblocks that pervade the open-road dream—and there *are* mirages and roadblocks—any belief in the horizon can only be self-defeating. I wonder, though, what else are we to do? Are we to tell Annie that tomorrow never arrives and vanquish her pitiable delusions of hope? Go ahead, tell her. I prefer not to because, quite simply, the open-road idea encourages a contrary and thus hopeful response to Annie's dream. Without apology, it embraces her unswerving push toward the future.

Now, give Annie a car.

CAR CULTURE AND THE AMERICAN OPEN ROAD

The American open road attained its most powerful expression with the coming of the automobile. Thus began a love affair that has been perpetually reinvigorated and reworked as a central practical and symbolic principle of the United States, a nation that continues to define itself as forever on the move. For over a hundred years, Americans have conducted most of their movement behind the steering wheels of automobiles, machines that encapsulate national cohesion and individual autonomy.

"Automobility" has become the accepted shorthand term implying all facets of a complex and nuanced culture instigated by and responding to the automobile as a transformative technology. And, as a result, it moves through the heart of twentieth-century American economic and social history. As dramatic changes in values and behaviors became more entrenched by the second half of the twentieth century, the idea of the road, likewise, became a more varied, accessible, and dynamic expression of national and individual dreams. The zeal for the open road is in the American grain like no other self-identifying concept, and the automobile has been its ideal implement of expansion. The arrival of the automobile did not create our cultural pursuit, of course, but it granted more autonomy and much more speed. Americans immediately loved the "lifestyle it promised," according to J. B. Jackson, primarily because it could make us "infinitely mobile."[8] In the increasingly chaotic energy of the twentieth century, a technology—the automobile—arose from that tumult to grant some defense against the seemingly overriding power of modernity and to allow us to reassert our autonomy in a mechanized world.

If the American road is "a mythic space of possibility," as Brigham puts it, then Americans carry an obligation to believe in it.[9] Mobility—physical and social—became the core of the American Dream and complemented the national image built around a frontier mythology. The grand narrative that reflects open-road sensibilities derives directly from westward expansion of Euro-American power. There is no way to escape that origin. The Euro-American narrative of westward movement and conquest has always been interwoven with the ideals of individual and national aspirations. This politically dominant history of the nineteenth century provides the essential backdrop to how vibrant car culture would become in the United States in the twentieth century and is drawn from the frontier mythology first and most concisely defined by Frederick Jackson Turner in 1893. His "Frontier Thesis" argues that the most pervasive social characteristic defining American strength in opposition to Europe came about from the movement ever westward by settlers.[10] Turner's argument is reductive and Eurocentric. Many other types of movements influenced development and cultural upheavals, but a vast majority of Americans in the nineteenth and twentieth centuries embraced the idea that the nation was shaped by the frontier, which demanded a ruggedness that defined the national character.[11]

It is therefore a story that provides the dramatic mythology for the "winning" of the American West, a construct that celebrates the political and social movement as an exceptional triumph of democratic ideals. The story is profoundly more complicated and reveals cultural conflicts that were tumultuous and at times even horrific. Therefore, in addition to being a singular narrative of victory, the historical reality is also tied to political and economic expedience and aggression; it is about war and genocide, suffering and loss. Although the concept of the American open road celebrates the theoretical freedom for all to pursue happiness, it has been, in fact, not fully open to all Americans. Despite the aspirational beliefs implied in the founding documents of the United States, the practical opening of American roads has been a tedious work in progress. This is the core paradox of the American culture of mobility. The resulting stresses, personal and political, are captured in the many varied narratives of automobility. American mobility is forever tied to a legacy of triumph and horror but still forever progressing toward all-too-distant ideals on the horizon.

The burgeoning car culture of the early twentieth century steadily altered frontier mythology into a more democratic catalyst for social change. Turner bemoaned the loss of the frontier and worried that the strength of the nation would wane without the dramatic goal of conquest to provide purpose for the society at large. His concerns were unwarranted. He, of course, had no way to envision how the automobile would extend frontier mythology into the twentieth century with the same transformative energy. The frontier closed by the end of the nineteenth century, but it was reborn and reconfigured. Turner's focus westward emphasized the overwhelming push of American political power away from European models but negated the broader dynamism of movement itself. The American open road never demanded a westward expansion or a culture steeped in the challenges of the frontier. Rather, it required an impetus and opportunity for mobility, the true totem of American energy. Increasingly, Americans aspired to reach the dreams implied by that mobility with their eyes forward and looking through the windshield of an automobile. In other words, with automobility the frontier as symbol of aspiration was no longer a line of political and social demarcation making its way to the Pacific Ocean. To the contrary, it became an ever-moving line of possibility just beyond the front bumper of an automobile.

With the coming of the automobile, the idea of the open road became a more democratic national ideal. This is not to assert a Pollyannaish notion that car culture fully realized the American dream by making mobility equal for all. Yet it expanded the potential for more people to embrace egalitarian ideals suggested by the open road like no other cultural transformation. The movement in terminology—if not in full practice—became a narrative no longer of nation building or the march of manifest destiny but one more directly defined by a dream and a car. The elasticity of such a narrative is its strength. That robust capacity for optimism fuels the American open-road narrative, making it adaptable through a range of contexts and challenges. The transition to a car culture was a phenomenon that spanned the twentieth century and has continued into the twenty-first. The post–World War II era defined car culture and solidified its centrality in the American experience.[12] The mythology of the road encourages the energy that drives it; popular culture—especially via writers and filmmakers—put car culture in the driver's seat of all things American.

Any commitment to one thesis-driven historical narrative limits appreciation of a complicated upheaval that informs and permeates the road narrative in popular imagination. Jeremy Packer, in *Mobility without Mayhem*, offers a useful summary of what he defines as the "two versions of the automobile's history." He notes that one version adopts a dark vision of how the automobile destroyed traditional value systems and organizing principles of civic mindedness and recklessly pushed the nation toward "individualism, conspicuous consumption, suburban sprawl, environmental destruction, highway carnage, and even oil-related military expansion." The competing version, however, touts the connection to Frederick Jackson Turner's frontier thesis and thereby celebrates automobility as a beneficial framework for a unifying force.[13] Packer correctly notes the validity of both accounts. I agree and further argue that these two cultural narratives exist symbiotically in our consciousness, each steadily informing the other. The whole narrative, employing elements of both visions, demands an aspiration for making an American into a "self-empowered mobile citizen," as Packer puts it. Americans in the cultural milieu have both an "opportunity and obligation" to "actualize [their] potential for mobility."[14] Americans, then, enjoy the ostensible opportunity to pursue happiness, but they also, in equal measure, carry the burden of engaging with that pursuit. American mobility must be expressed through comprehensive effort.

To realize such a vast pursuit required not simply cars but also myriad ribbons of asphalt. The roads that a nation builds are emblematic of culture and are a standard-bearer of the breadth and power of any nation. Phil Patton offers a logical model for gauging the vitality of the United States and its roads: ancient Rome. In his comparison, he notes a vital distinction: "In the Empire, all roads led to Rome. In America, all roads lead to other roads."[15] Considering Rome as an idea as well as a destination amplifies its centrality within a far-reaching empire. The point that Patton captures is an ideal expression of the open road in America—all roads lead to other roads, which lead to other roads, and so on. All are given meaning by individual choices and varied pursuits. Patton finishes his comparison appropriately: "While the Romans had their road map in the Forum, for Americans roads are themselves the Forum."[16]

At the close of World War II, Americans were poised to embrace this new machine of mobility as the ideal vehicle for a headlong push into modernity. Whereas Patton celebrates its core concept, claiming that his text regards "the special status of the road in the metaphorical landscape of the American mind,"[17] there are detractors, and cultural intimacy with the automobile is not without its problems. In *The Age of Asphalt*, Richard Davies shares his own ambivalence about car culture and its impact on our national ethos. One of many detractors of automobility to emerge in the 1970s, Davies questioned the wholehearted obeisance to automobility in the postwar era. His provocative work nonetheless acknowledges indirectly the power of the American love affair with cars. Though highly critical of the automotive industry at large, Davies offers a confessional of sorts that reveals the deep impact of automobility on the national psyche. In the preface, while clarifying his critical position against the interstate system and the American obsession with automobiles, he shares the following: "I own today, two gasoline-gobbling vehicles: a traditional American sedan, vintage 1971, that is virtually indispensable for the daily functioning of my active family; and an antiquated four-wheeler with which I would part only upon pain of death . . . for it holds the key to my infrequent escapes from the ravages of daily life into the backwoods of Arizona's incomparable and still primitive mountains where I can rest, relax, think great thoughts, and occasionally outguess a two-pound trout."[18] This is a marvelous passage. It conveys a refreshing self-awareness as Davies understands his hypocrisy as both a hater of automobiles and lover of *his* automobiles. His inner conflict is shared by many Americans. He convincingly notes that his dubiousness toward automobility is informed by his own ambivalent relationship with cars, complicating his strongly felt political belief that America needed to halt its uncritical dependence on them.

His revelation betrays the depth to which Americans love their cars. Davies regarded his family sedan as "indispensable." That adjective acknowledges practical necessity. His ownership is not a willing choice but simply a capitulation to a car-structured society. The second vehicle, however, exposes the crux of the dilemma. His emotional attachment to what he calls an "antiquated four-wheeler" belies the joy it provided. This vehicle, born of the same often burdensome automobility that mandated the "indispensable" sedan, rewarded him with a four-wheeled freedom buggy. His love for that machine should not be discounted or undervalued, neither for the madness of its irrationality nor for the depth of its passion. Here's the rub: Many people recognize the damage wrought by car culture, but many of those same people love their cars. We are caught in a love-hate relationship, a perverse codependency of perpetual annoyances and undeniable pleasures. Our mobility with automobiles is thus both exhilaratingly open and exasperatingly confining, freedom paired inextricably with bondage. John Urry puts it succinctly: "The car is immensely flexible *and* wholly coercive."[19] We are trapped by the breadth of car culture, so what is the best way to escape such stress? The answer is obvious: get in a car and drive!

This perverse love affair with automobility became centralized in the 1950s, not simply due to the booming optimism and the delayed desires of a generation but, more specifically, because automakers in Detroit played Cupid. In 1954, General Motors celebrated an important milestone: the production of its fifty millionth vehicle. A pamphlet celebrating that accomplishment goes far to illustrate both the historical progression of the company and how GM would solidify that success by ensuring that the automobile would be at the center of postwar economic and cultural development. The pamphlet, *GM Builds Its First 50 Million Cars*, opens with a cutout of a newspaper article with the dateline "Flint, MI, Nov. 23." The actual source is not identified, but the article notes that the fifty millionth GM automobile "rolled off the assembly line" that day. It identifies the actual vehicle as a 1955 Chevrolet Bel Air Sport Coupe, a fitting choice for the distinction. The Bel Air typified the expectations of middle America in the mid-1950s, a golden age in the nostalgic chrome-addled affections of baby boomers. That year, 1955, Detroit set records for auto sales, moving over seven and a half million vehicles off dealership lots nationwide.[20]

The content that follows in *General Motors Builds Its First 50 Million Cars* rejoices in the history of GM's growth into a massive industrial goliath tied to all facets of American life. It contains a section with the heading "All America built these cars" and follows that overview with a subsection—"Only in America . . . "—which weaves GM's fortunes with those of the nation itself. "Nowhere on earth, except in the United States, do you find a free market large enough to absorb 50 million cars. Only in America do you find the freedom to compete, the incentives to seek new ways of making better products at lower costs that are so important in the mass production process."[21] It is the United States, the text avers, that has made the building of so many cars possible. This celebration of GM is intrinsically and directly tied to the postwar potential of the United States itself and without qualification aligns the goals of GM (i.e., selling cars to ensure profitability) with those of the nation (i.e., social and economic mobility to ensure American success in the Cold War). The goals so aggressively asserted in the pamphlet demanded faith in automobility to achieve both.

The pamphlet has one moment of understatement that merits special attention: "The most obvious and dramatic change has been in our new mobility as a nation."[22] "New mobility" is an apt phrase. Car culture had been insinuating itself into the American cultural fabric for fifty years by the time GM reached this milestone of fifty million vehicles built, but it was in the 1950s when that transformation would be completed, fusing rapid postwar economic growth and pent-up consumerist desire to make the United States truly a nation on wheels. Americans in cars (and trucks and motorcycles, etc.) became the crux of our individual and social narratives as the culture adapted to the idiosyncrasies of new ways to move.

Roughly one hundred years after Walt Whitman asserted the lure of the open road, and sixty-two years before Swedish carmaker Volvo would invoke him in service to its S90 luxury sedan, General Motors implied indirectly a cultural and technological context that made the optimistic promise evoked in Whitman's voice feasible for a vast swath of middle America. According to GM, "The automobile has given us a personal mobility unmatched in any other country. It has made Americans the most traveled people on the face of the globe—and made them better acquainted with each other than any other people."[23] This rather bold assertion went well beyond a boastful company touting its prowess in the marketplace. It declared American exceptionalism, of course, but that distinction was also couched in the implied cohesion of the nation's people and their closeness to one another, all made possible by automobility. This statement was a declaration of national unity made possible by the design, production, and selling of the most individually alluring mode of transportation the world had ever seen.

The notion of the car as central to the American narrative becomes clearer in the next paragraph: "The automobile has become a symbol of the wide gap that separates the living standards of the average American family from those of people in other lands. For only in the United States do wage earners drive to work in their own cars. And only in America is the farmer able to take his products to market in his own truck." In a clear nod to the Cold War, this statement confirms the superiority of the American political and economic system because it allows workers and farmers to enjoy the products of their labor. Readers could infer from this narrative a simple message: people tempted to believe that the Soviet Union provides such an opportunity should perhaps drive a Soviet-made car first. The text goes on to associate GM's success with the inherent American character, wherein the advances in automotive production demonstrated that the "American people . . . had a positive genius for doing things in a big way."[24] This pamphlet lauded a company milestone, but it was far from simply being a scrapbook for the coffee table. It captured the energy of the nation at a critical juncture of its history—that moment when it faced an existential threat from the Soviet Union and also stood on the threshold of a complete cultural transformation into what GM calls the "Auto Age."

The personal connection to automobility is with not only the cars Americans drive but also the roads on which they move. Primeau makes a useful assertion that the American highway is regarded as "sacred space."[25] The use of "sacred," a term usually tied to religious discussions, is appropriate here in that it describes a necessary part of popular culture—both secular and religious—that demands faith in abstractions. As to whether any road—Route 66, for example—can be sacred in its most basic sense is uncertain, but the capacity of an idea—"Route 66," a place to "get your kicks"—to become so is self-evident. In this sense, a road, like a national shrine, can serve as an emblem for national values and aspirations and thus can become hallowed because, quite simply, we believe it to be so.

Consider a road that is special to you. Describe that road without using romantic imagery or, better yet, without referring to a story from your own past. It could be a major byway with a powerful historical significance: the multiple routes tied to the Underground Railroad and the Oregon Trail, and the Trail of Tears, as examples. It could be a road celebrated in popular culture: Highway 61 in Mississippi, A1A in Florida, the Pacific Coast Highway in California, the New Jersey Turnpike, and so on. It could be something much more personal: the secluded gravel road at the edge of town precious to so many teenagers, the street where you grew up, or even the spot where the car left the road and changed everything. Roads carry vehicles and freight and people, but most of all, they carry our lives. And those narratives can never be summed by practical realities alone. They require imagination. Our relationship to any given road, then, is inevitably and inextricably tied to our emotions, how we feel as the road rumbles beneath the wheels and how we respond to those moments of movement then, now, and forever. If it is personal, it can be sacred, and American roads are often very personal and thus consecrated ground.

SELF AND PLACE ON THE AMERICAN OPEN ROAD

The often-profound personal associations many Americans have had with their automobiles and roadways encourage a belief in the essential revelatory power of the open road. At this point, I would like to explore a theoretical framework for thinking about mobility to delineate how we experience all those cars on all those roads. Let us start with the basics. Geographer Tim Cresswell has produced a formidable body of scholarship exploring the range of human motion and its personal and cultural implications. In *On the Move* he notes that the basic representation of mobility must first be recognized in its broadest and simplest sense: as movement from point A to point B.[26] We must keep in mind that understanding mobility does not demand reckoning distance or speed. Rather, study of it requires appreciation of movement itself and how it informs all human experience. Therefore, those points A and B have innumerable applications. Consider these two examples: multiple journeys across the nation taking place over several years, as represented in Jack Kerouac's *On the Road*, and repetitive cruising back and forth along a "strip" of road by teenagers taking place on one night, as represented in George Lucas's *American Graffiti*. Both can be analyzed as road narratives informed by nuanced expressions of mobility.

The characteristics of the movement as it informs self and place are the essential focus. According to Cresswell, mobility is "socially produced motion" that can be understood via the intersecting energy of "three relational moments": (1) mobility as "brute fact"—that we move, (2) mobility as an idea with meaning—that we think about movement, and (3) mobility as phenomenon of experience—that we see ourselves as mobile beings.[27] There is always the core physical act of moving. For example, a chicken crosses a road, an actualized movement from A to B. Such "brute fact," as Cresswell phrases it, is inherently instilled with some meaning, typically implying intent or desire: a chicken crosses the road *to get to the other side*. But the meaning inferred by that crossing could be augmented by numerous additional questions: "Is the chicken escaping danger?" or "Has the chicken considered the speed of an oncoming vehicle?," for example. Any effort to answer such questions adds to our understanding of the fact of the chicken's motion and the many ways in which that act expresses the complexity of flightless avian experience. The same goes for flightless humans.

Road narratives are creative expressions tied to direct physical actions elaborated by complex mobility. Any movement from A to B carries the potential for a wide range of actions, values, and memories. It follows, then, that any discussion of road experiences must be undertaken in terms of complex interactions between *self* and *place*, the individual (an often-complicated self) moving through geographical space (an often-complicated place). We need to distinguish between "space" and "place" in this context. Place is any "meaningful segment of space—locations imbued with meaning and power."[28] For example, a large canyon in northern Arizona has specific geological features that can be observed, catalogued, and defined. Moreover, it has a specific location that can be charted, labeled, and so on. However, the particular canyon in question is formidable by all measures of understanding and carries an array of possible inferences tied to historical data and varied human encounters related to it. Many conjectures could be suggested by the name itself: the "Grand Canyon." Moreover, that designation implies much more than size. It also encourages the emotional responses to it as awe-inspiring, a remarkable physical reality firmly associated with nationalistic aspirations as well as personal desires. Seeing it holds value. Americans have agreed in large numbers over the generations that the Grand Canyon is a special place—a vast physical space that has been granted profound social meaning. Any movement of a self in relation to that place engages with multifaceted data points of meaning.

How is meaning tied to mobility drawn from such places and created on the page or on the screen? Sticking with the Grand Canyon example, consider two characters, name them Thelma and Louise and make them mobile. At a certain climactic point in their road journey, they approach the edge of the Grand Canyon in a Thunderbird convertible and then drive off the edge and into the vast openness of the canyon. This interaction between self (selves) and place evokes a world of meaning within the film itself and within the broader social history of the Grand Canyon in the American zeitgeist. Callie Khouri, screenwriter of *Thelma & Louise*, employs the iconography of the Grand Canyon for that purpose. The two protagonists, Khouri implicitly asserts, have earned both this final act of rebellion and also the location. Director Ridley Scott follows through with the intentions set out in the screenplay. The power of the scene is deepened by the cultural resonance of the Grand Canyon as a special place representative of the grandness, if you will, of American potential. In the rich moments of decision, the car is still. Then. The two women join hands, and Louise pushes the accelerator. They move into open space. This dramatic movement is full of emotional depth and arguably one of the finest dramatic moments of road film history. So it matters not that the scene was shot in Utah.[29]

Such mobile moments define the American open road in our imaginations. They are created by manipulation of mobile selves in reference to various places and given meaning via narrative. The places and the people captured by countless events on the road call on a wide range of experiences tied to the American landscape. In all cases, self and place are made dynamic by mobility. J. B. Jackson, in his discussions of landscape imagination, points out that there are legitimate conflicts regarding our understanding of how self and place interact. He notes that "a sense of place is something that we ourselves create in the course of time. It is the result of habit or custom." Others, he recognizes, take the contrary position and sublimate our creative role, believing that "a sense of place comes from our response to features which are *already* there—wither a beautiful natural setting or well-designed architecture."[30] Both are true. When we are told that Thelma and Louise are poised at the edge of the Grand Canyon, we believe it because the expectation has rightly been created in the film for the two lead characters as well as for the audiences in the theaters, but its value was also already powerful in the American imagination long before the making of the film.

Places are active and subject to the traveler's eye (or mind's eye) and thus fungible based on perception, an interaction that is perpetually "in process."[31] Cresswell's defining of place is crucial for mobility in that movement must always be referenced by and to space; therefore, mobility is given meaning by place, and the other way around. In this context, we can think of any given self-place encounter on the road as an "event" defined by "openness and change rather than boundedness and permanence."[32] Within a road narrative, the sense of self, the import of place, and the character of movement may all be in flux. In this context, a road narrative emerges from the steady reconfiguring of meaning caused by the interactions between self, place, and mobility.[33]

MODES OF ROAD MOBILITY: STABLE AND SUBVERSIVE

Despite the passion for mobility on individual and social levels, Americans nonetheless remain ambivalent about it, thinking in broad strokes that individual movements indicate "progress" and "freedom" but also, and in equal measure, "shiftlessness" and "deviance." This is an uneasy dichotomy. Americans both laud and distrust those who are mobile, and that uncertainty permeates road experiences. Aspirations for onward movement are often tinged with restlessness, and ambition paired with discontentment. The new mobility made possible (and, indeed, essential) by automobiles in the years after World War II carries forward an implicit contradiction between traditional mainstream and countercultural notions of mobility. On the one hand, the mainstream roadview avows thinking of personal road experiences in terms of national values and traditions. On the other hand, the countercultural roadview privileges highly individualized experiences. Two major modes of mobility represent seemingly contrasting world views, and I label these views as the stable and the subversive.[34]

The stable mode is marked by potential energy employed in service to specified goals and measured by the control of resources and management of experiences. Evidence of successful use of energy resides in material comfort, upward social mobility, and cultural respectability. This framework produces a point of view that can be characterized by its desire to assert a *stable* road wherein movement is in reference to rootedness and belonging. Therefore, I think of its mobility in terms of circular or concentric movements, all in service to long-term solidity for the nuclear family. This movement thus radiates outward, as if in waves, from the home as constant reference point, a perennial center. Purpose derives from seeking, building, and preserving the integrity of the circle while expanding its reach.

The subversive mode is marked by kinetic energy employed in service to often unspecified goals and measured by the release of control and the enthusiastic embrace of uncertainty.[35] Evidence of successful use of energy thus resides in novelty and experiences that are anathema to the materialism of consumer culture. This framework produces a point of view that can be characterized by its desire to assert a *subversive* road, ostensibly directly desiring spontaneity and often opposing stability. Therefore, I think of the subversive mode in terms of linear movements, all in service to short-term expressions of individual desires. This movement lurches forward as if a projectile with no clear or obvious reference point other than the road itself. Purpose derives from seeking and maintaining the energy of the projectile and its implied aggressive seeking of experience. This projectile, once launched, denies any restrictive tether or long-term securing of energy.

For the stable mode, mobility must exist in a specific and meaningful relationship to place. In its most simple terms, mobility encourages attachment to a secure homeplace and affirms the self's connection to the permanency that it affords. The implicit goal of any stable road expression is the power gained by social upward mobility and status, enacted most directly via material wealth—stylish and dependable cars, nice hotels and restaurants, and attractions legitimizing their efforts within mainstream values. All help to secure freedom from the stresses of unpredictability. The stable mode values persistence and patience in its efforts to include the road into its home-circle and expand its interdependent and tethered self. As a result, a road-narrative moment from a stable point of view must consider the degree to which travelers see themselves in relation to their homes and how that may change with mobile experiences.[36]

For the American family, freedom of the open road translated into issues related directly to convenience, speed, and efficiency.[37] More and better roads combined with the growing availability of automobiles to create an open-road mythology for mainstream America built around family travel—taking vacations and Sunday afternoon outings, driving the kids to baseball practice and dance lessons, and commuting to work from the suburbs. Movement extends influence, ripples radiating from a home pulse that also serves as a homing beacon. Expanded horizons are implied via a widening circle of identity. The stable mode frames experience in direct and conscious reference to the home-self, ensuring that road events are defined with that persistent touchstone, assuming all along the vitality of the home as a mobile entity. As E. Relph notes, "Home in its most profound form is an attachment to a particular setting, a particular environment, in comparison with which all other associations with places have only a limited significance. It is the point of departure from which we orient ourselves and take possession of the world."[38] Relph emphasizes home as the "point of departure," and thus it has a dynamic influence on how we interpret road events. In the stable mode, travelers seek to "take possession" of the road within the known circles of a home-self. Such movement built around the American suburban home celebrated the road as emblem of American prosperity and superiority.

For the subversive mode, mobility must exist in specific and meaningful relationship to movement itself. In its most simple terms, then, mobility encourages detachment from any referential and binding place to affirm the self's capacity for unencumbered movement. The implicit goal of the subversive mode is the power gained through autonomy of movement and absence of obligations, enacted most directly via immaterial evidence—novelty, "kicks," self-expression, and the joy of speed, among others. All help to secure freedom from the stresses of conformity. The subversive mode values resistance and verve in its efforts to associate with *any* place at *any* time to absorb an array of experiences into an independent self. The subversive mode encourages passion for individualized goals as most expressive of the national character. It expresses personal and immediate desire. Subversive roads suppose an experience projecting beyond the horizon and thus implying perpetual motion, the beacon drawing the traveler away from home. The impulse implies overcoming the horizon while also being cognizant of new horizons coming ever into view.

The subversive mode is the more obvious and declarative mobile identity, the one rendered sacrosanct in Kerouac's *On the Road*. The tone of the novel persistently captures the kinetic energy expounded by a rebellious point of view. It is evident in one of the most oft-quoted passages from the first chapter, wherein Sal asserts his devotion to its overriding philosophy. He notes, "The only people for me are the mad ones, the ones who are mad to live, mad to talk, mad to be saved, desirous of everything at the same time, the ones who never yawn or say a commonplace thing, but burn, burn, burn like fabulous yellow roman candles exploding like spiders across the stars and in the middle you see the blue centerlight pop and everybody goes 'Awww!'"[39] The madness Sal craves is subversive energy, and his poetic rapture evidenced by the style of the passage, as well as much of the most compelling segments of the novel, matches the assumptions inherent in subversive roads wherein all is given to the ever-present moment, as the passage implies with the claim that "mad" people are those who are "desirous of everything at the same time." Within this joyful assertion, however, is the perhaps unwitting revelation of the downside of subversive roads. The beautiful and endearing "pop," while being the culmination of a glorious self-exploration is also self-immolation. Fire consumes what it energizes. The subversive mode often rejects the stability of home and its commonplace things, defining it as simply confinement. It seeks road events that have a seemingly impromptu and exhilarating character wholly unchained from mundane concerns. The traveler therefore takes to the road as an outward-reaching peripatetic self, questing for experience.

The clichéd phrase "they rode into town" conveys a world of tension between stable and subversive mobilities. The stable mode sees home as central, the base from which mobility both emanates from and returns toward.

The outsider thus can only be a stranger and therefore a threat. An episode of *The Andy Griffith Show* titled "Stranger in Town" provides a useful illustration of this conundrum and its underlying tensions.[40] The basic premise of the teleplay is built around the comic results of a stranger coming into town and immediately presupposing familiarity. He talks to everyone as if he has known them for years. What the locals do not know is that he had met a man from Mayberry and after hearing stories about the town had fallen in love with the place. He learns more about the town by reading the local newspaper and eventually moves there, acting as if he were a longtime resident and adopting their home as his own. Despite his friendliness, he unnerves townspeople because he is an outsider, a subversive traveler, from their points of view, no matter his shared sensibilities. In short, he has *learned* about Mayberry as an idealized *place* but has not *earned* Mayberry as *home*.

Such tensions arise as we situate ourselves at any given road event in either a stable or subversive mode. We must negotiate our relationship to places and define our responses to them by privileging the mode that suits our desires at that moment. We are rarely easily ensconced in one or the other. On the contrary, we move in and out of modes of discovery and meld a more complicated road narrative than we often imagine. The key for our consideration is to recognize that road narratives slip in and out of these modes of thought in response to the nature of any given self-place event. The basic organizing principle for discussing road narratives derives from the tensions between stable and subversive points of view as they are revealed in discourse—not as a dichotomy but as an uneasy symbiosis wherein cultural conflicts are in a constant push-and-pull battle for common ground and distinction.

Although we most often consider the subversive mode as definitive of the American road narrative and dismiss references to the stable mode, a better way to read the road is to see the interlinking desires as coequal and observe that the more exhilarating burning of improvisation embraced by Kerouac is often matched by the countervailing humdrum of preparation. These opposing and complementary mobilities inform the American road mythology and thus serve as the overarching framework for the open road in American culture. The two modes of mobility are intertwined despite their inherent contradictions. Both are equally vibrant and compelling dreams of mobility, and we must consider the dividing line between stable and subversive imaginations and not only assess how and why they diverge but also consider how they often travel intertwining paths.

One of America's best known and beloved poems is Robert Frost's "The Road Not Taken." As with Walt Whitman, Robert Frost has earned a lasting place in the American imagination. His poetry serves as a cultural touchstone for a range of situations. "The Road Not Taken" may be one of the most referred to poems in his formidable canon. How many high school valedictorian speeches have in one way or another encouraged graduates to take roads "less traveled by"? It is appealing advice perfectly tuned to an occasion like a high school graduation. The message exploits a social imperative to maintain an independent spirit on life's journey. Those valedictorians, however, have misread the poem, which, like much of Frost's deceptively simple work, evokes a more complicated narrative. Consider the poem in full to see how it establishes a nuanced message that incorporates both stable and subversive modes of the American open road:

> Two roads diverged in a yellow wood,
> And sorry I could not travel both
> And be one traveler, long I stood
> And looked down one as far as I could
> To where it bent in the undergrowth;
>
> Then took the other, as just as fair,
> And having perhaps the better claim,
> Because it was grassy and wanted wear;
> Though as for that the passing there
> Had worn them really about the same,
>
> And both that morning equally lay
> In leaves no step had trodden black.
> Oh, I kept the first for another day!
> Yet knowing how way leads on to way,
> I doubted if I should ever come back.
>
> I shall be telling this with a sigh
> Somewhere ages and ages hence:
> Two roads diverged in a wood, and I—
> I took the one less traveled by,
> And that has made all the difference.[41]

In stanzas one through three, the speaker provides a relatively straightforward setup: a person walking on a path in "a yellow wood" encounters a dilemma when coming to a fork in the road. This poem is a standard bearer for using the road as a metaphor for life, and, in this instance, life's multiple roads imply life's multiple choices. The three stanzas share the speaker's thought process when faced with options defined mostly by unknowns, but, alas, one traveler means one path at a time. A decision is required. That does not stop us from trying to see as far down the road, as far into the future, as possible to help us make the better choice. Therein lies the tension along the road of life. What to do?

The speaker confesses that both paths are basically the same, so there is no clear choice here with implications for any stable future or subversive present. The effort to make the impending decision easier by asserting distinctive options has been in vain: "Both that morning equally lay." Choices mean opportunity but also uncertainty, confusion, and, of course, regret. Frost knew this quite well, and the poem, all in all, is not suited for valedictorians. The speaker obsesses over options that were *not* chosen. Trapped by regret, so much so that there can only be a "sigh" of resignation, the speaker is desperate to validate a personal road history. Most valedictorians ignore this bit of mundane information because acknowledging that point undermines their planned inspirational applause line that goes something like this: "No matter what, fellow graduates, be yourself! Take the road less traveled by, and make all the difference!" (Slow clap building into a standing ovation!)

* * *

On the surface, "The Road Not Taken" seems to celebrate a subversive mode, one that rejects mainstream values and encourages individual aspirations. But despite the triumphant finish, the speaker clearly assumes that misgivings will remain and that contentment may be hard to achieve. The only salvation rests in the creation of a story to control the uncertainty of self-place interactions. Frost invokes a nostalgic voice of age ("I shall be telling this with a sigh") to emphasize that the secret of the road in our understanding is revealed by narrative, by the interplay of memory and meaning, of expectation and desire. The history of the American road imagination is thus always a history of not simply what experiences arise from automobility but also how those stories are remembered and told. As we meld our stable and subversive dreams, we reveal all the while the cultural vitality of the narratives forever generated along the American open road.

2
Mapping Mobility

Roads, Automobiles, and Landscapes

AMERICANS DRIVE AN astounding variety of cars, trucks, and motorcycles on an equally diverse array of streets, avenues, highways, and interstates. Taken together, they form a remarkably complex matrix on the American landscape. What Americans think and feel about those vehicles and roads springs from a dynamic discourse energized by the new mobility that exploded in the years following the end of World War II. The concrete, physical elements of car culture mesh with the abstract impressions of imagination to evoke the roiling energy that permeates narratives of mobility. Toward categorizing that narrative context, I would like to establish three overlapping but distinctive frameworks for defining open-road experiences: the road imaginary; the automobile imaginary; and the landscape imaginary.

THE ROAD IMAGINARY

We should first consider our intimate relationship to the many roads we travel. In Kerouac's *On the Road*, the following ambiguous question is asked only once in the text but is implied throughout: "What's your road, man?"[1] The breadth of possible answers to that provocative question is vast simply in practical terms, much less in the loaded symbolic overtones intended by the question. Our experiences on the American open road must consider the impact of actual roads as well as metaphoric ones, all part of a complicated mosaic of mobility.

The American road system—national, state, and local—does not establish a wheel-and-spoke system even remotely like that of the railroad system, with a clear central authority and grand central stations. Rather, it implies a chaos of individual movement within a complicated social contract. Phil Patton writes, "Our roads are considered to be of equal importance at any given place: they assert democracy, the power of the people, the service of the public—and the statistical profile of the average driver, average consumer. The limo and the jalopy are equal in their sight."[2] This observation glosses over the persistent social differences that affect the road experience, but Patton correctly notes the inherent value of a system wherein individuals assert power on the road, no matter how many clear and present dangers may exist for them on any given road at any given time.

The building and using of roads, though profoundly influenced by social and political struggles, has not evolved from the focused business interests of railroad companies and the politicians who supported them. Roads can never reach everywhere, but from the beginning they have implied that such a thing was possible in a far more resonant way than railroads could match. Patton notes that "the automobile promised to put the positive power of transportation in individual hands and offered an escape from the dominance of the railroad."[3] That escape, however, required roads, and lots of them, and as the nation built a road system to meet the ever-growing demand, it would also construct ways for Americans to think about their roads that in turn would influence how they would view the nation and their places within it.

With the advent of the interstate highway system in 1956, the largest government enterprise of the late twentieth century, the interlacing of the open road both as ideal for individuals and as emblem of national power became complete in the age of the automobile. The name of the bill that appropriated the funds for highway construction makes the connection indelible: the National Interstate and Defense Highways Act.[4] Not surprisingly, to get enough members of Congress on board, the massive dose of government spending needed a justification beyond common sense. The "defense" rationale was to build a highway system that would facilitate military movement across the country as necessary and with all due speed. Moreover, the system would allow efficient evacuation should such a need ever occur. National security, the argument went, depended on good roads. To be sure, however, most people believed that more and better roads would benefit everyone. As Richard Thruelsen wryly noted in 1955 in the *Saturday Evening Post*, "Now, everybody loves a highway program. Like the Girl Scouts, better schools and Christmas, the better-roads program is a continuing institution which has no enemies."[5] The battle was over the details, not whether roads were needed.

Postwar prosperity made full use of the roads in the meantime, and the national landscape was transformed. Although the political maneuvering during the many years of discussions for road building in Washington had plenty of challenges regarding details, the project for building the interstate system enjoyed overwhelming support. Secretary of the Treasury George M. Humphrey, whom Richard Davies labels an "archconservative," gave his fiscal blessing: "America lives on wheels, and we have to provide the highways to keep America living on wheels and keep the kind and form of life we want."[6] Humphrey's line is helpful—"America lives on wheels"—and those wheels require an extensive and ambitious road system to keep them rolling to perpetuate the "life we want." Americans ran headlong and smiling toward that life, and the most powerful of our stories assess its effects over and over again.

Although the push for good roads had been an ongoing political battle since automobiles and bicycles started moving around urban centers and across rural areas, it was the postwar push that would be truly transformative. Only then would the political, economic, and social forces asserting a genuinely national and comprehensive vision take hold. The localized and regional battles for better and more roads had already resulted in many changes to the American landscape throughout the nation, including some limited-access highways in the form of toll roads and turnpikes. The 1950s provided the setting wherein arguments for a nationalized system and the money to make it happen could be secured and the dream realized. Automakers in Detroit played a significant role in popularizing the notion of an interstate system of "freeways," a name and policy intended to stand in direct opposition to toll roads like the Pennsylvania Turnpike and others. All cultural mythologies depend on a range of interests to solidify the popular imagination, and, of course, the major automakers had an obvious interest in encouraging an aggressive campaign for road-building across the nation. Nice, new cars are rather useless without nice, new roads. And "free" roads encourage more car travel, which leads to more car purchases.

From public service films to sales brochures, from magazine and newspaper advertisements to extravaganzas of entertainment events like Motorama and Powerama, automakers pushed to make their product central to the postwar American dream. In 1951 the public relations department of General Motors published a promotional pamphlet to correspond with an informational film in support of the push for a national road system. It was titled *Let's Get Out of the Muddle* (fig. 2.1). If any readers were perplexed by the rather odd title, the cover image most certainly provided clarity.[7] The message emphasizes a nation at risk due to an overcrowded and underperforming road system. This "muddle" could stymie national dreams of mobility and snarl it in traffic. Featuring pedestrians surrounded, even trapped, by cars whose drivers are likewise caught in a traffic jam, and a police officer seemingly overwhelmed by the mess, the image implies mobility rendered impotent by inadequate infrastructure.

Fig 2.1. *Let's Get Out of the Muddle.* General Motors Department of Public Relations, Detroit, Michigan, 1951. GM Heritage Center.

The introduction is written by Albert Bradley, executive vice president of General Motors and chairman of the National Highway Users Conference. He argues that "the American economy rolls on gravel, black top and concrete roads. Every day more and more people are on the road, more and more goods are moved from place to place." Bradley celebrates the fact that the United States has more roads and cars than the rest of the world combined and that core point of pride justifies the oft-repeated line he echoes: "We are a nation on wheels." However, that identity was under significant pressure, according to Bradley. He adds that "every snarl of traffic that slows our wheels, slows the work of the nation just that much."[8]

The postwar prosperity that was just gaining momentum could not be stalled by inadequate roads or, implicitly, by a lack of commitment to build for the future. In a nice rhetorical flourish, Bradley taps directly into the American mainstream family ideals by bringing the issue into the suburban home: "Well, let's get out of this jam—it's Sunday now . . . why not pack a lunch and take mom and the kids. Let's head for the *open road*."[9] Although he is obviously pushing for aggressive policies to build more roads, he deftly employs the dream of mobility in his rhetoric. He is not simply talking about protecting the movement of commerce or military vehicles. Rather, he is talking about basic mainstream values as illustrated by a Sunday drive with "mom and the kids." Bradley then closes the rhetorical trap: "What 'open road'? . . . Try to find one!"

General Motors also released a promotional film in 1954 titled *Give Yourself the Green Light*, which parallels the message of *Let's Get Out of the Muddle*.[10] The brief opening title sequence features an animated traffic light, which quickly fades to a live-action aerial shot of a limited-access highway, traffic moving smoothly, with the following voiceover: "This is the American dream of freedom on wheels, an automotive age traveling on timesaving superhighways." The film goes on to note that such highways are far too few in number and overall mileage to handle the needs of a robust nation on wheels. The current system could no longer manage what the voice calls the "the mounting traffic of our growing greatness."[11] *Give Yourself the Green Light* is a formidable artifact of the ongoing effort of GM to sway cultural debates over road building, a compelling film whose copy picks up on the same themes as the earlier pamphlet. Both argue for an active effort to redress overbearing traffic congestion. These public relations outreach efforts contributed to the consciousness of the political debates and added to the mythology of the open road. In both productions, the key emotional argument is one that defines the road as essential to freedom. The "growing greatness" of the United States has become inextricably tied to the strengthening of our commitment to automobility. Moreover, that greatness is directly aligned with individual mobilities: "Give *yourself* the green light" (emphasis mine).

Ford Motor Company followed a similar path and for the same reasons. Its major public outreach effort was a film and related book published in 1956. The title captures the point without ambiguity or subtlety: *Freedom of the American Road*.[12] The book is a collection of essays penned by varied authors, all promoting a national highway system. Containing a prefatory letter signed by Henry Ford II, the book was sent out to Ford dealerships with directions for dealers to make it available to their communities; *Freedom of the American Road* also went out to two hundred thousand prominent Americans. The book and the accompanying film are less artful than the GM efforts but follow the common goal and narrative theme reflected in the title.

Its introduction was written by renowned historian and literary scholar Bernard DeVoto, who had already demonstrated himself to be adept at exploring large cultural themes. *The Course of Empire* earned the National Book Award for nonfiction in 1953, and he followed that success as editor of *The Journals of Lewis and Clark* later that year. Much of DeVoto's work demonstrates a keen interest in the American West, which served him well in this corporate writing task. The introduction to *Freedom of the American Road* follows similar themes, echoing the grand narratives of his earlier works and unequivocally applying them to the postwar enthusiasm for automobility. DeVoto offers a compelling statement that captures the emotional aspirations of the project far better than the rest of the book does. The following is especially instructive: "There is no more fascinating experience than to watch the construction of a highway, and no more illuminating experience than to spend a few hours on a rise above one watching the most mobile people go by on their businesses and pleasures. One comes to perceive that the American road represents a way of life. . . . In no other nation is the motorized transport of people and freight so interstitial in everyone's daily life, in his business, his diet, his solvency, his recreation, even in his daydreams."[13] DeVoto's imagery here places the modern automotive landscape firmly in the traditions so prominent and effusive in nineteenth-century nature writing and landscape art.

Also a scholar of Mark Twain, the most beloved American writer of the late nineteenth century, DeVoto draws on the aspirational use of landscape to evoke a grand vision. He places readers on a hill looking over a modernized landscape of automobiles that echoes nineteenth-century preindustrial idylls expressed by Twain through the boyhood dream-visions of Tom Sawyer or Huck Finn. Likewise, this tableau evokes the landscape imagery made resonant by the paintings of Thomas Cole or Frederic Church. DeVoto celebrates the roadways of the twentieth century, suggesting without irony that the interstate highway system can be viewed on par with the great rivers of the earlier age, the Mississippi and the Hudson.

In his closing paragraph in which he describes the task of building a better road infrastructure, DeVoto muses that the new mobility provided by an interstate project would reveal the true unified potential of the nation: "It begins in front of our house but it will end by loosing the threads which bind the giant so that he can use his full strength—for the first time."[14] This rather ambitious imagery makes a powerful connection between our own driveways and the "giant" of American mobility itself. With the full measure of confidence earned by victory in World War II and heightened consumerist expectations emboldened by the previous twenty years of sublimated desire, Americans were eager to move. At long last, they had the economic, political, and imaginative power to do so in vast numbers and with ever-increasing speed. They would do so on bigger and better roads.

As automakers used ads and promotional media to encourage wide support for aggressive roadbuilding, and as political leaders, locally and nationally, wrangled over putting together road-building packages for America's "growing greatness," journalists engaged with the ongoing efforts as well. One of the most sustained attempts to follow the debate came from Richard Thruelsen mentioned previously, who wrote several articles for the *Saturday Evening Post* in 1955 and 1956, all analyzing issues surrounding impending federal highway legislation. In "Coast to Coast without a Stoplight," Thruelsen picks up on the same enthusiasm offered by GM and Ford and offers readers a substantive look at the promises of a robust limited-access highway system. In his opening paragraph Thruelsen writes, "Public Law 627, known as the Federal-Aid Highway Act of 1956, represents such a monumental conception of national public works that its accomplishment will literally dwarf any previous work of man."[15] He reflects the overarching confidence that the project elicited from many constituencies.

As the article moves on, he makes revealing comparisons in elaborating his claim that the roads will "dwarf any previous work of man." Thruelsen addresses the planned timetable for completion in fifteen years (1956–1972): "Does fifteen years sound like a protracted work schedule to you? It took the Romans 500 years to build the 50,000 miles of their famous single-lane highway system; in the Interstate System alone we'll be building some 150,000 lane-miles of incomparably superior road in about one fortieth of that time." He goes on: "If the crushed stone to be used for the base of the roads constructed under the new program were to be dumped in conical piles, you could form 500 pyramids, each the size of Cheops—four city blocks square and rising to the height of a forty-story building."[16] Thruelsen's optimism serves to exalt the inherent and persistent connections made in the public imagination tying automobility in the 1950s with the destiny of the United States. This message arises so often and in so many forums that it—like the phrase "open road" itself—becomes an irreducible truth that is self-evident throughout American culture at midcentury.

That a massive federal program remaking the land to accelerate the new mobility would transform the culture was accepted without real qualification by most people. Thruelsen was no exception. The stated assumptions granted much leeway to those envisioning a mobile future. The following passage is instructive as to the optimistic, even utopian, dreams surrounding the interstates and the blindness to the possible pessimistic view regarding how the system could affect the national landscape:

> Though cutting traffic corridors through the hearts of our cities may at first seem like a horrendous economic waste, the experience of highway planners to date has proved that such developments actually profit every section of the urban community. Property holders on the expressway sites are paid a fair sum for their equities, while land adjacent to expressways invariably increases in value. Most important, the combination of the inner-city expressways and the belt lines enables the city to spread its former boundaries of convenience and creates new realty values in all directions. A happy by-product of all these expressway developments is that they invariably do an excellent job of slum clearance as they knife through the poorer sections of the city.[17]

His uncritical dismissal of the potential negative effects of what he blithely terms "slum clearance" sounds obnoxious to readers more familiar with the contributions to urban decay made by dissecting many American cities by the end of the twentieth century. In his enthusiastic support, he unwittingly brings up key issues that have plagued urban development in subsequent generations, beginning most substantively in the 1970s—incoherence created by roads slicing through cities, profiteering by landowners with little benefits to others, and loss of neighborhoods, among other problems. He notes that roads "profit every section of the urban community" but discusses only landholders. Suburban sprawl and the expansion of the "boundaries of convenience" beyond the capacity of other facets of city infrastructure and financial coffers have had many catastrophic effects on cities. Detroit, not so ironically, is a perennial example. He calls the removal of poor people a "happy by-product." Though there is no way to deny the inattentive blindness revealed in the passage, it stands in evidence of the overall dream proffered by the interstate system on the whole.

The celebratory narrative becomes more evident as Thruelsen continues. He provides a list of transformations in several major American cities, each example indicating positive urban renewal: "Boston's circumferential expressway, Route 128, which loops around the city ten miles from its center, has created industrial and housing sites worth millions in what was formerly marginal farmland. Houston's freeway to Galveston has developments hugging its route far beyond the city limits, while the Los Angeles Santa Ana Freeway has spawned a whole complex of communities in the dry farmland to the south of the city. What this all proves, of course, is that it is travel time and not distance which governs the growth of urban and suburban areas. The projected expressways should create enough new wealth to pay for themselves many times over."[18] Viewing the interstate system and automobility writ large as simply "new wealth" without noting potential costs strikes later readers differently, especially as the social and environmental costs became much more apparent. The key point here, though, is that Thruelsen's vision of the mobile future had few detractors, and he faithfully captures a cultural optimism that helped to shape the open-road ideal. He closes the essay by noting that construction has already begun (the first official work began August 10, 1956, in Missouri), writing, "With a little luck and lots of cooperation from everyone, we'll be riding from coast to coast and from border to border without a stop light or a traffic snarl by 1972."[19] The dividends and the costs for the interstate transformation of the American road system were many. The essential point here is how Thruelsen captures an unfettered optimism as the nation looked forward with immense hope.

The road is a physical entity and a symbolic idea. Both components are essential to our perceptions. As physical phenomena, roads are constructed from varying substances—concrete and asphalt (to use the most generic terms). They also often include paint for lanes and essential and nonessential demarcations. They inhabit specific spaces (geographical) on the earth's surface. Moreover, they crumble and decay; they buckle in heat and become slick in rain. They go straight and wind left and right; they go up, down, and around hills; they begin and end. But that is not all. They are also complemented by a vast range of physical artifacts directly and indirectly related to their existence—signs, medians, rest stops, diners, gas stations, produce stands. Roads are meeting places for strangers eliciting many social interactions—friendly waves, gestures of anger, loud music or loud mufflers, the moments after a wreck or during a traffic jam, and so on. Roads are also places of isolation wherein drivers can be wholly self-absorbed while being surrounded by numerous similarly absorbed people. The road implies destinations and departures. We use them to go, to escape, and to return. Roads cross boundaries and connect places and peoples. Roads have lanes and lines and edges. Roads imply freedom of movement and choice, but they are constructed along a prefigured course. Drivers may choose *whether* to follow a road but not *where* it leads. The road is also a persistent metaphor, the road as life. This metaphor has no boundaries. Its strength is its simplicity. The road disappears in the deep back of the frame, but our dreams are on the multitude of horizons implied for everyone immersed in its inspirational message.

Yet there is also the cold, hard fact that the asphalt ends, or turns, or buckles, or collapses. There are roadblocks and exits, speed limits and detours, stops for gas and restroom breaks. And there is always traffic. Such uncomfortable realities do not erase the open-road dream. They demand consideration, however, for the dream to have any sustaining meaning for us beyond sentiment alone. This is not a challenge to open-road mythology, which is deepened by the physical limitations of our roads. We blend practical and metaphorical experiences. This perhaps uneasy conjunction is not simply tied to our roads but also to how we move along them. We may dream of horizons, but we must reckon with the actual road beneath the tires. Our emotional and physical attachments to roads—our road imaginary—exists, nonetheless, always in direct relation to our intimacy with automobiles.

THE AUTOMOBILE IMAGINARY

Automobility, as seen by many, restored the traveling autonomy that had been thwarted by the primary driver of the frontier dream, the steam-powered engine. The automobile promised a return to a more individualized travel—more akin to the romantic imagery of riding horseback—than did the routes and schedules required by trains and steamboats. Along these lines, Patton makes an important point: "The automobile arrived in a world already settled by the railroad, which had opened and then closed the frontier. While it quickly took on the same air of historical inevitability, . . . the automobile from its beginnings was not associated so much with a vision of some modernistic future, but with the restoration of old values—the values of the frontier and the individual. It was seen through the eyes of nostalgia as a way to return to lost freedoms and a lost sense of the discovery of America."[20] No timetables, no tracks, no tickets—the automobile allowed Americans to take control of the wheel and choose their own routes, their own timetables, and thus engendered into our imaginations the notion of absolute freedom. As a technology, as a consumer product, and as a way of life, automobiles would have no competition in the twentieth century. Even approaching the end of the first quarter of the new millennium, the car reigns supreme.

The centrality of automobility, though long recognized as inevitable, became the mainstream mark of normalcy in postwar America. *Consumer Reports* (*CR*) magazine, which has served as a measure of consumerism since 1936, is an especially useful window into the shifting culture. *CR* evaluates and validates material culture by providing ostensibly objective information to consumers for a wide array of products. A 1956 article, "20 Years in Review, 1936–1956," provides a brief overview of the trends in the first twenty years of the magazine's history. In a section called "Love that car," *CR* notes the following: "Probably no product, in its changed position, has had a greater impact on consumers and on the economy in the past 20 years than the auto. Americans become greater car lovers each year, a love which really bloomed with the sale blitz of 1955." The article goes on to note that car ownership has become a "hard necessity" for the American family. Citing the Automobile Manufacturers Association, the article asserts that "88% of the new car buying families use their automobile to drive to work" and also that just under a third of "new car buyers owned two or more cars."[21]

As the automobile became intrinsic to the daily lives of increasing numbers of American families, it likewise became intertwined with a vast portion of the entire economy and thus became formidable fuel for the postwar boom. *CR* made this point succinctly, noting that "American automobile production is the biggest manufacturing venture in the world."[22] By the mid-1950s, automobility was intricately associated with American economic fortunes and inextricably woven into the fabric of an emerging value system. The article also reasserts the accepted reality that the automobile had already become a practical necessity for a vast swath of Americans. Automotive sales set records in 1955, and, though they would ebb and flow in the ensuing decades, the transition to an American way of life devoted to automobility was completed in the mid-1950s, those golden years of bright colors and glorious chrome bumpers. Americans from hence forward would see themselves, see each other, and see the country in reference to automobiles. Harlow Curtice, president of General Motors at the time, while announcing formidable expansion plans to accommodate soaring demand, noted quite intuitively that the company's growth programs reflected "faith in our country."[23]

The faith was well placed. The increasing mobility of the nation was built around demographics and shifting paradigms. As *CR* notes, "What with more people moving into the suburbs, and with a sizable crop of teenagers coming along, two car families, say auto makers, will be behind the times soon. The up-and-coming thing, the trade press reports, will be a drive to put *three* cars into every garage."[24] Although the writers of *CR* may have been too bullish regarding three-car households, the facts bear out a clear movement to two-car households as a baseline standard for suburban America. The spreading out of American metropolitan centers made car dependence not just alluring but necessary. When General Motors, Ford, and Chrysler expanded operations, their faith rode on the mobile aspirations of the suburban American family more than any other portion of the population. And it is to this expanding group of consumers that the major automakers made their persistent pitches. In short, automakers made American car buyers believe in every facet of that new mobile faith.

CR reveals a clear understanding of the shifting cultural landscape and illustrates how Americans were building an intimate relationship with car ownership. In an article titled "The Two-Car Family," *CR* comments, "Two cars go particularly well with small-town or suburban living. The lady of the house who has a car of her own needn't wake up each morning with the bleak alternative of remaining housebound for the day, or else simultaneously making breakfast, preparing the children for school, and getting herself dressed so that she can drive the man of the house to work or to the railroad station."[25] This passage shows gender coding at work, with the "lady" of the house fully responsible for the running of the household, but the implication is nonetheless evident: mobility is freedom—the opposite of the "bleak alternative" of living trapped in the home in a culture built around the car.

A few examples from GM and Ford advertisements are instructive regarding how the automakers seized on the opportunities afforded by the suburban boom. In an ad promoting the idea of buying a second car, Chevrolet taps directly into the desire for suburban families to increase their mobility. Scheduled to appear in *American Weekly*, *This Week*, and *Parade* in April of 1956, the ad captures a typical suburban scene wherein two young boys are playing "cowboys" in their driveway, tying their mother to a tree as part of the play (fig. 2.2).[26] The accompanying text touts the virtues of buying a used Chevy as a second family car. The metaphor is not nuanced. The mother is trapped because she does not have a car. An "OK Used Car" can rectify this situation: "How much of your precious time is tied up 'back at the ranch' while you wait for your husband (or *you*, sir, wait for your wife) to return home with the car so that you can put *your* plans into action?" The suburban reality for many housewives could be confining, a condition that the image of her being literally tied up makes comically clear. Of what true value, it would seem, is a spacious ranch home in the suburbs if you cannot leave it at will?

Ford proved more aggressive than GM in selling the concept of two-car families in the mid-1950s. Its ads, developed by the highly regarded J. Walter Thompson Company, often featured the slogan "Buy 2 Fords," noting that two Ford vehicles could be affordable for many growing families. The two ads represent the overall strategy of Ford in the mid-1950s. The catch phrase for both is "Two fine cars for the price of one!"[27] The ads were scheduled to run in the late summers of 1955 and 1956 and be placed in popular magazines, including *Saturday Evening Post*, *Life*, *Time*, and *Newsweek*, with the potential of reaching over 14,500,000 readers (figs. 2.3 and 2.4). These full-page ads were geared for a broad swath of Americans and take their content from core assumptions tied to middle-class values and consumer expectations.

The ads feature families on the go. The first uses an empty garage, with only tire tracks indicating absent cars, and the text reads, "This Ford went to Market while this one went to the Club." The smaller inset images in the bottom half of the ad complete the scene, with the mother picking up groceries in a station wagon and the father at the golf club in a sedan. The second ad shows a family returning home from their outings, which we can safely

Fig. 2.2. "Meanwhile, back at the ranch . . ." General Motors Research Center, Sterling Heights, Michigan. Chevrolet Advertising database.

assume were conducted in support of household needs. The text touts the many benefits of becoming a "two-Ford family," noting that "when Dad goes golfing, Mother still can go shopping. When Dad heads for the office, Mother can get to her PTA luncheon." The automobile imaginary, as pitched to and eagerly embraced by middle America, was a total package, a transformative lifestyle. This cultural embrace of the new mobility was comprehensive and driven by governmental, corporate, and personal interests.

Fig. 2.3. Two fine cars 1. The Benson Ford Research Center, Dearborn, Michigan. Accession 19, box 32, 1955 T–Z folder.

Fig. 2.4. Two fine cars 2. The Benson Ford Research Center, Dearborn, Michigan. Accession 19, box 32, 1956 T folder.

Automakers, while most certainly the largest and most aggressive purveyors of mobility dreams, were by no means the only corporate players. Cars need roads, but they also need gasoline. The Ethyl Corporation's contribution to building the automobile imaginary paralleled the contributions of the automakers by providing advertisements in print media touting the happiness attained by being on the move. Their slogan was simple: "Drive More."[28] The campaign argues for a family life rendered fully mobile, wherein, as the ad suggests, families can "make every weekend an extra vacation." The text continues, "You can have forty-nine extra vacations a year! Just take advantage of your weekends. Get in your car and go . . . to see new places, new faces and enjoy extra hours of leisure and pleasure."[29] The new mobility represented the postwar dream of American prosperity as indicated by growing material wealth, technological advancements, and robust industrial output. Bigger and better vehicles were churned out of the assembly lines in Detroit, making their way to the driveways in bustling suburbs. To vacations, to jobs, to stores, to church, to PTA meetings, Americans were on the move in big cars and with big dreams, entering a world of tomorrow, their happiness ensured simply by driving more.

Implicit in the discussion above is that the ideal American car is the family sedan, with the key term being "family." By extension—metaphorically and physically—the station wagon would become the more stereotypical vehicle for family convenience. In both cases, the success of such vehicles arose from their clear and practical association with the needs of the nuclear family, the center of the stable mode of mobility. Although family-friendly vehicles drove the overall market and thus evoked the dominant portion of the automobile imaginary, other vehicles also competed for a place within the American imagination. The tensions therefore between idealized family cars and other types of vehicles, namely motorcycles and hot rods, illustrate the overarching tensions between stability and subversion. In short, we are what we drive. While automakers were busy promoting the building of more intricate road systems and of more family cars, other vehicles were also traveling those roads, and they were doing so for not-so-stable purposes.

Perhaps the best way to assess that dynamic is to consider the American relationship with a mode of transportation that serves as touchstone for conflicting cultural values: the motorcycle. To this day, the motorcycle enjoys (and suffers from) a paradoxical symbolic identity within road mythology. It is first and foremost the perfect motorized symbol of freedom implied by the term open road. Yet it is also a pervasive symbol of subversion antagonistic to stable postwar dreams. In other words, mainstream Americans love the idea of the motorcycle in theory but often fear those who choose to ride them. Likewise, many riders choose that mode of transportation not only as a statement of individuality but also as a more aggressive evocation of disdain for mainstream culture. Motorcycles elicit sharp differences of opinion from all parts of American culture.

As with automobiles, motorcycles began as playthings for privileged classes, a new vehicle for leisure-based adventure.[30] As automobiles spread in popularity and quickly became mainstream thanks to Henry Ford and the Model T, the motorcycle remained elusive and even dubious for most Americans—both too expensive and completely impractical for families.[31] Although always on the periphery of American consciousness, after World War II the motorcycle gained notoriety as increasingly anathema to middle America. From the late 1940s until the early 1970s, the motorcycle owner was most often presented "as a free-spirited white male wearing black leather, boots, and denim" who lived "a rebellious lifestyle that threatens mainstream American values."[32] The first non-leisure adopters of motorcycling were returning veterans who had been introduced to motorcycles during the war effort and were not inclined to settle down into a standard family life preferred by most.

In contrast, many young people took to the open road with a machine that emphasized their independence. As a result, a subculture of bikers developed that was decidedly male and in stark contrast to the domesticity being pushed by the culture at large in all facets of popular culture. Although these veteran bikers began as law-abiding citizens (and most remained that way), by the mid-1950s the stereotype interlocking motorcycles with scofflaw behavior was solidly entrenched.[33] We should keep in mind the Cold War context here that made mainstream Americans so reactionary to any subculture value system that implied disdain for their choices. In a time of profound fear of mass destruction both real and imagined, any contesting of dominant expectations could be easily inflated as a challenge to social order or even as a threat to national security.[34] Popular media helped push this fear through both sensationalized news coverage and popular entertainment. For most Americans, the activities of bikers were no longer simply rebellious but also dangerous.

One especially provocative article earned significant national attention when published in 1947. Appearing in *Life*—one of the most widely read magazines in the nation—a short article told of trouble caused by roving gangs of bikers in Hollister, California, during the town's Fourth of July celebration. The story, "Cyclist's Holiday," had a significant impact on the growing negative opinion of bikers, which carried much more sinister implications than the title implied. According to the *Life* article, more than four thousand bikers descended on the town and wreaked havoc. "Police arrested many for drunkenness and indecent exposure but could not restore order."[35]

The key phrase is "could not restore order," a message carrying unsettling implications. An unseemly photograph accompanied the article. It featured an apparently drunken man perched precariously on his bike and facing the camera while holding a beer bottle at the ready. Strewn on the ground around the bike are numerous broken bottles and crumpled cans of beer. The photograph, which was staged, helped to solidify unflattering images of motorcycle enthusiasts in the mainstream mind. By all subsequent accounts, the photograph and the content of the article grossly exaggerated the menace to society posed by bikers. The story nonetheless indicated broader potential for chaos, made more problematic by the apparent inability of the forces of law and order to handle the threat.

"Cyclist's Holiday" had an impressive capacity for reincarnation. A few years later, another prominent story in a national mainstream publication further fueled the growing fear of biker culture. A short story written by Frank Rooney and titled "Cyclists' Raid" enthralled readers by telling about a roving band of bikers who rode into a peaceful town and terrorized its citizens. Rooney's rather mundane work of fiction derived from the Hollister incident. For a quick example of how such media events can evolve, we should note that the original *Life* article was titled "Cyclist's Holiday," and Rooney in his fictional account opts to replace "holiday" with "raid." Although a fictionalized narrative appearing in *Harper's*, the story nonetheless carried significant heft in affirming the public's fear of biker subculture. One of the readers of Rooney's short story was filmmaker Stanley Kramer. Inspired by the bikers-gone-wild story, Kramer produced one of the most iconic American films of the 1950s, *The Wild One*, directed by László Benedek and starring Marlon Brando. Although not an immediate popular success, the film further agitated many Americans and solidified the stereotype of bikers as the film gained a stronger foothold in the American grain and as Brando's own fame increased. His brooding angst played well on a motorcycle.

Although there were numerous media representations of outlaw bikers before *The Wild One*, it defined the outlaw image like no other. According to Chris Hodenfield in *Cycle* magazine, "Overnight every motorcyclist in America acquired a mean and shifty reputation."[36] An iconic subversive star was born in Brando, but it was the motorcycle that was most assuredly typecast as a dangerous force on the American road. The film opens with a warning for viewers: "This is a shocking story. It could never take place in most American towns but it did in this one. It is a public challenge not to let it happen again."[37] Despite the qualifier that "it could never take place" everywhere, the message carries the opposite implication: chaos can rumble into *your* town at any time. For mainstream drivers, the same roads that allowed culturally affirming, stable travel could also support culturally subversive travel rumbling into any town. The basic plot frame for the film undermines the core positive assumptions of expanding national road systems. The image is reversed, emphasizing not the expansion of stability but the intrusion of unwelcome Americans into those now-vulnerable small towns.

The opening sequence was particularly effective, as leather-clad bikers filled the screen. Though for twenty-first-century viewers, they come across more comic than dangerous, viewers in the 1950s were expected to see a clear and imminent danger headed their way. This effect is accentuated by the directorial choice to film the bikers moving directly toward the camera, implicitly moving into audience space. By the mid-1950s, the motorcycle had become a powerful wedge revealing the split in an American culture built around the generation gap, class tensions, and ideas of "normalcy" and "deviance." *The Wild One* exploited an uneasy strain between the ambitions promoted by mainstream culture, on one hand, and the rejection of that push for conformity, on the other. The two dominating and often contradictory strands in American open-road culture—the stable and the subversive—are themselves evidence of a paradox. The road as an idea is a unifying concept, but it encourages priorities among its devotees that imply disunity. The stable dream is one of mainstream adherence to shared values and fears; the subversive dream rebuffs deference to rules that restrict individual will. The stable road leads to prosperity and order; the subversive road leads to autonomy and spontaneity. These words, however, carry both positive and negative implications for everyone: order means stability but also control; spontaneity means free-flowing choice but also chaos. The core dichotomy in American culture is revealed by the two modes.

The overarching challenge to stability represented by the motorcycle is evident in its basic design. As discussed above, the phrase "family sedan," though pervasive, is nonetheless redundant. Everything about its design and style is geared toward stability. The motorcycle stands in complete opposition to the characteristics of a sedan in that it does not stand on its own at all. A Chevrolet Bel Air sedan is in perfect balance and can sit in a driveway steadfast. On the other hand, a motorcycle, without a kickstand, falls over. Moreover, the motorcycle, though it can accommodate a passenger, is built for an individualized experience, an exhilaration fully offered to the driver alone. Add to this existential fact of design the cultural use of the motorcycles as a hyper-individualized mode of transport in media and art—wherein riders gather not in families but in gangs—and an inescapable fact becomes clear: in the automobile imaginary, the motorcycle typifies subversion.

Automobility draws meaning from how we understand the roads we travel on and the vehicles we travel in (or on). We assert ourselves and determine how we see the world and how the world perceives us. Roads and vehicles (cars and motorcycles) are practical and metaphorical. A third imaginary is crucial to road narratives and equally dependent on perceptions. We also define the spaces we pass through in negotiation with those vehicles and roads. Our surroundings become places vital to our mobile existence. We move perpetually in intrinsic and intimate contact with ever-evolving landscapes of imagination.

THE LANDSCAPE IMAGINARY

The American landscape has often been tied to human aspirations. It therefore plays a vital part in defining the American open road, granting an appropriately vast and variable setting for mobile experiences. Ronald Primeau writes, "Space on the road is not a passive background or a completed scene travelers merely pass through but is itself an evolving interaction of the pastoral landscape and cultural symbols."[38] The creation and appreciation of landscape imagery has long been central to mobility, as it provides the moment of discovery and meaning for all who travel into the unfamiliar—explorers, emigrants, and tourists alike. Thus it forms the third imaginary of American automobility.

Even in an age of motorized travel often at high speeds, the landscape remains an active component in road mythology, not simply as background but also as a dynamic space. It completes a crucial interaction that combines physical and symbolic tensions for travelers and the places they briefly inhabit. Edward Relph writes that "character and meaning are imputed to landscapes by the intentionality of experience." What we want from landscape affects what we find. He continues, noting that the natural surroundings along the road are "therefore always imbued with meanings that come from how and why we know them."[39] Landscapes are in a constant push and pull regarding our expectations emanating from automobility. The physical environment that surrounds us, both natural and human-made, is experienced as we are moving. A place, therefore, is not simply defined by a static image, a postcard from the edge of the road. It is also a blur of space encountered as we speed past. Landscape, as a framed image of our surroundings, comes into focus when we stop, but it also may be given meaning by the very fact that we may not stop at all. In all cases, the landscape related to any given road or vehicle provides more than a backdrop or setting; it is also catalyst.

All road encounters arise from our perceptions of self and place, catalyzed by mobility, so "experiences of perceptual space are fleeting and unexceptional," according to Relph, and "no less important for that, for it is these personal experiences of space that are the basis for much of the meaning that environments and landscapes have for us."[40] When "fleeting" moments are represented in narrative, they become lasting both personally and socially.

They become cultural productions that translate directly into the creation of iconic images and formulaic moments of discovery. These otherwise "fleeting" impressions always have the potential to carry profound implications as settings for human drama. Often such moments participate in a longer cultural narrative that has determined the value of that place along with how we should respond to it. To harken back to the earlier discussion of the Grand Canyon, individuals experience personal interactions with the space they encounter while also being influenced by the cultural assessment of that place; the Grand Canyon is a national park hosting millions of visitors annually with a publicly recognized name that asserts its value as "grand."

The personal is always intersecting with the public, rendering interactions with individually new but culturally familiar places complicated. The landscape is forever imagined space as well as physical phenomenon. It is a place; the road is a place; the vehicle is a place. All are in flux and *becoming* moment after moment along the road. Automobility as presented pervasively in advertising by the automakers in the mid-1950s again provides a useful guide to cultural assumptions defining American mobility. Although one would expect that ads would feature the vehicles in question, of equal importance to the narratives implicit in such ads is how the American landscape is depicted. In a telling, consistent pattern, the imagery dominant in print advertising harkens back to a pastoral America. It steadily draws on longstanding popularity of grand panoramas representative of the grand potential of the United States itself.

The iconography of the American landscape became fully established in the nineteenth century and remained a vital part of the public imagination.[41] Our natural surroundings have always served as emblems of national greatness and potential, and that context became especially popular in the mid-nineteenth century with the work of painters like Thomas Cole, Frederic Church, and Albert Bierstadt, among many others. Such painters, along with other graphic artists in various mediums, cast the vastness and fecundity of the American landscape as representative of the social and political potential of the growing nation. The so-called Hudson River School painters, as well as Romantic literary figures and travel writers of the nineteenth century, framed the American landscape and demonstrated how Americans should see it—infused with spiritual implications and political ideology and always undergirded by powerful emotion. The paintings, taken as a whole, while offering much variety of scene and individual style, are also highly formulaic, marked by conventions that resonated with audiences. If Americans struggled with insecurities regarding their place in the world, especially in comparison with Europe, the potential implied by the natural landscape served to assuage those fears.

Romantic visual artists and writers gave Americans a way to interpret landscape in direct relation to a sense of destiny for the nation at large. When American landscape painters embraced romantic framing conceits, they infused them with a cultural and political resonance tied to American optimism and expansionism. The paintings can be seen as inextricable from the political ideals expressed in shorthand as manifest destiny, landscape becoming a primary actor in human drama. They became chroniclers tracking the course of empire over a land whose romanticized vistas ultimately supported that hopeful progression. Although the practical infrastructure tied to roads, rails, and rivers allowed Americans to move and consume picturesque landscapes as an ideal experience, the aesthetics of paintings, as well as popular literature, was most crucial in promoting landscape iconography.

Mobility in the nineteenth century ensured the popularizing of landscape as representation for American progress. John Sears, in *Sacred Places*, an especially compelling study of tourism in the nineteenth century, asserts that tourism "demands a body of images and descriptions of those places—a mythology of unusual things to see—to excite people's imaginations and induce them to travel."[42] Writers and artists, he goes on to note, "informed Americans of the nature of these places and encouraged the touristic habit of consuming scenery as a series of views."[43] The aesthetic and the practical are both necessary to create the American landscape as an emblem for the hopes of the nation. Such imagery was interwoven into the fabric of American culture well beyond art and literature and into every facet of life. The characteristics of this romantic imagery and the overarching cultural implications of their popularity carried into the automotive age. For the mid-twentieth century, the same ideals were adapted to the new mobility as Conestoga wagons and trains were replaced by automobiles. Artists followed well-established tropes as they incorporated the automobile and the paved road seamlessly into the grand scale of the American landscape. Such imagery is not incidental or showy backdrop filler. To the contrary, it is central to the imaginary, securing automobility within the public desire. Note, for example, a full-page ad by Chevrolet from 1955 (fig. 2.5).[44]

Complementing the graceful lines of the newly designed bright yellow sedan is the wonderfully detailed panorama afforded by the prominent vantage point. We gaze over a vast, fertile valley in the middle distance and forested land running up the frame into a lake situated in the foothills, then a mountain range framed by billowy clouds in the far distance. This image evokes not only the vastness of the nation but also its productivity popularized in the nineteenth century. The bisecting four-lane highway modernizes this verdant scene: the land, the road, the car—all integrated components of open-road mythology.

Fig. 2.5. 1955 Chevy. General Motors Research Center, Sterling Heights, Michigan. Chevrolet Advertising database.

Ford also tapped into landscape power for its midcentury publicity. In October of 1955, a full-page ad was scheduled to run in mainstream magazines including *Saturday Evening Post*, *Life*, *Colliers*, and *U.S. News & World Report*, with the potential of reaching over twenty-three million subscribers.[45] To promote the 1956 models, the ad incorporates the landscape imaginary (fig. 2.6). The tableau presented perfectly harmonizes the beauty, power, and safety in the design of the Ford vehicles, the smooth efficiency of the new highways, and the ever-bountiful American landscape. This Ford ad squeezes other models into the scene, a station wagon and the popular Thunderbird sports coupe, but they are additional elements of the symbolically rich natural imagery presented here.

Fig. 2.6. New '56 Ford. Benson Ford Research Center, Dearborn, Michigan. Accession 19, box 60, 1956 J–N folder.

The panoramic landscape is a substantive part of the persuasive intent of the imagery. The long road trailing behind the car and curving pleasingly into a pastoral rural scene and the peaceful foothills rolling endlessly are seemingly reaching toward the horizon. Likewise, the stylized vehicles, by suggestion, move smoothly along a limited-access highway. These are all elements of American iconography of nature complementing the sales pitch of the advertisement. GM and Ford are focused, first and foremost, on selling their vehicles. The two corporations are engaged in an intense corporate battle, yet the ads agree about one assumption: the idyllic landscape is an emblem of American greatness and thus a fulcrum on which each sales pitch depends.

Automotive advertising captures the optimism of the 1950s like no other part of American culture. Within its clichés and tropes is the energy that drives the open road in the popular imagination. Of course, the goal for all such ads is the same: to sell cars. But cars, second only to homes in the typical family budget, are sold by ensuring that the machines are alive within our dreams of contentment. To this day, the same images, with only slight variations of the theme, permeate the print and video promotions of the many automakers. The cars are stylish and technologically advanced, the highways are efficient and free of congestion, and the landscape is a marvel.

* * *

The narratives emanating from the new mobile culture that exploded in the American popular imagination in the postwar years explore the constant interplay between road, automotive, and landscape imaginaries. The experiences that would be represented in a range of narratives created for page and screen immersed audiences into this imaginative framing to modernize the road for an age defined by automobility. The stories of the American open road assert individual dreams in response to the tensions associated with stability and subversion, but they also reflect the interplay between self and place as enacted on an increasingly mobile stage. The resulting narratives, therefore, adopt and expand familiar patterns and conventions that merit consideration so we can better understand the stories we tell along the open road.

Part II

Conventions of Road Narrative

3

Seeing the Horizon

The Liminal Road

DEFINING THE ROAD NARRATIVE

The previous chapters established the open road as an idea with imaginative power and practical connections to the rise of automobility in those crucial years following World War II. The task now is to delve into the patterns of the road narrative as a vibrant response to that transformation. The American road narrative as a literary and filmic genre resists easy definition.[1] That is both its challenge and a reason for its ongoing popularity. The open road—as physical reality and as expansive metaphor—is wonderfully adaptive to a wide range of personal and political contexts. It is useful for artistic expression in that it allows for and encourages intimate and panoramic ways of seeing the world. The profound grip that road stories have on American culture indicates how persistently Americans embrace the open road and its varying narrative expressions.

Travel writing, with its formidable history, provides the overarching structure of the road narrative, which freely adopts its patterns and assumptions. Stories that follow a person on the move combine a range of rhetorical approaches, including elements of fiction, journalism, memoir, autobiography, history, and philosophy.[2] The road narrative likewise mixes a little bit of everything, with the potential for shifts in form and content as often as the ground shifts underneath a motorized point of view. That does not mean that only travel in internal combustion engines apply. Rather, it simply means that such vehicles are the dominating norm within the culture explored by any narrative in question, and mobility is thus framed by the centrality of car culture. By way of illustration, let us consider a few quick examples.

Jack Kerouac's *On the Road* manipulates core expectations of automobility throughout the narrative, but we often see Sal Paradise, the narrator, in motion, but not in automobiles. Yet when he walks along the highway, he is still very much a part of car culture, always looking for a ride. The meaning implied by any walking or bicycle-riding Sal performs derives from how such acts contrast to the automobility that defines his world. In the film *Forrest Gump*, based on the novel by Winston Groom, the titular character embarks on a jogging odyssey across America. Despite the fact that he does not drive, he moves on roads paved for the use of automobiles and thus in direct association with and in conscious contrast to a culture dominated by automobility. He gains notoriety due to his unintentional subversion of automotive norms. In Cormac McCarthy's *The Road*, we encounter a post-apocalyptic America wherein cars no longer function, but the roads remain, degraded and in disuse. The horrific new normal of the United States is defined by the comprehensive loss of automobility but also the ongoing desire (need) to keep moving along the crumbling road system nonetheless. In another apocalyptic film, *The War of the Worlds*, Steven Spielberg's updated take on the H. G. Wells classic, we see a similar context.[3] The desperation caused by the wholesale destruction of automotive infrastructure defines much of the action and reveals the growing horror of the alien invasion. In the early escape from the New York metropolitan area, protagonist Ray Ferrier (Tom Cruise) has the only car that works, a stroke of luck in sharp contrast to the dominant fact of highways clogged with immobile vehicles.

Just because a narrative has cars and roads, however, does not mean it is a road narrative. Because automobility is so central to American culture beginning in the second half of the twentieth century, few are the narratives that do not reflect that reality to some degree. The defining characteristics of road narratives, therefore, must rely on the significance of automobility to any given narrative. The presence of mobility as plot device only—the equivalent of showing an airplane take off and then land to reset a scene—does not grant a text road-narrative status any more than the inclusion of someone riding a horse means that the story should be considered a Western. Other factors must be considered.

Assessing the character of any given narrative, therefore, must depend on its commitment to the road. Toward that goal, I wish to stipulate three categories—tiers—that qualify the varying levels of dependence that any given narrative owes to open-road ideals. Tier 1 includes narratives that are easily identifiable because their comprehensive structure falls unequivocally within assumed road constructs.[4] Tier 1 road narratives would include the following: nonfiction—William Least Heat-Moon's *Blue Highways*; fiction—Jack Kerouac's *On the Road*; film—*Thelma & Louise*. Such narratives are permeated by road experiences central to plot and character development. This fact is unambiguous. Because tier 1 narratives are wholly committed to and dependent on open-road tropes, they merit the most analytical attention and respect. They are not, however, the only cultural expressions of the American open road worthy of attention. Many other narratives employ significant facets of road mythology and represent the wide reach of its ideals and patterns.

Tier 2 road narratives carry more ambiguities and demonstrate less commitment to the road itself, yet they depend on it to illustrate vital issues within the broader narrative structure. This tier draws from highly varied works of literary and cinematic art making substantive use of the road in engaging ways. Such narratives have the same characteristics as those inferred by tier 1 but may devote only a portion of its thematic focus or structure to automobility. Examples include the following: nonfiction—John Howard Griffin's *Black Like Me*, Hunter Thompson's *Fear and Loathing in Las Vegas*, and Jessica Bruder's *Nomadland*; fiction—Flannery O'Connor's *Wise Blood*, Mona Simpson's *Anywhere but Here*, Neil Gaiman's *American Gods*, and C. J. Box's *The Highway*; cinematic works—*It's a Mad, Mad, Mad, Mad World*; *Rain Man*; *My Own Private Idaho*; and *Zombieland*. In such examples, the road content is often subservient to a more prominent narrative mission but nonetheless offers meaningful and extended content deriving from road conventions.

Tier 3 represents works that employ a key segment or theme dependent on open-road assumptions. The relative content may be embedded within or appended to a broader narrative or may even be tangential. In any case, it asserts a substantive meaning within the narrative and depends on audience awareness of road tropes. Included are prose works like Arthur Miller's *Death of a Salesman*; Ralph Ellison's *Invisible Man*; Donn Pearce's *Cool Hand Luke*; Stephen King's *The Stand*, *Christine* and *Desperation*; and cinematic works like *Dazed and Confused*, *The Graduate*, *Crash*, and *Barbie*, among myriad others. Tier 3 works may serve as the most wide-ranging evidence of the impact of the open road in the American imagination. They demonstrate the omnipresence of the conventions so vital to its popularity. Though the open-road mythology makes up small or seemingly incidental portions of an overall narrative devoted to other forms, its presence nonetheless indicates the broad acceptance of road-narrative patterns. Tier 3 works thus merit attention.

Road narrative conventions appear with depth and meaning in a range of creative works that have different levels of devotion to the road. By asserting a tiered system, I hope to clarify the most important characteristics of these conventions as they are realized in a variety of contexts. Tier 1 narratives offer the most substantive examples of *the* road narrative. Other stories (tiers 2 and 3) also illustrate the reach of narrative patterns. Designating tiers insists on making important distinctions while also allowing for a wider application of the subject as it appears in varying intensity in a plethora of narratives. How writers and filmmakers invoke those patterns is instructive, both to the cultural dynamics at work at the time of production and to the persistent power of common motifs and themes. Characterizing conventions does not measure clichés; to the contrary, it demonstrates the fluidity and vibrancy of the road in popular imagination. Conventions appear with meaning and depth in all tiers of road narratives, and those patterns can be defined and thereby appreciated.

ROAD NARRATIVES AND LIMINALITY

The most comprehensive convention of the road narrative arises from devotion to the experiential development of the person in motion. How a primary character engages with automobility and changes as a result of that experience is the essential narrative process. Any person in motion is in perpetual flux as determined by both the movement itself and the narrative structure that serves as the explicit rationale of each moment. In this context, the road is liminal space wherein experience is defined by a transitional state of consciousness. In his seminal study of ritualistic behaviors, *The Rites of Passage*, Arnold van Gennep establishes a three-stage process essential to the structure of rituals.[5] He refers to "rites of separation from a previous world" as "*preliminal*"; rites tied to a "transitional phase" as "*liminal* (or *threshold*)"; and rites arising from ceremonial "incorporation into the new world" as "*post-liminal*."[6] A simpler way to state these stages of liminality is as follows: (1) separation, (2) transition, and (3) incorporation. Someone on the move is in a constant state of mutability, a condition that repeatedly aligns with someone performing a cultural ritual who "wavers between two worlds."[7] This phrase is especially applicable to the inherent liminality of the road narrative, which explores not only the practical representation of people moving along roadways but also their emotional and intellectual shifts from one level of awareness to another.

The most important road narrative convention, therefore, is the presence of liminality. Unlike most ritualistic behavior, the essential liminality of the road creates a potential repeating of transitions as automobiles move and as the exigencies of narrative demand ever-changing perspectives. A person driving or riding along the road exists in a continuous liminal state, and road narratives must evoke this experiential condition. Jack Kerouac, in the tier 1 novel *On the Road*, provides an especially powerful suggestion of this context. During his first cross-country trip, Sal Paradise describes a particular moment of rest wherein he senses a transitional event. Alone in a hotel room, he awakens to an eerie feeling of confusion:

> I woke up as the sun was reddening; and that was the one distinct time in my life, the strangest moment of all, when I didn't know who I was—I was far away from home, haunted and tired with travel, in a cheap hotel room I'd never seen, hearing the hiss of steam outside, and the creak of the old wood of the hotel, and footsteps upstairs, and all the sad sounds, and I looked at the cracked high ceiling and really didn't know who I was for about fifteen strange seconds. I wasn't scared; I was just somebody else, some stranger, and my whole life was a haunted life, the life of a ghost. I was halfway across America, at the dividing line between the east of my youth and the west of my future, and maybe that's why it happened right there and then, that strange red afternoon.[8]

This passage is a particularly appealing evocation of liminality. Kerouac exploits the centrality of this idea by using Sal's geographic location to match two psychological selves, the East as past self and the West as future self. His confusion stresses his emotional unsettledness. He has lost a heretofore assumed sense of self by moving his physical self. The awakening (actual and metaphorical) occurs at the national geographic boundary between East and West but also at a moment of transition between youth and adulthood, a shift that defines many rituals. He is "halfway across America" and senses that he is on a threshold of change, a "stranger" somehow no longer able to look at his life as anything other than something belonging to a "ghost."

Likewise, in another seminal tier 1 narrative, *Blue Highways*, William Least Heat-Moon draws on the essential quality of liminality that informs experiences on the open road. "Blue highways," he explains, are the "back roads," as delineated in old maps in blue ink. More importantly, Heat-Moon imbues them with metaphoric meaning as well, claiming that in those moments just before dawn or dusk, the actual asphalt takes on "a mysterious cast of blue," wherein "the open road is a beckoning, a strangeness, a place where a man can lose himself."[9] This description found in the epigraph echoes the emotional response that Kerouac employs. Heat-Moon uses idiosyncratic phrases in this passage, choosing to write "a beckoning" and "a strangeness" rather than a more expected phrase like "a strange place beckoning us forward." He thus emphasizes the road as infused by uncertain power most evident during transitional times of day. The overall effect celebrates the essential changeovers of liminality as inherent in the open road. The "pull" is strongest just before dawn or just at dusk, those times of day denoting the flow between light and dark. The narrative that follows this opening keeps this central motif as the narrator responds to a series of similar moments, some profound, some incidental, and all tied to an evolving self.

The potential for change represented by liminality is the overarching attribute of the road narrative. As illustrated in practical and symbolic ways, how we see the world from the road is manifested in motifs made familiar not only by repetition but also by effectiveness. Distinctive perspectives elicit a range of reactions from travelers and help to reveal the complex interplay between varying points of view in expressing liminality on the road. The fundamental roadviews are: *the windshield* (the road ahead); *the mirror* (the road behind); and *the side window* (the surrounding landscape).[10] Windshields typically provide aspirational framing for implied futures. Mirrors provide retrospective framing for the past. Side windows provide ever-present framing for concurrent spatial awareness. All views are dynamic responses to the catalytic effects of mobility and the exigencies of narrative.

Though the phrasing here is drawn from the design of cars, the three roadviews take meaning from three distinctive ways of seeing from any motorized vehicle. To safely move along a road at relatively high speeds, we need to see ahead, around, and behind. To turn that movement into narrative, we need to see the same through our consciousness as well. These ways of seeing the road are all tied to and expressive of experiences that are by their very nature liminal and are thus expressed in narrative most often via emotional vibrancy.

THE WINDSHIELD ROADVIEW

The windshield is a symbol and a rhetorical device. Of the three main roadviews, the windshield is the most directly applicable to movement, the occupants looking forward. This point of view evokes the present but does so in connection with the future. It suggests, first and foremost, the road ahead with its inherent potential and associations with the horizon; the narrative "I" gazes forward but keeps referential grounding in the present moment. If all mobility is defined most simply as the movement from point A to point B, the windshield thus represents the most direct way of seeing that movement while being focused with intentionality and intensity on point B. The windshield view thus privileges destination while also being conscious of the steady alteration of self. Providing a transparent barrier between two worlds, a windshield suggests the constant state of liminality.

The windshield view invokes the metaphorical space just beyond the windshield or, in some references, the space at the front edge of the vehicle—the front bumper of a car or the front wheel of a motorcycle. In any case, the same idea extends the self to the vehicle with both in motion as one. That space immediately in front of the self is the cutting edge of experience. It is often used to emphasize the liminal moment of becoming for the road traveler. The windshield roadview has two perspectives: *looking out* and *looking in*, the first capturing the view of the protagonist(s) looking forward, and the other adopting a view from the outside of the vehicle and directed into the eyes of the protagonist(s). Though these two points of view create differences in perspective, they nonetheless assert intimacy between protagonists and audiences.

Two juxtaposed screenshots from the film *Vanishing Point*, a tier 1 road narrative, illustrate the basic applications of the windshield roadview. Marketed as "the ultimate car chase movie," *Vanishing Point*, directed by Richard Sarafian, offers a substantive narrative of liminality well beyond that of typical chase films.[11] Occurring at the end of the film, the transitional moment suggested in the first screenshot finalizes a tragic narrative. The bulldozers, shown via a looking-out windshield roadview, dominate the frame to imply total obstruction and thus represent the end of the journey. The horizon is no longer available but for a glimmer of light between the forbidding shovels of the two machines. The looking-out shot combines with the audience's awareness that the car is traveling at a high rate of speed to suggest a catastrophic moment of impact as future and present collide (fig. 3.1). In contrast, the second image employs the looking-in view to allow audiences to see directly into the face of the protagonist in a crucial moment. In general, this windshield framing is intimate, allowing voyeuristic access into the thoughts of the character in frame. In this example, Kowalski (Barry Newman) speeds toward a tragic or triumphant collision. Cutting back and forth between the two shots, Sarafian increases the suspense of the impending crash as Kowalski chooses his "vanishing point," the narrow space between the two bulldozers. We know from the looking-in shot that Kowalski embraces the moment and makes his transitional choice with a sense of purpose and contentment, and even relief (fig. 3.2). In the approach, he wavers between two worlds.

Perhaps the most well-known and provocative uses of windshield framing to suggest liminality occurs in *Thelma & Louise*, a transformational film directed by Ridley Scott based on the screenplay written by Callie Khouri. Windshield framing appears often and for varying intentions. Let us consider two shots capturing crucial threshold moments for the titular characters. In an evocative sequence, Thelma and Louise engage in a vital conversation that begins with a typical road question: "You awake?" The brief discussion that follows is far from mundane and serves as a key statement of liminality within the film. Louise responds initially as if the question simply referred to fatigue. As the conversation continues, much more significance becomes evident. Thelma begins a brief testimonial of her altered state of consciousness. The moment is rich with the expression of Thelma's emotional evolution.

Fig. 3.1. Bulldozers in *Vanishing Point*. DVD, Twentieth Century Fox Home Entertainment, 2003. Author's screenshot.

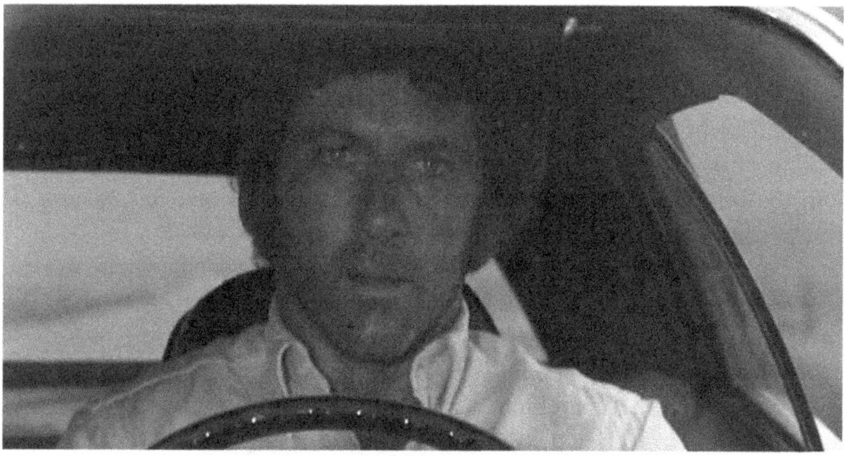

Fig. 3.2. Windshield in *Vanishing Point*. DVD, Twentieth Century Fox Home Entertainment, 2003. Author's screenshot.

> "I feel awake." (Thelma)
> "Good." (Louise)
> "Wide awake. I don't remember ever feeling this awake. Know what I mean? Everything looks different. Do you feel like that too? Like you got something to look forward to?"[12]

During this scene, the camera almost exclusively sticks with looking-in shots, allowing audiences to watch the faces of the two women as they express transitional experiences. We look directly at Thelma as she explains a new awareness (fig. 3.3). She has transitioned into a new identity, and as a result "everything looks different." Although both women have evolved during the narrative, Thelma represents the most significant development for the simple reason that she was the most "asleep" at the beginning of their journey. Being on the run has granted her the opportunity to recognize her previous life of stasis and reject it. She makes these statements as she looks through the windshield toward a horizon of possibility that she has never imagined before embarking on this road journey.

The conclusion of *Thelma & Louise* is the most essential liminal moment, and it is established by a final looking-out windshield view. Thelma and Louise choose to drive into the Grand Canyon, to "keep going." This is a powerful windshield roadview, and it corresponds to the similar willful moment in *Vanishing Point*. The two women commit to mobility and the freedom it implies. In this moment, director Scott opts for windshield framing, with the audience behind the characters as they clasp hands and move forward to their newly defined horizon (fig. 3.4).

Fig. 3.3. *Thelma & Louise*, awake. DVD, MGM Home Entertainment, 2004. Author's screenshot.

Fig. 3.4. *Thelma & Louise*, keep goin'. DVD, MGM Home Entertainment, 2004. Author's screenshot.

The windshield roadview is a conventional tool easily ascertainable in road films. Although directors often use windshields as frames for scenes within a car, in road narratives such moments are likely to carry significant import beyond basic staging convenience. The usefulness of the windshield is not limited to formidable and serious-minded road journeys like *Thelma & Louise*. We can also note its value in works like *National Lampoon's Vacation*, a wildly popular film parody of the American family road vacation—that ritualized expression of the stable mode.[13] The Griswold family performs, to the best of their limited ability, the idealized road narrative, a circular journey affirming mainstream respectability. They are motivated by their privileged position within the American middle class.[14]

The windshield image grants director Harold Ramis the opportunity to exploit the experience of failed expectations as the family bungles their way across the American West, following roughly the westward course of empire of the nineteenth century in a comedic vein. As a technique for expressing the aspirations of the Griswolds' journey, the windshield represents a hope for the horizon as symbolized by the destination, "Wally World," a thinly disguised reference to Disneyland. They are on the road to perform a task that has been defined culturally as essential to the family experience. Two direct windshield images not only exploit comic failures but also illustrate the potential of the windshield roadview to engage audiences in the narrative.

In an especially instructive moment, Ramis makes use of the looking-in windshield roadview. The shot is extended for full comic potential, but it also serves to undermine the capacity of the father to assume full power behind the wheel (fig. 3.5). A few moments before the screenshot, the car is moving at highway speeds as the camera pans the inside of the car to show each family member, the children and the mother, all sleeping comfortably. The camera then moves at last to the father in close-up. Viewers are most certainly prepared for the joke coming a mile away, so to speak. Few are prepared, however, for the full-on sleeping posture of Clark Griswold, who seems to be not simply nodding off but crashed out completely. The camera then pulls back for the full windshield view—the glorious shot of a family oblivious to their own precarious mobility. Ramis stretches this scene out quite a bit, with shots of the chaos of the car out of control spliced with returns to the still-sleeping family. Clark awakens just in time to swerve into a parking spot at a motel, the fitting end to the day for a mainstream American family on the road.

In an extension of this joke, the windshield again becomes a window into the dysfunctional family and its clumsy mobility. This second example adopts the looking-out perspective. In this case, the father is not asleep but simply clueless and overconfident. The film in scene after scene undercuts

Fig. 3.5. *National Lampoon's Vacation*, sleeping. DVD, Warner Bros., 2003. Author's screenshot.

that unearned complacency. As they search for the Grand Canyon ("the biggest goddamned hole in the world"), an essential family vacation stopover on their way to California from Chicago, they become lost and fail to see the "detour" signs. The screenshot provided shows the moment just before the family station wagon crashes through the barriers and sails over a gulch. It is not the Grand Canyon but an open space big enough to stop the family station wagon (fig. 3.6). In the moment before the vehicle takes flight, the image is framed by the looking-out windshield roadview to convey the significance of the moment. Indeed, the road is closed.

As the ever-popular example of *Vacation* makes clear, a road narrative can

Fig. 3.6. *National Lampoon's Vacation*, road closed. DVD, Warner Bros., 2003. Author's screenshot.

effectively mock mainstream modes of travel and utilize the symbolic and practical applications of the windshield view. The same can be used with a much darker tone. Consider for a moment the opening driving sequences in the film *Psycho*, directed by Alfred Hitchcock.[15] The film qualifies as a tier 3 road narrative in that, even though Hitchcock is much more concerned with psychological terror caused by an unhinged motel owner, he incorporates a substantive manipulation of road conventions crucial to setting up the primary narrative. In a remarkable three-minute sequence, Hitchcock makes full use of the windshield view as Marion Crane (Janet Leigh) drives toward the end of her road. As she grows more stressed, we hear the supposed conversations of the people she has left behind who are slowly realizing that she has stolen money and has absconded. Marion Crane is on the run.

The voice-over narrative provides the back story, but Hitchcock keeps viewers focused on the increasingly difficult conditions Crane faces as she tries to maintain her mobility. The scene implies a full day's drive, and the close-ups evoke a growing weariness. Traffic increases as night falls, the weak headlights limiting her capacity to see the road ahead. It starts to rain, rendering her view treacherous, as the windshield is an almost constant blur of water and glare. She must stop. Her fatigue combines with the horrible road conditions to force her to take refuge in the supposed safety of a roadside motel. The way Hitchcock subverts the idealized windshield view of the road ahead demonstrates its archetypal power. The more she drives, the more her horizon shrinks. The traffic, the darkness, the oncoming headlights, and the storm combine to erase the view ahead. The screenshot provided (fig. 3.7) serves as a sample of numerous similar moments. Despite its brevity, this opening sequence to *Psycho* is a meaningful component of a remarkable film. A woman's recent history plays out with verbal flashbacks as she falters under the pressure of that guilt, all while driving. When she pulls off the road at the end of a torturous day on the road, she looks through the windshield and sees a sign of hope: the Bates Motel. The road-narrative part of *Psycho* has come to an ominous stop.

As the examples suggest, filmmakers make practical and profound use of the windshield. Literary artists can adapt it as well. For prose representations of the windshield view, authors suggest such framing via physical descriptions and emotional introspections expressed. Often writers establish a visual clarification that the driver is looking at the road ahead, but that is often simply assumed. In all cases, though, the same idea applies with the looking-in and looking-out windshield roadviews stated overtly or by implication. William Least Heat-Moon in *Blue Highways* captures in the following example the mundane concerns of the road. Traveling a lonely highway in the vast spaces of Montana, Heat-Moon writes, "The clamor of the wind

Fig. 3.7. *Psycho*, windshield glare. DVD, Universal Pictures Home Entertainment, 1998. Author's screenshot.

numbed my ears; the fever made me woozy. *Pock-pock*. First the highway held me, then it entered me, then I was the highway. *Pock-pock, pock-pock*. Prairie hypnosis. I drove miles I couldn't remember, and the land became a succession of wet highway stripes, and I wished for a roadfellow. I sat blindly, dumbly like a veiled stone sphinx. Finally, to dispel the miles, I stopped, got out, and held my face to the rain. I shook myself. But, once more on the road, I again became part of the machine: generator, accelerator, humanator. I knew nothing. A stupefied nub on the great prairie."[16]

Though writers, unlike filmmakers, do not have the luxury of showing fatigue and emotional strain via the direct shots looking in to weary drivers behind the wheel, they can describe such moments in methodical detail to guide readers. In the passage, Heat-Moon drives along the prairie, enduring stress that matches the intensity of that shared in the discussed example from *Psycho*. Human, machine, and road meld in Heat-Moon's consciousness, as he notes that the road "entered me, then I was the highway." Eventually, even after trying to awaken from the fatigue- and space-driven "hypnosis," he loses his selfhood: "I knew nothing." Driving across the open spaces of Montana challenges notions of self, place, and mobility as the physical and emotional toil undermine all confidence. Heat-Moon conjures a haunting image for readers: a lone driver staring mindlessly ahead through the windshield, questioning choices with each moment, the dulling repetition emphasizing the tedium of distance and the pressure of an uncertain future.

Later in his journey, this time in Maine, Heat-Moon again uses the windshield roadview to evoke a loss of selfhood and an uneasy consciousness affected by monotony. In this sequence, he asserts the liminal implications of the ever-changing self within an amorphous landscape: "Although I was still miles from the ocean, a heavy sea fog came in to muffle the obscure woods and fly over the land like a sheet of dirty muslin. I saw no cars or people, few lights in the houses. The windshield wipers, brushing at the fog, switched back and forth like cats' tails. I lost myself to the monotonous rhythm and darkness as past and present fused and dim things came and went in a staccato of moments separated by miles of darkness. On the road, where change is continuous and visible, time is not; rather it is something the writer only infers. Time is not the traveler's fourth dimension—change is."[17] This passage combines notions of space and time with the traveler's use of the windshield as a metaphor for looking forward while also implicitly using the rearview mirror to view the past. Both come together as Heat-Moon immerses his readers into the repetitiveness of nighttime travel complicated by harsh weather to reflect his emotional stress. He thereby evokes a windshield roadview to reassert the defining liminality of such travel.

The windshield is perhaps the most obvious and widely used framing device for road experiences. First, of course, it is convenient. As a result, the windshield-as-frame is pervasive in any context wherein filmmakers or writers wish for audiences to see a protagonist in a car. More important are the meanings implied as they relate to experience and the ever-present mobility of the narrative. As the examples used above demonstrate, the windshield is a crucial window into road experience as defined by liminality, but other views are essential as well and often complement or even contradict the forward-looking windshield. With equal intensity, we also gaze at the road behind.

THE MIRROR ROADVIEW

Mirrors are those wonderful practical features of automobiles that allow us to see what is behind us. That view is most often irrelevant to the decisions we make on the road, though when such information is needed, it can be crucial indeed. Sometimes that view is gained by turning around, but most often the mirrors are essential. All time frames can be relevant, but the mirror most often invokes the past. Perhaps a classic comic moment in the Steven Spielberg film *Jurassic Park* best illustrates that point. When the T. Rex first chases the protagonists, Spielberg gives audiences a shot of the predator within a side mirror with the text common on vehicles made in the early 1990s: "Objects in mirror are closer than they appear." The "object" in this case has very large teeth. The past asserted here is closing in fast on the present, which does not bode well for the future.

For a road narrative, the mirror roadview becomes much more important as it not only captures practical information for drivers but also serves as a mirror into the soul, to use a dramatic but meaningful phrase. At all points a road narrative has an implied past—the road behind, the life behind—that insinuates itself into the present. The mirror brings the past forward into our consciousness. It therefore becomes an essential practical reminder of and a metaphorical comment on the more dominant forward-looking aspirations. Such moments may simply confirm the progress made but may also complicate the ongoing narrative. The mirror roadview is introspection and thus a view into self-doubt and pride, regret and comfort. The mirror roadview provides an essential moment of awareness and, as such, represents liminality as a reflective device conjoining two time frames. It connotes a space between the protagonist facing forward to the road ahead and also looking backward to the road behind. The present moment is pressed between the two.

Perhaps the most common trope of this time interplay is the driver's eyes captured in the mirror. The symbol is convenient but nonetheless powerful when employed at the right moment. Kerouac provides a useful example of the significance of the backward glance in *On the Road*. In the following passage, he notes the often-conflicted feelings implied by leaving someone behind or in moving away from one's past, the core conceit of the mirror roadview. He writes, "What is that feeling when you're driving away from people and they recede on the plain till you see their specks dispersing?—it's the too-huge world vaulting us, and it's good-by. But we lean forward to the next crazy venture beneath the skies."[18] Looking into the rearview mirror rhetorically, Sal experiences the pathos of moving forward while others remain in place. In this instance, the mirror roadview acknowledges that the people we have met and even loved "disperse" as we move forward. For Sal in the subversive mode, the road must always be ahead, and refusing to embrace the windshield roadview fully could cause stasis. To avoid the potential pitfalls of a too-intrusive past, a quick embracing of a windshield view can maintain mobility, so Sal keeps his mirror moment brief and chooses to "lean forward."

The mirror roadview can also demonstrate a conflicted or troubled self as the driver finds no comforting view and the mobility forward is under distinct stress. Steven Spielberg provides a useful example with his directorial debut *Duel*, a tier 1 narrative based on a short story by the same name written by Richard Matheson, who also wrote the screenplay.[19] Spielberg makes significant use of the three roadviews, and his manipulation of the mirror roadview is especially effective. In a sparse narrative of survival, the protagonist, David Mann (Dennis Weaver), is tormented by a truck driver intent on killing him. The mirror roadview captures increasing desperation and fear, as the road behind refuses to recede into memory. It keeps haunting Mann's progress. The paired images included capture the two ways to stage the mirror roadview, both employing the practical frame of the rearview mirror itself. In the first screenshot, audiences see the protagonist within the rearview mirror. In the second screenshot, audiences see what the driver sees, that looming danger, the beast that cannot be appeased (figs. 3.8 and 3.9). Spielberg jumps between the two mirror roadviews to heighten the intensity of the chase and to emphasize the whiplash-like mental stresses that Mann faces in an existential battle for survival.

A similar use of the mirror roadview occurs in "The Hitch-Hiker" episode of the *Twilight Zone*, a wonderful twenty-two-minute tier 1 road film.[20] Nan

Fig. 3.8. *Duel*, Mann in mirror. DVD, Universal Pictures Home Entertainment, 2003. Author's screenshot.

Fig. 3.9. *Duel*, truck in mirror. DVD, Universal Pictures Home Entertainment, 2003. Author's screenshot.

Adams (Inger Stevens) is heading for Los Angeles from New York City on a classic cross-country vacation. She has an accident in Pennsylvania, and from that moment on her journey is plagued by a hitchhiker who appears, inexplicably, at multiple points along the road. The episode uses the natural combination of windshield and mirror roadviews to accentuate the haunting presence of the hitchhiker, who becomes increasingly intrusive. Rod Serling's teleplay is firmly rooted in open-road mythology and maintains the overarching metaphor that the road is life. In this allegory, the hitchhiker is death, the end of Nan Adams's road. Because Adams does not stop for him, he kindly waits. As with *Duel*, "The Hitch-Hiker" juxtaposes windshield and mirror views to evoke the emotional battle waging in her mind as Adams drives in a desperate, if unconscious, effort to escape death. The episode operates in the stable mode in that Nan Adams is on vacation, enjoying a break from her normal daily life. As we can infer from the background narrative Serling provides in his introduction, she fully intends to return home and thereby complete a circular road-trip affirming her middle-class status. This is supposed to be a stable journey, but something goes horribly wrong on Highway 11 in Pennsylvania. She is involved in a fatal wreck. The remainder of the journey explores her struggle with liminality as she is trapped between life and death, wavering between two worlds in the "twilight zone."

Widely regarded as one of the most compelling episodes in the *Twilight Zone* canon, "The Hitch-Hiker" owes much of its artistic success to the archetypal power of the open road as cultural reference point. In one of the most intense scenes, Adams comes to a stop, waiting for an oncoming train to pass. The hitchhiker appears on the other side of the tracks. In a panic she moves forward onto the tracks, eager to speed past him. The car gets stuck and stalls. So there the car sits, straddling the tracks. This moment is a wonderfully concise evocation of road liminality. Between the road ahead and the road behind, she is on the verge of crossing over into death, at that moment represented by the hitchhiker on the other side of the tracks. The oncoming train is getting closer. Turn the key, turn the key. At the last moment, she gets the car started and pulls into reverse just as the train thunders by.

Nan Adams momentarily escapes, but eventually she acknowledges that she can no longer flee. Upon this realization, she notes, "Ahead of me stretch a thousand miles of empty mesa, mountains, prairies, desert. Somewhere among them, he's waiting. Waiting for me." She decides to stop moving. Getting back into her car, she adjusts the rearview mirror to reveal the face of the hitchhiker, now in the backseat. With a simple half-smile, he states, "I believe you're going my way." The mirror has merged with the windshield to force acceptance for Nan Adams. Her transition is completed on the American open road, sometime around twilight (fig. 3.10).

Fig. 3.10. *Twilight Zone*, hitchhiker in mirror. DVD, CBS, 1960. Author's screenshot.

THE SIDE-WINDOW ROADVIEW

Side windows allow motorists to look around as they move. Whether those peripheral glances and glares result from the necessities of maneuvering between lanes or from engagement with the surrounding landscape, drivers take their eyes away from focusing on the road ahead and consider their environment. That opportunity is central to road experiences. The lateral or peripheral sightlines offered by the side-window roadview privilege space as entity aligned with road experience perceived mostly as a series of self-referential places in a constant blur of movement. The side-window roadview is deeply tied to the landscape imaginary and thus provides context, situating travelers within the cultural and/or personal understandings of place. As with the other views, it offers the opportunity for introspection and definition, but it is the most relevant roadview for the present moment in any narrative. It may occur as a brief look to the side or as a more prolonged engagement with surroundings. In contrast with the other roadviews, the side window emphasizes the immediate surroundings to offer some answer to the implied question: "Where am I?"

The primary purpose of the side-window roadview is to provide texture to movement as characters demonstrate awareness of the world outside of the vehicle and beyond the road itself. Equally significant, however, is the capacity for this roadview to embrace a contrasting stillness to deepen the implications of mobility. It encourages travelers, in some cases, to stop. The side window creates the opportunity to embrace the landscape imaginary as more than scenery. In motion, the side-window roadview results in cursory, blurred perceptions; when stopped, it can offer a deepened road experience, a chance to step into the framed image from the window and explore the present environment. To be sure, stopping must be temporary, but such moments often produce the most common incantations of liminality in the road narrative. Whether the moment of transition occurs while in motion or while stopped, the road experience is intensified by awareness of and engagement with surrounding life.

William Least Heat-Moon provides a concise example of how this view can appear in a prose narrative. In this example from *Blue Highways*, he exploits a side-window roadview as he travels at night through the American Southwest. He comments on his relationship with the surrounding world as he notes his own reflection, writing, "A mirror may not reflect mind, but a man's response to landscapes, faces, events does. My skewed vision was that of a man looking at himself by looking at what he looks at. A man watching himself: *that* was the simulacrum on the window in the Nevada desert."[21] In this confessional moment, Heat-Moon accentuates the relationship between the peripheral roadview as window both to the outside (the landscape he is passing by) and to the ego (the emotional effect of his perception). Heat-Moon acknowledges his self-absorption, wherein the self—the face, blurred but not erased—gazes outward at the landscape being traversed. Even the standard phrasing we tend to use in such moments captures the illusion created by mobility. We typically refer to the passing landscape when, in actuality, we are doing the passing. The key, though, is how we perceive the environs in an unapologetic reference to ourselves. Heat-Moon is revealed by what he chooses to see and remember.

The side roadview is by necessity impressionistic. It gives context to movement as protagonists cover space. Though often arbitrary and fleeting, it makes possible deepened awareness of the essential interactions between self and place. Myriad examples illustrate such contact, as writers and directors employ seemingly chance encounters to elaborate on characters or on the journey itself. *American Graffiti*, directed by George Lucas, makes practical but often meaningful use of the side-window roadview. An exploration of the automobility of American teenagers in the early 1960s, the film focuses on one night, the last one of that roiling transitional summer between high school and college for the protagonists.[22]

American Graffiti focuses attention on conversations carried on from car windows as teenagers cruise up and down the "strip," a bustling of energy and anxiety defined by an often rowdy, if repetitive, mobility. The film has many examples, but the screenshot below occurs during an especially provocative encounter that establishes a quest narrative for the main character, Curt (Richard Dreyfuss). He sees a mysterious and alluring blonde woman in a white Thunderbird, as both cars sit side by side at a stoplight. The woman smiles at him and mouths "I love you." He does not fully understand and becomes animated by the implied promise of her words, but he cannot respond to her because his window is rolled up. As he finally manages to roll the window down, she pulls away, so the conversation is truncated. In an additional complication, he is in the backseat and has no power to direct the vehicle. Unable to convince his friends to follow his "vision, a goddess," he is powerless. He can only bemoan his condition in the backseat, all the while daring to hope that "someone roaming the streets wants me." The remainder of his night is dominated by efforts to find her, a dream of happiness in a white Thunderbird always just out of sight (fig. 3.11).

Fig. 3.11. *American Graffiti*, T-Bird. DVD, Universal Pictures Home Entertainment, 1998. Author's screenshot.

Richard Linklater, writer and director of *Dazed and Confused*, follows the patterns established by Lucas to evoke a similar immersion into teen mobility, in this case during the 1970s.[23] Relying often on the side-window roadview, he captures the dynamism of mobile interactions. The screenshot below shows passengers looking out from the vehicle as the cultural landscape of their youth bustles around them (fig. 3.12). Whereas the long-view goals of both films focus on the windshield views toward the horizon of American youth, the bulk of each film depends on the lateral engagements via the side-window roadviews that define current road experiences. These are the moments of mobile life thoroughly focused on the present tense and therefore so palpable in an American teenager's heart. Though the characters in the screenshot are together in one vehicle, each is immersed in a singular view and, by implication, engaged with individualized moments of thought. Participating in a ritualized act, they are together in the car yet focused on personal dreams. Implicitly, they are going somewhere, but exactly where in this context is yet to be established and hardly important to the ritual itself. Whether or not they find a place to go (or stop) matters little in that the night is defined by their continual openness to any experience they find, a subversive road dream.

Fig. 3.12. *Dazed and Confused*, side window. DVD, Universal Pictures Home Entertainment, 2011. Author's screenshot.

* * *

There are many ways to see the world from the road. The three primary roadviews—the windshield, the mirror, and the side window—offer ways to frame and interpret nuanced characteristics of mobile experiences. These primary ways of seeing illustrate the centrality of liminality on the road. With repetition in varying narrative forms, these views have become conventional but no less compelling in most instances. They emanate from the basic physical facts that have governed the design of automobiles, namely, in this case, the need for windows so that drivers can travel safely by looking forward, backward, and to the side. As invoked in narratives inextricably tied to liminality, such acts also carry metaphorical associations as writers and filmmakers try to elucidate the range of road experiences emanating from the ongoing interactions between self, place, and mobility. The roadviews defined above convey distinct but overlapping encounters with the omnipresent state of liminality that defines the open road. The core moments of transition persist from all points of view and at all points in narrative time. We look ahead; we look behind; we look around. At every moment, we move along the road forever on the threshold of change.

4
Building the Journey

The Emotional Road

STAGES OF THE ROAD NARRATIVE

The overarching presence of liminality in the road narrative is best illustrated by considering the multiple ways Americans see the open road as they move on it. As discussed in the previous chapter, three roadviews—windshield, mirror, and side window—emphasize the ever-present transitional potential made possible by the steady interactions between self, place, and mobility. Other staple characteristics merit attention as well, as we continue to define the most instructive conventions of the genre. This chapter explores the essential stages of the road narrative as it adapts the archetypal structures of the heroic quest along the American open road.

The stages of the hero's journey, exploited in varying forms by writers as long as narratives have existed, complement the liminality central to road experiences. The thinker in the Cold War era most responsible for placing the traditional heroic quest into the American popular vernacular is Joseph Campbell. His *The Hero with a Thousand Faces* has encouraged substantive dialogue on the mythic structures permeating popular culture, and his work remains vibrant.[1] Employing the work of Arnold van Gennep to develop the connection between ritual liminality and mythic journeys, Campbell succeeded in making the social underpinning of heroic quests more accessible and, as a result, more evident in modern cultures. His work allows for a logical application of his broader observations on the hero's journey to the more specific subject of American road narratives. Campbell laid out seventeen "elements" of the journey, some of which can be understood as stages and some as characteristics.[2] I have chosen to simplify the elements into four broad stages that serve as a structural formula for the American road narrative: departures, collisions, awakenings, and reframings. Tracing the progression through these road stages illuminates the underlying and essential patterns that animate the American open road.

DEPARTURES

Any removal from home asserts a significant emotional weight on an individual. It implies, within the stable mode, a temporary separation from security with the long-term goal of strengthening the attachment to home. For the subversive mode, on the other hand, departures typically reflect a desire for separation and thus rejection of a home base. In all cases, however, the decision to move requires dedication to implied or stated goals in direct juxtaposition to the self at home. The traveler must, as Campbell phrases it in reference to the hero's journey, "accept the call to adventure" in preparation for any departure.[3] Therefore, the first step in going anywhere in any mode depends, quite simply, on someone deciding to go.

Why go? The answer to this question provides the catalyst for any road journey, and most road narratives offer some explanation as a way to engage readers and justify the narrative that follows. In traditional travel writing, this is obligatory in order to establish a clear rationale and authority. In a genre marked by intense competition for reader attention among writers who were often covering well-trod ground, readers were often assured directly that the text was an honest account from a humble, trustworthy narrator.[4] For the road narrative, the same pressures apply, though the need for humility has subsided almost completely. More important is the assertion of a purpose that must be stated or implied. A reason to depart must be believable and compelling. In short, travelers must offer a plan.

Although *On the Road* is best known and loved for its spontaneity and subversion, Sal's beginnings are characterized by pragmatism. He chooses to take to the road as a break, a vacation of sorts from his primary career as a writer. He hopes to travel across the United States and subsequently around the world, working as a merchant seaman. His goal is to return home, as he states it, with "enough money to support myself in my Aunt's house while I finish my book."[5] These passages clearly place Sal's narrative opening within a stable mode. His journey has no overtly romantic quest features. To the contrary, he asserts a standard, mainstream plan for concentric travel to solidify his commitment to his book . He seeks a break as a way to affirm long-term stability, not reject it. Sal Paradise seems to have a reasonable plan. Kerouac writes, "I'd been poring over maps of the United States in Patterson for months, even reading books about the pioneers and savoring names like

Platte and Cimarron and so on, and on the roadmap was one long red line called Route 6 that led from the tip of Cape Cod clear to Ely, Nevada, and there dipped down to Los Angeles. I'll just stay on 6 all the way to Ely, I said to myself and confidently started."[6]

The supposed plan is not a good one. Sal finds himself stranded and flustered immediately, having a miserable first day on the road and making no progress at all. This setback is more than simply a cosmic demonstration of the truism regarding the best laid plans of mice and men. It also captures the inherent challenge of maintaining the subversive mode because, even in *On the Road*, the pull for stability never leaves our consciousness. Sal is desirous of following madness but is also drawn to pragmatic planning. He twice calls himself a "damn fool" and ends up retracing his route, forced to start over. However, that failure pushes Sal to reform his departure, free of the encumbrance of a planned route. After he takes a bus to Chicago to recoup the time lost on that first day, his narrative begins to follow a more subversive mindset, and his heroic journey begins.

A few years after *On the Road*, in one of the most successful American road narratives, *Travels with Charley*, John Steinbeck prepares for his road quest with a similar devotion to stability. He explains his rationale in the opening paragraphs, which echo the departure plans of Sal Paradise. His opening paragraph confesses that he has always suffered from wanderlust and that age has not thwarted the desire to move (he was fifty-eight when he made this trip). Using phrases like "once a bum always a bum," "the itch" to move, the "fever" to take to the open road, the "urge to be someplace else," and "the disease incurable," Steinbeck claims that a romantic sense of inevitability girds his quest. In justifying his choice to take to the open road, Steinbeck follows traditional travel writing patterns but also adopts a personal desire for adventure more typical of late-twentieth-century road narratives established so firmly by Kerouac. He writes, "When the virus of restlessness begins to take possession of a wayward man, and the road away from Here seems broad and straight and sweet, the victim must first find in himself a good and sufficient reason for going. This to the practical bum is not difficult. He has a built-in garden of reasons to choose from. Next he must plan his trip in time and space, choose a direction and a destination. And last he must implement the journey. How to go, what to take, how long to stay. This part of the process is invariable and immortal."[7] Though his overall narrative proves to be firmly within a stable mode, he asserts nonetheless a youthful energy tied to the romantic desires of a "wayward man," as if, in his heart of hearts, he remains a subversive. In this manner, he fashions himself a modernized (and decidedly older) version of Mark Twain's Huck Finn who, in support of his own longings, states,

"All I wanted was to go somewheres; all I wanted was a change, I warn't particular."[8] Steinbeck's claim implies an acceptance of the "call to adventure," to refer back to Joseph Campbell's phrase. In addition, he suggests a heroic quest to find America, as the subtitle makes quite clear: "In Search of America." His decision to move, then, derives from a selfless desire to explore the nation and discover its true characteristics—"to rediscover this monster land."[9]

This opening is compelling and wonderfully conventional. It follows patterns with skill and energy, all the while blending stable and subversive claims. Unlike Huck Finn, Steinbeck *is* quite particular. His departure is well planned and clearly justified and matches that of Kerouac's Sal Paradise in its assumption of order. Steinbeck writes, "For weeks I had studied maps, large-scale and small, but maps are not reality at all—they can be tyrants. I know people who are so immersed in road maps that they never see the countryside they pass through, and others who, having traced a route, are held to it as though held by flanged wheels to rails."[10] He confesses an inconsistency, fully aware that as he adopts the stable conceit of making practical plans and conforming to patterns he is also inhibiting spontaneity and the sense of adventure implicit in a subversive mode. Sticking to a map as a factual delineation of movement instead of sticking to the road as a place of mythical possibilities destroys the implicit heroic potential of a journey. As Steinbeck understands, refusing to choose one's own routes is simply traveling by rails, wholly foregoing individual will and whim.

Most tier 1 road narratives, fictional or nonfictional, literary or cinematic, establish rationales for departures; and, as in the examples above, the intentions, in the end, may not mesh with the journeys actually encountered. Many departures are altered by circumstance, often diverging from an assumed or hoped-for experience. Consider the following examples: in *Rain Man*, brothers Charlie (Tom Cruise) and Raymond (Dustin Hoffman) embark on a cross-country trek wherein Charlie hopes to regain his father's inheritance from his autistic brother, Raymond; in *Smoke Signals*, Victor (Adam Beach) and Thomas (Evan Adams) depart their Coeur D'Alene reservation home to retrieve the ashes of Victor's father in Phoenix, Arizona; and in *War of the Worlds*, Ray (Tom Cruise) endeavors to get his children safely to Boston from New York.[11] The characters in each of these examples find very different roads than expected, and such is the case for most odysseys. Myriad reasons can send Americans on the road, whether they assume roles as heroic figures or not. They may be eager or reluctant to begin, and they may struggle with inherent conflicts between stable and subversive goals, but the key for all is what happens once they start moving. Adjusting to problems, therefore, though it is celebrated in the subversive mode, is always in one way or another a requirement of all road journeys. Expectations collide with the unknown that lurks around every curve in the road.

COLLISIONS

Turn left or turn right; speed up or slow down; stop here or stop there: the simple choices of the road face us constantly. More complicated ones inform our road narratives. If the primary question informing departures is "why should I go?," then the related question for subsequent decisions is "why should I keep going?" Any answer might infer a more pointed concern: "*Can* I keep going?" The varying obstacles that provoke such introspective questions provide tension in all road narratives. Every choice made can lead to a seemingly endless line of what I choose to call "collisions"—encounters with physical and emotional obstacles to mobility. The traveler, in any collision with a force that may deter the heroic journey, must make substantive choices that define the road ahead. Any impact may affect the probability of failure or success. Collisions not only threaten the quest but also create opportunities for development and renewal. In moments along the road, the hero protagonist must inevitably collide with an obstacle that might have the capacity to thwart forward movement briefly or forever—a stop sign, a boulder, a stranger, a wreck, or, to employ a metaphorical foil typical of heroic quests, a dragon.

In this discussion, the term *collision* implies a multistep process. Therefore, it does not just refer to initial impact but also to the adjustments evident in the associated aftermath. Collisions demand responses, so this stage must include the careening caused by the initial encounter. At any moment on the road, a challenge may force a difficult choice and then a crisis. A driver sees a deer crossing the road. The driver reacts, choosing to swerve left, which forces an oncoming vehicle to swerve as well, resulting in the second car hitting a tree as the first driver recovers and pulls to the side of the road. What now? In pure physical terms, this brief scenario summarizes a near collision, but in narrative terms the implications of "collision" remain in play. We have a potentially emotional and dramatic impact, a crisis moment wherein the first driver (perhaps being inebriated or in the midst of an unrelated distraction that affected driving) now faces another dilemma. Much could be at stake in this rather common occurrence, and such events may arise at any point along the road. In a few moments of stillness—liminal space—everything may change. Eventually and with possibly profound implications, however, someone must respond. Someone must move.

A collision may be minor or major, but the key element is the response of the traveler. Joseph Campbell uses the phrase "the road of trials" to help define the "initiation" phase of the heroic quest. He goes on to state, "Once having traversed the threshold, the hero moves in a dream landscape of curiously fluid, ambiguous forms, where he must survive a succession of trials."[12] A collision forces a trial, and the result always has the potential to alter mobility. Collisions as narrative moments therefore pivot between the desires of travelers and the characteristics of obstacles. Often such confrontations force crises of conscience, transformative moments wherein existential challenges put into question the will of travelers to move ahead.

Collisions take many forms. Perhaps we should harken back briefly to the departure comments in *On the Road* discussed above. On his first day, Sal is forced to turn around and start over. Two things collide in this example. The misguided plan that derived from a false assumption that he could follow one convenient road across America meets with the fact that Sal has chosen a lonely road with almost no hitchhiking potential. Collisions are pervasive by the nature of narrative, and any related action makes up the vast middle of all road journeys. If movement on the open road offers an ever-present series of liminal moments, then, likewise, the collisions influence the characteristics of the ensuing transitions. These collisions test the capacity of travelers to keep moving, and they are thus rightly considered as "trials." How do characters respond to and define those experiences in relation to their desires?

William Least Heat-Moon in *Blue Highways* is keenly sensitive to exploring the metaphysical challenges he encounters. Early in the narrative, still close to home, Heat-Moon faces a morning of self-doubt that threatens his journey. He writes, "One week on the road—a week of clouds, rain, cold. And now it was snowing. Thirty-four degrees inside the Ghost, ice covering the windshield, my left shoulder aching from the knot I'd slept in."[13] He emerges from the van to clean the snow from the windshield, a physical act that also carries symbolic resonance tied to the windshield roadview: "Clearing the windows, I wondered why I had ever come away to this place and began thinking about turning back. Could I?"[14] The rhetorical question is omnipresent on the road. The unknown energizes the narrative forward, creating a lurking uncertainty that grants compelling power to each movement. Heat-Moon continues, "I cranked the sluggish engine. Four lanes of easy interstate from Morristown to Missouri [home]. One day. The engine fired, sputtered, and caught. I listened as I did every morning. Smooth but for the knocking waterpump. I moved out. A red light at U.S. 11 East. Home was a left turn, right was who knows. . . . I took who knows."[15] Although it happens early in the journey, this moment of uncertainty—a liminal moment of choice—represents a potential existential threat to Heat-Moon's quest. Readers must take him at his word and recognize that a journey, despite the seeming certainty of desire, can end in its nascent stages. Heat-Moon here must reassert his commitment and choose to move into the unknown.

The essential structural motif of *Blue Highways* emanates from a steady reenactment of this basic choice for Heat-Moon. Repeated collisions followed by sometimes grand, sometimes mundane, decisions to continue. Much later in the book, in one of his most important collisions, Heat-Moon reaches a crisis moment that shifts his overall perspective, resolving the inherent question—keep going?—by leading him to define his journey in more metaphysical terms. He begins asking a deeper question: What does going mean? He writes, "At any particular moment in a man's life, he can say that everything he has done and not done, that has been done and not been done to him, has brought him to that moment. If he's being installed as Chieftain or receiving a Nobel Prize, that's a fulfilling notion. But if he's in a sleeping bag at ten thousand feet in a snowstorm, parked in the middle of a highway and waiting to freeze to death, the idea can make him feel calamitously stupid."[16] For the moment, this collision stops Heat-Moon. Even if he wanted to move, the situation forbids it. Moreover, he faces a profound challenge to his idea of the journey. His physical predicament forces a turning point, a threshold event within the narrative. Heat-Moon struggles with his mobility in a carefully orchestrated scene that places him physically in the middle of the road—symbolically a liminal space—not simply stifled by circumstance but also by indecision. Trapped by a winter storm, he faces physical danger. He is also in a precarious situation regarding his selfhood, suffering from self-loathing ideas that question the integrity of his entire life. He describes the emotional careening resulting from the collision: "The whole night I slept and woke, slept and woke, while the hail fell like iron shot, and thunder slammed around, and lightning seared the ice."[17] Heat-Moon is at risk of an annihilation of self.

No matter the specific characteristic of any given collision on the road, whether a minor inconvenience or a gut-wrenching moment of crisis, the essential question as to whether the traveler will continue remains the same. This cycle may appear multiple times in any given narrative, each encounter being informed by others. If mobility survives, if the self finds the capacity to affirm the journey, then, and only then, does the next stage become possible. The hero can awaken to substantive change.

AWAKENINGS

The road narrative does not demand that the hero conquer a beast or foe other than the self, though the ever-present foe in the mirror is often paralleled by the physical barriers that pop up along the road. For the series of collisions endured and conquered to have substantive meaning, the hero must experience a lasting change, what I am calling "awakening," a profound expansion of the self that arises from a conquest. By overcoming their weaknesses or demons, behaviors, patterns, and/or expectations, heroes awaken to a broader understanding of their world and their power. This shift of the self can be identified by alterations in thinking or acting or by a clearly defined new awareness, as in the case of Sal Paradise regarding Dean Moriarty in the closing scenes of *On the Road*. It may also be the completion of a simple task rather than an epic battle, as in the case of Bobbie Ann Mason's *In Country*, a tier 2 narrative, wherein the protagonist completes a planned journey to achieve emotional closure regarding the painful legacy the Vietnam War left on her family. It may be a growing capacity to see a broader narrative picture of one's life, as in Robert Pirsig's *Zen and the Art of Motorcycle Maintenance*, a seminal tier 1 narrative. In all cases, the awakening has been made possible via the traveler's response to collisions along the road.

As discussed above, in *Blue Highways*, Heat-Moon faces a crisis as he's trapped by a blizzard atop a mountain. His reckoning leads to a clear awakening, a way off the mountain practically and symbolically. Though Heat-Moon continues his journey around the United States, completing his planned circle, he achieves his most significant transition at this narrative moment—roughly two-thirds through his overall trip—and the remainder of his road narrative steadily reaffirms this awakening.[18] This crisis moment therefore pushes him through the threshold and significantly alters his consciousness. The symbolism is familiar and universal. Heat-Moon comes down from the mountaintop after this ordeal, emerging as a new self, a formidable step in his emotional development. Following this ordeal, he meets a young man who introduces him to the traditional concepts of selfhood within the philosophy of the Hopi nation. This section also reveals the girding visual symbol employed throughout the book, the graphic image that adorns all chapter headings. It is the ancient symbol for emergence drawn from Hopi mythology.

Likewise, *Thelma & Louise* derives much of its narrative power from its thematic focus on the awakening of the two protagonists. In a particularly compelling nighttime sequence, an awakening takes place, making possible their ultimate decision to "keep going" in the final moments of the film.[19] Director Ridley Scott creates a montage of both women sharing the driving duties as they cross through, as implied, the iconic landscape of Monument Valley. The sequence effectively conveys the passing of time and space, but the close-ups on Thelma and Louise individually employ a looking-in windshield roadview, creating a nicely choreographed evocation of liminality. In a film that stays in a realistic mode for most of the action, this nighttime drive sequence is artfully romantic as the lighting creates a glowing effect for the women and the car as they enter the landscape imaginary (fig. 4.1).

Each takes her turn behind the wheel, but the sequence emphasizes shared awakenings by blurring time and dissolving between the images of each woman driving. The exaggerated interior lighting that Scott employs creates an aura of thought symbolizing the transition underway for both women. The awareness of the self extends beyond the vehicle to include the broad landscape itself. The symbolic result creates a dream vision appropriate for this moment, wherein the expansiveness of the open road is demonstrated by the inherent contrasts between the physical reality and the dream reality. The fact is that two occupants inside a brightly lit car interior see virtually nothing beyond the windshield made reflective by such lighting. In this dream-vision moment, however, the bright interior implies a connection to the surrounding space as a place of human imagination tied directly to the two women's souls. Under this emanating orb of light, Thelma and Louise move not simply within the safety of the car but also within the iconic American landscape of possibility.

When they stop the car and step physically into the landscape, a side-window moment of awareness, they complete the liminal transition. The light previously emanating ostensibly from the dashboard now comes from the headlights but to the same purpose—the light sanctifying the awakening they have earned (fig. 4.2). The impressionism that defines the sequence evokes a peace that they have been unable enjoy as fugitives. Ridley effectively emphasizes a spirit of awakening, a sense of peace paradoxically arising from isolation and interconnectedness at the same time. Thelma and Louise are at home with the car, the road, the surrounding landscape. This night drive carries them through a threshold moment that renders the closing sequence an inevitable and self-assertive act rather than one of powerless desperation.

Because of the ongoing potential for transition on the road, travelers may learn from collisions endured and, as a result, grow as they move ever forward. In each such case, the road alters the narrative self, but mobility continues in some form nonetheless. Although awakenings imply a level of completion in the narrative, the hero's journey is not over without some type of inferred or stated revision of how mobility will be defined. An expanding self must come to grips with a new way to be expressed, a new road story to be told. Awakened, the traveler must refigure the road ahead. The question then becomes this: Where now?

REFRAMINGS

No matter the modes of travel employed—stable or subversive—mobility must be reframed in the end to complete the narrative. All road trips end. After all the departures, collisions, and awakenings, what is left to do? That is

Fig. 4.1. *Thelma & Louise*, night windshield. DVD, MGM Home Entertainment, 2004. Author's screenshot.

Fig. 4.2. *Thelma & Louise*, nightscape. DVD, MGM Home Entertainment, 2004. Author's screenshot.

the profound question to be resolved. This conundrum is rather pesky. The answer, it seems, derives from how the narrative wishes to reframe implied future mobility via the characteristics of the closing movements. One would expect for the stable mode to demand a full-stop return home and for the subversive mode to opt for unambiguous continuation. Should the traveler come home renewed or defeated and complete the circle or continue moving away from home in an ongoing series of departures?

How mobility comes to a close, of course, is determined by the overall goals of any given narrative. American literary and cinematic traditions have always exhibited a penchant for ambiguity or even obfuscation. As such tendencies have been adapted to road-narrative structure, the dominant approach to ending stories along the American open road is to stubbornly refuse to acknowledge full-stop endings altogether. Travel narratives overwhelming adopt a practical or metaphorical framing that allows the journey to end without stopping. The assumption that a stable narrative ends at home and a subversive narrative keeps heading down the road is a faulty one. As we will see at greater length in subsequent chapters, road journeys rarely reside in one mode or the other. To the contrary, they lurch into one mode or the other or even surreptitiously vacillate between the two. Overwhelmingly, however, road narratives end by giving the impression that protagonists hold on to an ever-mobile identity.

A brief rundown of a few endings can illustrate this paradoxical motif. In *On the Road*, after two years of manic rambling around the country, Sal Paradise returns home and rejects Dean Moriarty's mobile madness, yet as he does so, he is in motion, cozy in the back seat of a Cadillac. John Steinbeck returns home in *Travels with Charley*, having failed to complete the auspicious stabilizing journey he had conceived, yet he remains in his car, lost within a mile of his home. He has more driving to do. Captain America and Billy the Kid die violently at the roadside in *Easy Rider*, but the closing shots of the film nonetheless force attention to the nearby river that keeps rolling along. In *Zen and the Art of Motorcycle Maintenance*, Robert Pirsig's narrator achieves a unified vision of his life as he nears home but is still in motion. The Griswolds—much worse for the wear—make it to Wally World in *National Lampoon's Vacation* and fulfill their quest, but are still moving raucously, this time on a rollercoaster, as the credits roll. William Least Heat-Moon completes his circuit of America and finds himself whole in *Blue Highways* but not yet home as the narrative ends with his filling the gas tank. Thelma and Louise fly into the liminal space of the Grand Canyon, triumphant as the screen fades to white. Victor brings his father's ashes and his yellow pick-up truck home in *Smoke Signals*, but the film ends with the spreading of the father's ashes into the constantly flowing river. The unnamed narrator of Cormac McCarthy's *The Road* finds relative safety for his son as the boy walks toward a new home. In *War of the Worlds*, Ray reunites his family in Boston, proving his stable value, but remains in the middle of the street.

I would like to add a focused reading of the concluding sequence of a film not normally discussed in a road-narrative context to illustrate the complexity of any so-called end of the road: *The Graduate*. The film employs road tropes in its closing segment, and it thus merits recognition as a tier 3 narrative.[20] The film depends on a chase of sorts as Benjamin (Dustin Hoffman) embarks on a desperate drive to stop the wedding of Elaine (Katherine Ross). This quest is marked by several collisions and is expressed with manipulation of multiple roadviews. The road is hard, and he is short on time. He runs out of gas and continues down the road by running. He struggles to reach his destination and has had little time for any growth in response to collisions. The lack of genuine awakening is a crucial missing part of his journey. He arrives at the church and makes his way to the balcony overlooking the congregation below. Separated by glass windows (similar in this moment to a windshield roadview), he sees Elaine facing her betrothed and thus sees his future without her. He bangs on the glass repeatedly and shouts her name. In one of the most dramatic liminal pauses in film, he awaits affirmation. Elaine turns to see him and calls "Ben!" She thus grants permission for him to continue down his mad, manic road. They run toward each other.

Both the crusading knight and the damsel work together to escape the church and its implied stasis. Having succeeded, the star-crossed lovers escape a fate of mundane, plastic domesticity and start a new subversive journey together. They make their way to the road, climb aboard a public bus, work their way to the back, and collapse into the last row of seats. The film as romance should end here, but the shot holds as the bus moves ahead, and the film ends purely within road-narrative framing. The loving couple is mobile, heading down the road toward an uncertain but exciting future. They face forward into the camera. Though they are in the back of a bus, the frame is nonetheless a looking-in windshield roadview. What do Ben and Elaine see in the road ahead?

We watch their faces, their eyes gazing forward toward the horizon with all its promise. The tension becomes increasingly palpable as the shot lingers and as the bus begins to move. Despite the pleasure of their vibrant, spontaneous energy, the ambiguity of the open road chips away at their euphoria. Their smiles begin to falter. The confidence of their dramatic action wanes, an emotional movement from exhilaration to uncertainty. The shot then shifts, and the camera turns to become, in effect, a looking-out windshield roadview, our eyes seeing from outside the bus over their shoulders as they move toward the horizon. The bus gains speed, the camera briefly keeping pace. The bus starts to pull away when the camera stops, in effect, at an intersection. The film ends with protagonists moving toward the horizon. What are Elaine and Ben feeling? Are they hopeful or fearful? Who knows? The narrative is over, and the bus fades into the middle distance.

The road narrative struggles to find either the way home or the way ahead, but it nonetheless seeks some equilibrium in the roiling possibilities of mobility. Endings seem reluctant to signal a clear end to the road. To the contrary, they choose, quite stubbornly, to suggest that the road must always remain in some way engaged. The traveler has changed, having reckoned with the other stages of the journey. The road remains, however. Stable modes and subversive modes align to support a similar desire to accentuate movement as perpetual. Though narratives must inevitably work toward conclusion, they do not have to concede the horizon.

PLEASURE AND PAIN, LIFE AND DEATH

The stages of road trips are archetypal, tied to human narrative history and updated to investigate and continually renew American automobility. Other equally significant narrative tropes inform the road narrative and appear with a sustained frequency and thus merit scrutiny within any discussion of the conventions of the genre. Key moments tied directly to physical stimuli define the road narrative and cannot be snugly tied to specific stages of the heroic journey. They nonetheless serve as pervasive elements of the road experience. They are related to the complex physical interactions between self and place revealed through strong emotion. The most comprehensive interaction between mind and body that figures in the road narrative emerges from the core dualism of human experiences: pleasure and pain. How we respond to each on the road is often presented in conventional but compelling terms that foreground the experiential nature of life on the move.

The first essential pleasure of the open road is tied to personal power, the autonomy of mobility wherein we decide, for the most part, where to go—turn left, turn right—and how to go—speed up, slow down. We love the power we assert in controlling the steering wheel and the accelerator. We draw significant power from the machine itself and blur distinctions between the mechanical and the human. When we make our choices, we not only determine movement but also affect a growing self-actualization. Kris Lackey makes this point succinctly, noting that automobility "has inflated our sense of individual power, will, and significance."[21] He continues, "The automobile was a machine so perfectly responsive to individual whim that it assumed the neutrality of a prosthesis. . . . And because it is sometimes metaphorically linked to the body, it could function as a machine while its mechanical attributes were naturalized, made to seem part of nature."[22] This is an apt assertion of how the car alters the self-image of the traveler whose body extends symbolically to intertwine with the machine. The idea that the machine is connected intimately with the traveler is a vital component of automobility and how we tend to define ourselves in motion.

We enjoy the power of choice inherent in driving. We extend our sense of self to the machine to imply that the driver and the car are one entity. We also adopt a complicated relationship with the surrounding environment that is both logical and counterintuitive at the same time. The point of contention pivots on our overlapping notions of public and private space. We believe the following with great vigor: the car is our private space. We must also be aware that the car always moves in shared public space. John Brinckerhoff Jackson observes this crucial contradiction: "The automobile allows one to travel almost at will anywhere in the public domain while remaining in a completely private world unequivocally defined by physical boundaries."[23] This distinction supports the inherent tensions between the public and the private on the road. Drivers often regard the vehicle as self. The car is the body going at inhuman rates of speed, which offers a sense of outsized power and security for the human controlling it. Such movement is often exhilarating but also terrifying. Automobility is never simply the merging of human and machine as revealed in concrete physical action; it is also always deeply tied to intangible but powerful bursts of emotion initiated by that interaction. In the road narrative, driving (and riding to a lesser extent) must be an intimate emotional experience emanating from a seeming cooperation between human and machine toward goals that are imaginative as much as they are practical.

The pleasures of automobility permeate American cultural history, and narratives often express the inherent joy that movement affords. A few examples should suffice to capture this crucial component of the American open road. If the most expressive pleasure assumed within automobility is movement itself, then speed is often the most enthralling characteristic. One particularly evocative example occurs in *On the Road*, wherein Dean Moriarty's obsession with speed serves as a continual and unswerving expression of joy. Any time Dean is behind the wheel, there is speed (both rate of movement and illicit drug). We witness often how Kerouac develops Dean's mobile character through his intimate interactions with varying vehicles. In one of the most compelling sequences, Dean's power behind the wheel is manifest. Kerouac writes, "Dean headed pellmell for the mighty wall of Berthoud Pass that stood a hundred miles ahead on the roof of the world, a tremendous Gibraltarian door shrouded in clouds. He took Berthoud Pass like a June bug—same as at Tehachapi, cutting off the motor and floating it, passing everybody and never halting the rhythmic advance that the mountains themselves intended, till we overlooked the great hot plain of Denver again—and Dean was home."[24] This passage conflates several vital ideas. First is simply the unfettered, seemingly magical freedom of movement captured here. Though the use of "pellmell" evokes confusion and recklessness, that is the underlying point of such speed within the novel, especially as tied to Dean. It is the joy of the rollercoaster as the car moves with the constant hint of danger and uncertainty, the jerks and jolts pulling at readers and their sense of balance. It reasserts the use of rhythm to describe the road experience, especially the road tied to a subversive dream that finds joy in the movement.

The passage also reasserts Dean's power and grace as a driver who moves along the road with confidence, sitting behind the wheel of a car. In particular, the factual revelation that he cuts off the engine and coasts along the roadway provides an evocation of symbiosis between the road, the car, and Dean himself. In effect, when the vehicle is turned off, it accentuates the oneness of these road elements—human, machine, road—in a way that celebrates the unity of the experience. In addition, Kerouac pushes this point by implying through Sal's voice that the landscape is part of the synchronicity, suggesting that the mountains *intend* such movement. Sal goes on to state at the closing of the chapter that "the road is life."[25] The imagery reveals the ritualistic movement that implies a connection between all elements of modern life along the American open road, all conspiring to produce its essential pleasure.

This smooth blending of automobility within the landscape can be made more pleasurable with an idealized car. In another example, Sal and Dean drive a 1947 Cadillac in one of the most energetic sequences in *On the Road*. The Cadillac in the United States during the midcentury represented the ideal automotive machine. The "standard of the world" was an advertising tagline that few consumers in mainstream America would have questioned. When Sal and Dean get the opportunity to drive this Cadillac from Denver to Chicago, indeed they embark on a smooth stretch of road that most people would envy. The excitement is palpable as the two get this remarkably fortunate opportunity. Kerouac writes, "At the travel Bureau there was a tremendous offer for someone to drive a '47 Cadillac limousine to Chicago." Thus begins a segment that encapsulates the overarching joy derived from moving at high speeds, enhanced by the grace and beauty of the perfect vehicle. "It was a magnificent car; it could hold the road like a boat holds on water. Gradual curves were its singing ease. 'Ah, man, what a dreamboat,' sighed Dean. 'Think if you and I had a car like this what we could do. Do you know there's a road that goes down Mexico and all the way to Panama?—And maybe all the way to the bottom of South America where the Indians are seven feet tall and eat cocaine on the mountainside? Yes! You and I, Sal, we'd dig the whole world with a car like this because, man, the road must eventually lead to the whole world. Ain't nowhere else it can go—right?'"[26] This passage represents the subversive dream. Although Dean's vision is that of continual movement beyond the boundaries of the United States, what makes that idea resonate is the presence of material wealth and the economic stability inferred by the Cadillac. Dean revels in the promise of "a car like this," and happiness emanates from his emotional response to it, never mind the practical challenges of putting it into action. The expression of pleasure made possible by a machine called Cadillac drives the dream. Such moments are elemental to the ongoing appeal of road narratives.

Although *On the Road* is in many ways a record of degradation and heartache, its overriding spirit of joy serves as its defining characteristic. The novel captures the explicit joy of moving fast on America's roadways. It is simple. As Kerouac writes in yet another of the many excursions, "We all jumped to the music and agreed. The purity of the road. The white line in the middle of the highway unrolled and hugged our left front tire as if glued to our groove."[27] The "purity of the road" is tied to rhythm, and that beat rolls along the refrain of white lines passing underneath the car and giving metaphorical grooves to the vehicle, the pulse of a happy human heart. Throughout the narrative, Kerouac effectively ties the ever-present quality of the road to the spontaneity of music, particularly bebop with its improvisational energy. Here, everyone in the car is tied together in joyous celebration.

In another compelling sequence, Sal and Dean are riding in the back of a travel bureau car shared by others. Within this car we see a microcosm of the American open-road mythology, wherein the people in the front seat represent stable values, and the characters in the backseat, Sal and Dean, represent subversive values. "We had completely forgotten the people up front who had begun to wonder what was going on in the back seat. At one point the driver said, 'For God sakes, you're rocking the boat back there.' Actually we were; the car was swaying as Dean and I both swayed to the rhythm and the IT of our final excited joy in talking and living to the blank tranced end of all innumerable riotous angelic particulars that had been lurking in our souls all our lives."[28] The ambiguous "IT" implies recognition of the overarching joy of the present moment. As with references to music, the discussion between Sal and Dean rocks the vehicle and matches the rhythm of the road. Though the driver finds the energy emerging from the backseat unnerving, the joy is given physical impact on all occupants of the car. Sal and Dean's subversive mode seems odd, even threatening, to the others who are assuming a stable mode of travel: one car, two road experiences.

The pleasures asserted in the above examples from *On the Road* are present in myriad examples among all tiers of road narratives. In this place, however, I wish to draw on one image as illustrative of them all, partly for convenience but mostly for the joy this screenshot offers. It is taken from the film *Ferris Bueller's Day Off*, written by John Hughes, a tier 2 narrative built largely on a one-day road trip into Chicago from the suburbs.[29] Moreover, the most vital subplot of the film revolves around the tense relationship Cameron Frye (Alan Ruck) has with his father's car, a 1961 Ferrari 250 GT

California Spyder. The three teen protagonists drop off the Ferrari at a parking garage, unwittingly handing it over to an attendant who has just clocked out of work. He drives the car around the corner of the garage, picks up a friend, and pulls out into the city streets, thus beginning a wholly subversive joyride for the ages. In a short sequence showing glimpses of their adventure, the film captures perhaps the best shot of road happiness in American cinematic history (fig. 4.3).

Fig. 4.3. *Ferris Bueller's Day Off*, joy ride. DVD, Paramount, 2017. Author's screenshot.

Pleasure on the open road takes many forms, but it is always the driving force of human desire that perpetuates its revelation with automobility. The smattering of examples suggests the types of applications that express the inherent joy of mobility, but such moments tell only part of the emotional story of the open road. Yes, the road brings pleasure, but it also brings pain. The same imaginative power that conjures untold joy along the open road also portends unspeakable emotional devastation. Any journey may end in tragedy. If the road narrative stands as a metaphor for life, it must also inevitably suggest death.

In *Anywhere but Here*, a tier 2 narrative, Mona Simpson is conscious of this discomfiting fact of the road. She writes through the introspective voice of her young narrator, Ann, about the haunting presence of death associated with automobility: "All my life I'd imagined one death—slow motion, a clear day, pale blue sky, white clouds and a dull gray highway, a yellow stripe, the long bounce off a rounded blue fender, then the soft fall, dead, then nothing. All in sunlight. I'd never told anyone and I wonder if every person carried their own death with them, like something private and quiet, inside a small box."[30] This passage places the specter of death for Ann within an automobility context ideally suited to demonstrate her inner conflict. The passage evokes the inherent contradictions. Though Ann explains her imagined death on the road, there is no violence. Quite the contrary, it is dominated by positive descriptions: "clear day," "pale blue sky," "all in sunlight." Moreover, the crash itself is softened, "a long bounce off a rounded blue fender, then the soft fall."

The most frightening portion of the passage, however, resides in the confining, coffin-like image of the car. Both the vehicle of this dream and the idea of death itself for Ann derive from the same basic, simple description often used for both coffins and cars—a box. Though the explicit assertion of the open road as a positive, indeed "open," symbol dominates the road-narrative history, the corresponding idea of the road as a foreboding force remains a powerful undercurrent and thus merits attention as vital to understanding its conventions. The imagery is not always directly applied to death, but it taps into the powerful fears of the traveler that mobility itself will be stopped, a symbolic death, within the road narrative. Likewise, threats to the continued progress along the open road are thus ever-present and can range from simple inconvenience to horror.

In a direct counterpoint to the overarching tone of optimism defining the road horizon, the specter of death can also define mobile experiences. The road ahead can be ominous, something to demand trepidation from the traveler, as already inferred in reference to the opening segment of *Psycho* and in the *Twilight Zone* episode "The Hitch-Hiker." Another use of the road ahead as a menacing and constant threat comes from David Lynch, a master of this type of cinematic horror on the road. The cult sensation television show *Twin Peaks* used a swinging stop light, illuminated red, as a suggestive warning in its opening credits and often dramatized tumult and violence on roadways. It is the redux, *Twin Peaks: The Return*, however, that draws on road imagery most adroitly, even obsessively.[31] Viewers, as always with Lynch's work, struggle to understand what the hell is going on, but they are often rewarded with powerful explorations of the existential madness of human existence.

Twin Peaks: The Return makes extensive use of road mythology. In one of the most haunting uses of this imagery, Lynch simply forces viewers to gaze into the darkness of the road ahead. We peer through a looking-out windshield roadview but can discern very little, as the car's headlights reveal only a small portion of the frame. The remaining blackness is almost unbearable, a symbol of the abyss. This sequence is repeated throughout the series to suggest an impending catastrophe. Lynch lingers on the shots in each instance, forcing viewers into extended moments of tense uncertainty. The effect is unsettling as we try to reckon with the terrifying unknown ahead while also being forced to associate our perspective with the unhinged driver with whom we share the windshield view. We want to turn away or to stop but can do neither. This version of the windshield roadview carries no hint of optimism for a future, only dread. But death is not the only fear haunting the open road. The dangers of the road can also challenge our mobile psyche. Uncertainty in numerous forms haunts mobility. Our openness to experience suggests many opportunities for emotional upheaval on the road.

* * *

The emotional impact of mobility thus moves from extremes—joy to despair, life to death. Both poles of experience demand relevance. Examples of pleasure and pain provide a useful paradigm from which to think about our responses to a textured mobile experience. We move from exuberant expressions of bliss to devastating moans of anguish. Such content within the road narrative exists not simply to elicit emotional development but also to represent the wide range of encounters the road brings. The road is life; the road is death—and a plethora of pleasurable or painful experiences in between. The unbridled optimism of the road as life must be balanced by the uncontrollable fear of the road as death, and the emotional tumult that emanates from varied encounters serves as an essential convention of the road narrative. Nonetheless, as our road adventures reveal, we move at the threshold of change, ever-lurching from one moment to the next and perpetually telling the stories of our heroic lives.

5

Finding the Heroic Self

The Epic Road

THE SECOND HALF of the twentieth century was a golden age for the American open road, as varying narratives arose from the dynamism created by this era. This chapter focuses on the seminal literary and cinematic road narratives of this period. Four formidable best-selling prose narratives captured the specific context of their decades: Jack Kerouac's *On the Road*; John Steinbeck's *Travels with Charley*; Robert Pirsig's *Zen and the Art of Motorcycle Maintenance*; and William Least Heat-Moon's *Blue Highways*. In addition, this chapter also examines two cinematic road narratives: *The Long, Long Trailer* and *Easy Rider*. These tier 1 narratives enjoyed enviable marketplace success and critical respect and have thereby earned an enduring presence in American culture. Three other films—*National Lampoon's Vacation*, *Thelma & Louise*, and *Smoke Signals*—also deserve seminal distinction, but I place them in chapters 7 and 8, which focus on persistent gendered tensions. In this chapter, I remain attentive to thematic pairings: *On the Road* with *The Long, Long Trailer*; *Easy Rider* with *Zen and the Art of Motorcycle Maintenance*; and *Travels with Charley* with *Blue Highways*. By examining these crucial narratives in this manner, I hope to tease out their connectedness and explore the dialectics of the stable and subversive modes as they play out in these epic journeys.

ON THE ROAD AND *THE LONG, LONG TRAILER*

Jack Kerouac's *On the Road* is the cornerstone narrative of the American open road after World War II. That is an easy and—to a degree—obligatory statement to make. The novel captivated readers in the late 1950s and continues to hold sway as the shortcut assertion of the American road narrative well into the twenty-first century. Though there are better road narratives, none are as influential, and *On the Road* remains the measure of the postwar open-road idea.

Its centrality, however, most often comes from the belief that it establishes the ideals of the subversive road narrative. This is a misleading reading of the novel. *On the Road*, like all road narratives, employs facets of stable and subversive modes, and its success is deeply tied to the ever-present tension between the seemingly oppositional modes of the American open road. *On the Road* is seminal critically not because it defines only a countercultural road ethos but because it captures the struggle to balance our often-conflicting desires for both stability and subversion. In an especially useful discussion of the novel, Lars Erik Larson considers these competing influences as they are reflected in the struggles of Sal Paradise to define his road.[1] Larson correctly asserts the importance of the evolving ethos of the interstate system as a backdrop to reading the novel. Whereas Larson argues that the primary appeal of the novel has been how it presents the American open road as "granting deliriously liberating social, sexual, philosophical, and spatial freedoms," he also notes that Kerouac "stages a backlash against many of these liberations."[2] The novel thus reveals the complementary and oppositional perspective of the road tied to powerful cultural forces demanding conformity.

Kerouac's exploration of the cultural split in defining the open road in the 1950s is the strength of *On the Road.* Sal's journeys reveal intertwining and often contradictory notions of mobility. Roads can be travelled with a range of intentions. They provide opportunities for some travelers to escape and others to infiltrate, and for some to reject conformity and others to embrace it. Along these lines, Larson uses the terms "the ludic" and "the suspicious" to characterize the social schism and the inevitable pressures on the American psyche. In an era of containment thinking so prominent during the 1950s within its Cold War contentiousness, an open road is always a potential threat. Larson goes on to define the bicameral roads that result from this cultural tension, categorizing them as roads of containment and roads of promiscuity. These terms, and their underlying reasoning, correspond almost directly to the stable and subversive modes that I prefer, though Larson's interest is purposefully narrower. He notes the importance of what I am calling the stable road in *On the Road* and discusses the significance of "circular" mobility, with home as the point of departure and return.[3] The use of stable and subversive suggests a broader sweep and a more symbiotic association. Containment and promiscuity as framing terms, it seems to me, reduce Dean to an id character and Sal to a befuddled witness. The two characters are stronger representations of overlapping cultural desires than such nomenclature allows. Therefore, the adventures of Sal Paradise and Dean Moriarty create a more nuanced expression of American open-road mythology than is typically considered.

The subversive tone is set up early in the narrative as Sal celebrates his association with "mad" people in a passage referred to earlier, wherein he craves proximity to people who are "desirous of everything at the same time"[4] There is no better literary expression of the girding desire for the subversive mode, and every characteristic of the passage celebrates it while also acknowledging its tragic brevity without irony. He infers that madness is simply subversion, a fight against stagnation and boredom, a release of energy that inspires all those who seek it to express awe. Of course, Sal is often a tagalong soul desirous of association, but he is also one who struggles to wholly embrace madness, as he uses the term, as a primary actor. He seeks to be inspired by the burning but to do so without getting burned, and therein lies the complex mobility in the novel. Sal never claims to be mad.

Before exploring its meandering among stable and subversive modes, I would like to place Kerouac's novel in a comparative framework with another prominent American road narrative of the 1950s, one that earned a massive audience and that has unjustly been shuffled away from critical attention. Appearing a few years before the publication of *On the Road* and its subsequent sensation, *The Long, Long Trailer*, a film released in 1954 starring Lucille Ball and Desi Arnaz, was based on the travel book of the same title written by Clinton Twiss.[5] *The Long, Long Trailer* provides a provocative complementary text for *On the Road*. Taken together, the two successful narratives provide a more complex expression of the ideals of the open road in the formative 1950s.

The most popular American road narrative of the 1950s featured fictionalized versions of Lucille Ball and Desi Arnaz, not Jack Kerouac and Neal Cassady. America loved (loves) Lucy. *The Long, Long Trailer*, despite its success among readers of travel books and viewers of film comedies, however, has earned little attention in the critical world, and placing these two narratives side by side may seem odd. The juxtaposition is nonetheless rational and necessary to demonstrate the constant overlapping of the two modes in the American consciousness. *The Long, Long Trailer*—burdened perhaps by the length of its title as much as by the length of the trailer itself—is a substantive tier 1 road narrative, especially if we consider both of its versions. In fact, the differences between the travel book and the film are instructive. Twiss's book, a tier 1 narrative in its own right, is presented as a nonfictional narrative deriving from an elaborate road trip encircling the continental United States. It adopts a comic tone throughout. Though the book has been lost to readers since the original success, it is an ambitious journey around America that anticipates the more substantive narratives that would follow.

The Long, Long Trailer, in its original prose version, offers plenty of comic situations with much potential, but as a travel book it remains rather sparse line by line, mile by mile. Twiss's idea is much stronger than his literary follow-through. General readers at the time, however, found little to complain about. The novel went through eight printings in two years and encouraged much interest in Hollywood.[6] Before moving along to the film, which had a much broader reach in American culture, I wish to consider the book's structural and thematic breadth. Twiss understood the marketplace potential of his idea. The journey is ambitious, as the protagonists go from Southern California across the Southwest and South, including Florida, then up the entire Eastern Seaboard into Maine, then turn westward through upstate New York to Chicago, and finally head back to Los Angeles. This is a weighty American journey built around an arguably subversive idea: a middle-aged, middle-American couple opts out of the aspirational model for attaining the American dream. The idea behind taking to the open road is by no means anti-consumerist. To the contrary, the Twisses simply adapt the stable mode to the road by making the home mobile. The narrative structure is set to answer the basic question: What happens when a suburban home has wheels? The plan is to live on the road for two years, a conscious and intentional alteration of suburban life but not a rejection of it.

The film version, however, makes a significant shift away from this midlife adventure and builds its narrative around a young newlywed couple firmly committed to the material ideals of the American dream. The protagonists respond to the exigencies of the husband's job by making the homestead mobile. This road trip is not one of escape from domesticity but of immersion into it. Nicky (Desi Arnaz) is a road engineer, a career that forces him to move around from project to project as needed and thus be away from home often. Tacy (Lucille Ball) insists that they purchase a mobile home so that she can be with him. Her idea is that they are obligated as a newlywed couple to perform proper domesticity, and that can be assured only by providing him with a home to return to after a hard day's work. Moreover, unlike the case in Twiss's book, the couple in the film is at the beginning of their married life, and the journey, though not circular as the standard stable-mode journey, supports the idea of the home base as the definer of their mobility. The two use their honeymoon to travel to his first job assignment, moving the home from Southern California to Colorado, and the full film narrative tells that concise journey.

This significant alteration made by the screenwriters, Albert Hackett and Frances Goodrich, sets up a formidable tension between the original text by Twiss and the film version. We have no information regarding Twiss's thoughts on the film because of his tragic death in 1952, soon after the publication of the travel book and before the initial release of the film in late 1953. The film, to its credit, makes successful use of the comic scenes spread throughout Twiss's narrative, and the screenplay is perfectly suited to the stars of the film version. Arguably, the film is much better at fleshing out the humor under the well-established skills of Hackett and Goodrich and the direction of Vincente Minnelli. But the altered framing feels like a bowdlerization of the original work and thus a misrepresentation of it. It seems, quite frankly, that MGM purchased the book to surgically remove scenes rather than to embrace the scope of the original narrative. This is not surprising in that the enterprise was embarked on to take advantage of the enormous popularity of Lucy and Desi due to the success of their runaway hit television show *I Love Lucy*. A quick look at the promotional material for the film clarifies this mercenary context. Throughout the trailer for the film, the protagonists (Tacy and Nicky) are baldly referred to as "Lucy" and "Ricky," their *I Love Lucy* identities, "America's favorite comedy couple."[7] Audiences are assured that the new movie offers the same type of hilarity that has defined Lucy and Desi on television, and the film delivers solidly on this promise.

The core concept of taking a mainstream American "home" on the open road remains in both versions, and they both thus explore comically the inherent collisions caused by this melding of stable ideals with an extended journey. Comedy ensues because of that core incongruity, and the travels provide a quixotic sequence of events that, in the end, sets up plenty of failures, pratfalls, and misunderstandings. The film exploits an increasingly desperate effort to realize the dream of domestic mobility. As in the best episodes of *I Love Lucy*, the most pleasing segments of the film feature Tacy and Nicky easily overmatched by the perpetual—mile-by-mile—challenges of road life. Their flawed dream is compounded practically by the sheer size of the "long, long trailer" and symbolically by the inescapable absurdity of a home on wheels controlled by two people who have no experience with handling such a gargantuan load. In this sense, the screenwriters' choice to cast the protagonists as newlyweds was a stroke of genius because they have no experience in married life either. Their confused mobility is matched by their confused domesticity.

But their dream is pure and firmly rooted in the postwar boom wherein confident optimism ruled all. Fearful of being unable to establish a proper mainstream home for her new husband, Tacy pushes the idea of a trailer-home as the logical solution that will allow the new couple to fully establish middle-class respectability. She states, "If we had a trailer no matter where we went, I could make a home for you." This is a simple, seemingly obvious statement of normalcy to ensure that Nicky will be successful. In an especially poetic scene, she goes on to express the postwar dream of mobility in epic terms: "Can't you imagine what it would be like? Some of the most beautiful country in the world is between here and Colorado. The whole trip would be just like a dream. We go where we please, when we please. If we saw a beautiful spot beside a brook or a mountain lake, a lovely wood, and we'd stop there, and we'd be all alone. It would all be for us, moonlight and sunsets and the sound of tree toads."

As Tacy captivates Nicky with the poetic imagery and the inherent hope of the plan, they look off screen into the middle distance of an idealized American horizon. As the passage makes clear, this sales pitch asserts the American celebration of mobility central to both modes of road mythology. The statement—"we go where we please, when we please"—captures a subversive ideal, choosing experiences as opportunities arise. The stable component alters such a statement in that the spontaneity inherently implied is thoroughly grounded by the presence of a home. More importantly, their mobility derives from family decisions shared by the newlyweds. They both seem mesmerized as her voice trails away, immersed in a reverie. The moment is completed with the suggested sounds of tree frogs. The scene shifts abruptly into a contrasting setting. A gaudy neon sign appears: "Annual Trailer Show." The simple dream moves headlong into the marketplace.

What follows serves as a counterbalance to the later version of the open-road dream exploited by Kerouac's *On the Road*. Once they attend the Barnumesque bonanza that is the trailer show, the aspiring stable couple is thrust full throttle into consumer culture. As emerging participants in the mainstream middle-class values burgeoning in the 1950s, they are seduced by the larger trailers on display. During the purchasing process, they opt for a deeper entanglement with debt, which complicates the dream voiced above and makes their mobility fraught with economic peril. Freedom of mobility, as the balance of the film reveals often, is far from free. A few key scenes demonstrate the ironic underpinnings of the newlywed couple's corrupted hopes. Not only do they buy a trailer larger than intended, but they also buy a new, larger car capable of towing it. Moreover, they must customize that vehicle to ensure that capability. The implicit dangers to the couple, especially Nicky, are evident from the beginning, as he hits his head on first entering the trailer at the Annual Trailer Show. It gets worse.

As he tries to understand the practicalities of driving a "long, long trailer," Nicky reveals his underlying fears of being overwhelmed by the massive machinery. He learns quickly that taking a "home" on the open road is nothing less than terrifying. In the original book, Twiss ultimately names the entire rig "monster." The first drive with the trailer in the travel book is instructive.

As he embarks, Twiss notes the following as he looks into the rearview mirror: "In the mirror the trailer looked like a huge monolith, bearing down on us at break-neck speed. Quickly I looked away. It gave me quite a shock—I didn't realize the thing was so close. The faster I went, the faster the trailer followed. Again I got the feeling that the trailer had taken over. We were no longer towing *it*—*it* was pushing us!"[8] The impression of the trailer as constant threat, a "huge monolith" forever bearing down on the couple in the car, is formidable for Twiss as driver. The passage creates an effective comic image of a chase scene in which the desperate couple is unable to maintain control over their mobility as they are being, in effect, pushed by the trailer.

The awareness of such a threat to mobility carries over successfully into the film. In one of the most comic and telling segments, the mechanic who installs the trailer hitch assembly on the new vehicle instructs Nicky on how to drive the complicated rig. He emphasizes that Nicky must always remember the extra length that greatly alters every choice he makes on the road. The mechanic in the film version advises Nicky to consider that the trailer is like "forty feet of train" that is always behind him. In this sense, the "long, long trailer" is an apt image to evoke the burdensome nature of the updated American dream of mobility for mainstream America. In a voiceover, Nicky questions whether he pulls the trailer or the trailer pushes him, the omnipresent thought drawn directly from the original narrative.

The consumerist version of the road dream is what ultimately renders mobility treacherous for the newlyweds. The sheer size of the trailer (and its associated costs) makes their movement along the open road mostly miserable. This is foreshadowed before they ever take to the road when Tacy and her female friends pack the trailer as if it were a midsized ranch home. Again, the problem is best illustrated by the effects on Nicky, who is pushed around within and ultimately pushed out of the trailer altogether, thus out of the home. The comic treatment of Nicky parallels standard gendered dynamics as he is reduced to the traditional roles of financial provider—writing the checks—and manual laborer—driving, parking, and securing the trailer.

The film, more so than the travel book, uses the failures on the road to provide a steady and playful undermining of the aspirations of the young couple. Along that narrative line, the climactic scene becomes the treacherous ride up a mountain, a scene that occurs rather early in Twiss's book. For the film, the ordeal of climbing to eight thousand feet of elevation along a narrow road without guardrails becomes a comic nightmare that matches the overall instability of the newlyweds. The formidable challenges of negotiating dangerous driving conditions collide with the complementing stresses of matrimony, and the dream collapses under the strain. Throughout the tedious sequence, Minnelli presents the couple via windshield and

Fig. 5.1. *The Long, Long Trailer*, windshield. DVD, Warner Bros., 2018. Author's screenshot.

Fig. 5.2. *The Long, Long Trailer*, side window. DVD, Warner Bros., 2018. Author's screenshot.

side-window views, often looking like characters in a Hitchcock movie. They participate in idle chitchat as if they are not on the verge of disaster with each hairpin turn (figs. 5.1–5.2). To Minnelli's credit, the scene forces patience in viewers as they trudge ever-higher with a slow, methodical, death-march pace, an exacting sequence of comic terror as Nicky and Tacy teeter above the abyss.

After reaching the top of the mountain, the couple, though safe, suffers an even more significant setback. Before the tortuous climb, Nicky had asked Tacy to discard the canned vegetables and, more importantly, the souvenir rocks she had gathered during the trip. He was desperate to reduce the overall weight of the trailer. He discovers after the torturous climb that she had chosen not to do so, and, to his mind, the drive had been more difficult than necessary. The scene closes with a marital conflict more similar to those found in *Who's Afraid of Virginia Woolf* than anything audiences had ever seen from Lucy and Desi. The conflict includes implied violence from a man on the edge of madness who has been driven (pun necessary) into a rage. He takes rocks and throws them from the open door of the trailer as Tacy screams for him to stop. In any other context, this scene would be very troubling for audiences. This semi-comic, semi-tragic confrontation on the mountaintop sets up an emotional collision for the couple. The crisis is devastating, and they separate as a result. The scene confirms the failure of the journey to find domestic bliss on the road, and the protagonists are stopped cold.

This harsh ending to the dream-vision of America's couple does not stand for long. Nicky tries to find Tacy in an effort to repair the damage done by the grueling journey and the argument. In the down-pouring rain, he eventually finds her, and they reconcile, thus achieving the mainstay of American film history—the happy ending. The trailer had been parked as husband and wife apparently went their separate ways. When Nicky finally finds her, they meet in the doorway of the long, long trailer. Following the formula of a romantic comedy at this point, the two newlyweds are reunited after a horrible misunderstanding, and love conquers all. Tacy and Nicky embrace and kiss just inside the threshold of the doorway as the wind from the storm repeatedly blows the door open and shut, open and shut. As was typical of the situation comedy done so well in *I Love Lucy*, the story ends with a claim of normalcy restored and does so without any substantive investigation into the long-term implications of what has happened. Viewers must trust that they move forward with renewed confidence and solidarity. They embrace, after all, inside the trailer. The door is in motion, and the visual effect creates a liminal space of change—open, shut, open, shut—for the young couple. The narrative has stopped, but it does so by emphasizing ongoing transitions for the protagonists. They seem in motion toward stable unity at home and on the road. Standing at this liminal moment, they are together, and audiences can hold on to the safe assumption that they will stay in the home together and secure the door.

At roughly the same time that Clinton and Merle Twiss were traveling around the United States in their long, long trailer, gaining the experiences that would later become the travel book and then the wildly popular film, Jack Kerouac made several trips across the country as well. His experiences in those trips from 1947 to 1949 would eventually become *On the Road*, published ten years after his original journeys. It was a fortunate delay in that by the late 1950s, the appetite for a subversive open-road celebration was huge. *On the Road*, however, is far from a one-trope narrative of the joys of spontaneity and irreverence. Rather, it is more like *The Long, Long Trailer*, a narrative with pervasive ambivalence regarding the stability of mainstream American road ideals. Kerouac's novel is defined throughout by the inner tensions plaguing its narrator, Sal Paradise, regarding the long-term prospects of the subversive mode, even as it revels in the ever-present moment any time vehicles are in motion.

Sal's interest in "mad" people affirms his essential subversive road ethos. This affinity is confirmed in the closing statements of the opening chapter. As he attaches himself to Dean Moriarty, Sal's "life on the road" begins as a stance firmly against stability. An avatar of subversive mobility, Dean offers for Sal "a new horizon."[9] Sal goes on to state his confidence in this mode of travel, noting, "I was a young writer, and I wanted to take off." He expects that the road life would meet his expectations and the "the pearl would be handed" to him. No wonder so many readers were excited by this energy and confidence. Yet readers often blur over the fact that the hunger that Sal has for the open road has been set up by the failure of his attempts at mainstream stability.

The chapter opens with the crucial background information that Sal's marriage has failed and he has been ill, suffering from an emotional breakdown that has rendered the world "dead," as he puts it. This is the first assertion of identity in the novel that is wholly self-referential and separate from Dean's shadow of influence. Yet even this information comes seemingly sublimated to the first clause of the novel: "I first met Dean." Whereas by the end of the chapter Sal is firmly rooted in Dean's road mythos, readers should not forget the failed stability asserted in the opening sentence regarding Sal's domesticity.[10] Dean provides a way out of Sal's doldrums, but Sal is never wholly disconnected from stable desires. His clamoring for subversive kicks is always tempered by a long-term yearning for a home.

Sal Paradise, while being enamored of Dean's madness, is also very much like Clinton Twiss, the prose narrator of *The Long, Long Trailer*, the middle-aged discontent who seeks a two-year Thoreauvian journey away from the mundane. In both cases, the men leave home with significant levels of discontent. A real man (Clinton Twiss) and a fictional character (Sal Paradise) exist on the page with a significant point of comparison; both are disenchanted by the promise of stability. Perhaps Twiss's and Sal's individual decisions are tempered by their individual experiences. The aging Twiss, making choices from within a successful marriage, has no option for an individualized odyssey. The younger Sal, reeling from a failed marriage, has yet to establish a new home of his own. In *The Long, Long Trailer* (the book), the goal is to maneuver a home along the open road and thus make the subversion, in the end, stable—to escape without leaving home. In *On the Road*, the goal is to purge the subversive desire via aggressive immersion and thus make possible the stabilizing acquisition of a home in the end. Madness, as defined by Sal, is always intended to be glorious but temporary.

Within Sal's narrative, we can see this underlying tension in two instructive moments of bliss. In a lengthy episode characterizing what he calls "the greatest ride in my life," Sal shares a perfect example of the subversive open-road ideal and the joy it offers.[11] He has joined a group of men on the back of a flat-bed truck speeding through Nebraska on the way to California. The "two young blond farmers from Minnesota" are in the cab, and they pick up "every single soul" they encounter. The scene becomes an energetic celebration of American freedom of movement defined by speed, camaraderie, and carefree exuberance. Sal explains, "I yelled for joy. We passed the bottle. The great blazing stars came out, the far-receding sand hills got dim. I felt like an arrow that could shoot all the way."[12] This one-way dream of moving like an "arrow" is perfectly matched to the subversive mode. Though Sal is headed for California, the emphasis here is pure mobility as the essential element of experience, stars blazing as if in agreement. Invigorating and infectious, the energy of the passage matches the spontaneity of the subversive ideal. It is a pleasure that arises from pure chance and a willingness to take experiences as they come.

Contrast that moment with an equally poetic expression Sal later provides in San Francisco. He finds a vista from which to view the city and describes a compelling landscape image of hope and contentment. He comments, "I spun around till I was dizzy; I thought I'd fall down as in a dream, clear off the precipice. Oh where is the girl I love? I thought, and looked everywhere, as I had looked everywhere in the little world below."[13] Unlike the image of himself moving as an "arrow" speeding across the landscape, here the movement is circular, and there are hints of a stable road-wish. In response to a landscape view and images of contentment within "the romantic city in white," Sal describes himself as spinning as he takes in the scene, his emotional longings sparked by his turning around. He laments for a woman—"the girl I love"—who, it seems, could steady his dizzying mobility at the edge of a precipice. This description, too, defines his movement and is a vital part of his road life, a dream of stability that never departs from his consciousness.

The novel follows a departure/return format throughout, and this is not simply a matter of structural convenience. It is central to the overall concept of the open road Kerouac explores. Though readers have been much more inclined to celebrate the departures, with their manic vibrancy, they all occur within an equally significant reframing of Sal in a domestic context via persistent returns to stability. There is a constant push and pull of subversive and stable inclinations for Sal, and these vacillations are instructive. The fulcrum, of sorts, for Sal is his aunt's home. The ending of part 1 completes a circular movement, a return to that home and thus to normalcy: "I had my home to go to, my place to lay my head down and figure the losses and figure the gain that I knew was in there somewhere too. . . . When I got home I ate everything in the icebox."[14] The clarity of a homeplace allows him to assess the experience overall. In short, the meaning of movement can be defined only when girded by the stability persistently available in his aunt's home. His perambulations are consistently grounded by a place of stability with a full icebox.

All five parts of *On the Road* carry this basic complementary relationship with departure and return, and it even reveals itself in smaller scenes and interactions. As a complementary pairing to illustrate this concisely, we can simply note how the end of the novel parallels the end of part 1, the same dynamics in place and, of course, the same impulse for Sal to return home, this time for good. The road into Mexico presents many challenges to readers, especially those readers who are growing quite tired of the arrogance of the protagonists and the pervasive condescension to women who are steadily placed into subservience. However, the road into Mexico forms a cohesive symbolic extension of the open-road dream within the context of the novel. The narrative in Mexico disintegrates quickly, and despite the subversive joy expressed while mobile, the actions of the protagonists undermine any productive aspirations tied to road mythology. The segment descends into debauchery, and Sal ends up miserably sick in Mexico City.[15] The dream has fallen apart, and Dean ultimately abandons Sal, revealing the actual rationale that led to the incursion into Mexico: to get divorce papers to end his marriage to Camille. As he ditches Sal, Dean says, "Gotta get back to my life."[16] Dean Moriarty, the seemingly unswerving devotee of road pleasure, the man who aggressively acts as if animated by the subversive dream, is going *home*. This absurd turnaround has been actually evident all along as again and again Dean forges delusory home-lives that ironically mock stability. At long last, doubled over in pain and delirious with fever, Sal is in a liminal moment that blurs the distinctions between reality and dream. Exhausted but renewed, Sal awakens.

The experience in Mexico allows for the final separation, which occurs in New York, wherein Sal, in a moment of self-assertion, rejects Dean and thus the subversive mode. Unable to share the ride with him this time, Sal describes the last image of Dean. Sal is sitting in the backseat with his new girlfriend, Laura, as they are going to dinner as part of a night of respectable socializing. Dean has no place within this context, and for the first time Sal accepts that incongruity and honors the wishes of his other companions in the car. The juxtaposition of the haggard Dean on the street, on the one hand, and the comfortable Sal in the back seat of a luxury automobile, on the other hand, is a crucial framing scene of contrasts: "The Cadillac was parked and ready to go. Dean stood outside the windows with his bag, ready to go to Penn Station and on across the land."[17] This is a tableau of the stable (Cadillac "ready to go") and the subversive (Dean "ready to go") in one frame, the moment frozen just before the two men move in opposite directions. Just as the energy of this moment moves from potential to kinetic when the car pulls away, Sal changes.

The physical positioning in the moment for both men is significant in that it shows the altered states for each as well as their implied futures. Sal has chosen a stable road, and Dean illustrates the effects of his manic, speed-driven perversions of both stability and subversion, once again rambling across the country but heading back to a home. Dean asks for a ride, but Sal cannot help him anymore. Remi, who has rented the vehicle, refuses to allow Dean inside. "So Dean couldn't ride uptown with us and the only thing I could do was sit in the back of the Cadillac and wave at him. . . . Dean, ragged in a motheaten overcoat he brought specially for the freezing temperatures of the East, walked off alone, and the last I saw of him he rounded the corner of Seventh Avenue, eyes on the street ahead, and bent to it again."[18] In this last image, the focus is yet again on the road, but Dean is bent over, cold, and on foot, a posture far removed from the fluidity so often infusing his movements. Sal's days of subversive travel are over, and it appears that he may be on the verge of obtaining the mainstream dream that has undergirded his mobility. Sal's position in the moment is crucial: he is in the back of a Cadillac on his way to a Duke Ellington concert at the Metropolitan Opera. He will listen to jazz standards (not bebop) that will smoothly fill a glorious concert hall, everyone dressed in their finest. This sounds like a wonderful night of mainstream respectability. It is, of course, a far cry from the sweaty and grimy club scene that appears so provocative and engaging in earlier moments of the novel. Sal is not enthusiastic for the evening ahead, but he is moving toward it nonetheless.

The glorious final paragraph of the novel, a testament to the landscape imaginary, emphasizes movement yet one more time, a convention of the road narrative. Sal is perched on an "old, broken down river pier" looking toward New Jersey but in imagination taking in the whole of the continent and the nation westward. He celebrates the land that "rolls on in one unbelievable huge bulge over to the West Coast, and all that road going, all the people dreaming in the immensity of it."[19] The phrase, "all that road going," must be read as expressive of both stable and subversive modes. Though seemingly at home or at least at rest and content, Sal holds within his consciousness the dream of Dean in its most appealing version, tinged with nostalgia for those early roads. All in all, Sal reasserts a dream of mobility that is a hopeful statement for us all and our ever-present desire for and potential to change. The closing mood denotes liminality in a scene that begins as the sun goes down, always a threshold moment. Sal continues with his image of the nation writ large, noting that "the evening star must be drooping and shedding her sparkler dims on the Prairie, which is just before the coming of complete night that blesses the earth, darkens all rivers, cups the peaks and folds the final shore in, and nobody, nobody knows what's going to happen to anybody besides the forlorn rags of growing old."[20]

Kerouac's *On the Road* is most celebrated for its manic energy in stark contrast and in conflict with the mainstream respectability so dominant in late 1950s America. Kerouac's novel is nonetheless deeply tied to the stable mode as well. Throughout, Sal struggles between the push and pull that each mode represents. He vacillates between intense desires to move and equally powerful desires to create a home. The rewards for both are seductive and equally tenuous. To read *On the Road* without both modes is to read half a novel, and to vault Kerouac's fiction as a celebrant only of subversion is to mischaracterize the road mythology in the bustling decades following World War II. In the last line, he avers that "nobody knows what's going to happen" other than the persistent, plain old fact of aging, so the uncertainties of our roads ahead are always shared, no matter our mode of "road going."

TRAVELS WITH CHARLEY AND *BLUE HIGHWAYS*

John Steinbeck took to the open road with well-established heft in the American imagination. When he published *Travels with Charley* in 1962, the same year that he earned the Nobel Prize for literature, Steinbeck was arguably foremost among living American writers both for his critical reputation and for his popular appeal. *The Grapes of Wrath*, his most famous work, which earned the National Book Award and the Pulitzer Prize for fiction, was firmly in the American grain. The novel and the subsequent film, directed by John Ford and released in 1940, captivated audiences and evoked a road weariness definitive of Depression-era America.[21] The idea in the early 1960s for a literary giant like Steinbeck to embark on a journey around the United States was publishing gold. For Steinbeck to find a robust readership at that point was a given, and he stands alone among the seminal road-prose narratives in that regard. The man on the move in this instance did so as a celebrity. *Travels with Charley* provides an instructive example of the complexity of the road narrative and its relationship not only to the conventional interactions between self and place but also to how mobility impacts travelers with ambivalent feelings for the open road.

The formulation of the narrative idea is especially important. The subtitle, "In Search of America," asserts its grand thesis, a task perfect for Steinbeck. Add to that setup the inclusion of a companion dog, and all things are in place for a best seller. However, *Travels with Charley* is a problematic text that challenges critical appraisal. Since Steinbeck presents it as a travel book, an ostensibly nonfictional narrative recording actual travels, it is open to more scrutiny than a fictional account would garner, no matter his fame and no matter, to be clear, the readability of the book. Make no mistake about it: *Travels with Charley* is a good read. It seems, though, that Steinbeck played rather loose with the facts and, in many ways, created a unreliable text.[22] I have no interest in getting mired in the associated debates on this issue, quite simply because *Travels with Charley*, regardless of any questions of legitimacy, remains a tier 1 road narrative and a compelling reading experience. Though he committed sins as a travel writer, his road narrative is beloved and a vital component of American road-narrative history. To ignore it would be folly. It remains a tricky text, however, due to its content, so I will address some of its failings as a road narrative simply because doing so may help illuminate its open-road imagination.

Anyone examining travel writing as a vibrant genre blending multiple forms of literature must account, on some level, for the literary license enjoyed by writers. A travel writer cannot claim the wide latitude afforded by fiction and still maintain the credibility inferred by the writing of fact, yet to assume that a travel narrative does not include fabrication is naïve. It is a thorny sliding scale. One of the best travel writers ever produced in the United States is Mark Twain, who is also one of our best liars. Twain employed much fictionalized content in his travel writing, so readers should be careful to consider "Mark Twain" within any given narrative as a persona existing within that narrative only. Twain's readers always fully understood and loved his manipulation of any given situation for its comic and satirical potential or even simply for its convenience. I should add that reading Twain's travels is a wonderful way to spend time. Steinbeck, to the contrary, never established such a context for manipulating his narrative voice, and there is nothing in the presentation of experiences in *Travels with Charley* that implies otherwise.[23]

Steinbeck's scope is grand and serious. He sets up an elaborate frame for his work to match the idealistic search for America. He names his van "Rocinante," the name of Don Quixote's horse, a rather romantic choice that gives his narrative a self-consciously quixotic feel.[24] In addition, he travels incognito as a buffer against his fame, which could have altered how people reacted to him. When he began his perambulations, Steinbeck was fifty-eight years old (sixty at the time of publication) and well off financially. As he drove around America, he endured, we can assume, the many discomforts of age along with the many comforts of money. Both influenced choices made on the road and at the writing desk. Steinbeck did not travel like the Joads, the desperate family of *The Grapes of Wrath*, though it would be disingenuous for Steinbeck fans to deny that he conjures up such authenticity within the text. This is the choice of an author with a keen sense of creating compelling characters and rewarding readers with interesting content.

A crucial component of any travelogue is how authors justify their travels. In short, authors must explain what prompts their departures and what purposes drive their journeys. The subtitle, "In Search of America," is a rather lofty claim for Steinbeck to make, though it is also a rather generic one. To assert a desire to see and *know* America is always at the heart, implicitly, of any nonfictional travel narrative in the United States, and many travelers take to the open road with that goal in mind. The second component is equally important: *how* the travels occur or, rather, what mode of transportation defines the experience. For *Travels with Charley*, the vehicle is a modified pick-up truck camper, a home on wheels that locates Steinbeck's journey firmly within the stable mode. Though he implies that he is a romantic traveler tilting at cultural windmills, his vehicle is more accurately a tool for him to emphasize the grounding importance of home on the road. Steinbeck in effect merges *The Long, Long Trailer* and *On the Road* by keeping the metaphorical sense of home as he moves around the country while also implying that he makes his choices of where to go with a subversive glee. He implies that readers may need to help set the scene because at times he may not. Often, as a thoughtful man, he follows his imaginative inclinations with no direct connection to what may be happening on the road. He writes, "While these discussions go on you are to imagine me bowling along on some little road or pulled up behind a bridge, or cooking a big pot of lima beans and salt pork."[25] This is compelling imagery that conjures a genuine world for Steinbeck's travels reminiscent of the Depression era. He taps into the authentic simplicity of the Joads but without their constant, desperate struggle for survival.

Steinbeck rejects the inclusion of facts and figures, especially details of specific road and highway designations and other map-related information. He observes correctly that writers cannot include everything, nor should they, but this also assumes permission to be suggestive rather than reportorial. He provides a rough outline of his travels but notes that he does not like doing so: "I can report this because I have a map before me, but what I remember has no reference to the numbers and colored lines and squiggles. I have thrown this routing in as a sop and shall not make a habit of it."[26] Steinbeck's disdain for the dry facts and figures found on a map harkens back to Kerouac in a way that allies *Travels with Charley* with *On the Road*. Kerouac, through Sal, demonstrates clearly that dependence on maps restricts openness to legitimate road experiences, as assumed by the subversive mode. Steinbeck seems in full agreement, and he goes on to write a lovely passage, sharing heartfelt engagements with places rather than pedestrian renderings of facts and figures: "What I remember are the long avenues in the frost, the farms and houses braced against the winter, the flat, laconic Maine speech in crossroads stores where I stopped to buy supplies. The many deer that crossed the road on nimbling hooves and leaped like bounding rubber away from the passing Rocinante."[27]

Travels with Charley offers many such passages demonstrating Steinbeck's skill for creating introspective awareness of life as viewed from the road. Such abstractions can be critiqued for a lack of specificity, but the passage summons a depth that resonates for readers. Here and in many other examples, Steinbeck employs a side-window view focusing reader attention on the places and people he encounters. Such road moments demonstrate a key understanding of the genre and its tropes. This passage is evocative of why anyone should desire the open road and, for that matter, why readers love Steinbeck. There is little doubt, however, that he hedges his bets as his experiences evolve into narrative. He writes, "I cannot commend this account as an America that you will find. So much there is to see, but our morning eyes describe a different world than do our afternoon eyes, and surely our wearied evening eyes can report only a weary evening world."[28] This observation is perfectly true and beautiful, and it is indicative of much of the content of *Travels with Charley*. Steinbeck gives readers rewarding road experiences throughout the text. Each moment has the capacity to invoke a consciousness substantively tied to the interaction of self and place. No matter where each of us may stand on the legitimacy of *Travels with Charley* as nonfictional, the fact remains that the book does not reach its potential. Yes, his misrepresentation of his travel itinerary is a problem, but that issue is separate from what is most important for consideration here.

Travels with Charley has faults aside from the authenticity problems, and they warrant scrutiny here because they undermine the representation of narrative and imagination on the road. The real problem is that the book is incomplete and thus fails to sufficiently fulfil the conventional promises of a road narrative, especially as tied to the liminality of the heroic quest. The journey as promised is not realized on the page, and readers encounter too many partially explored moments on the road and, most importantly, a narrator who does not awaken. Simply put, Steinbeck runs out of energy for both the traveling and the writing. On the way back from California, for what logistically should be the second half of his odyssey, he chooses to rush to an end and provide only a glimpse of the Southwest and what he calls "a sampling of the Deep South." His failure to engage with the whole journey undercuts the liminal value of the open road. That is a shame, for the writing, even in this portion, is excellent. The truncated second half of the narrative makes *Travels with Charley* an unfinished quest.

A few representative segments illustrate this complication. As he turns back east, he foreshadows that he will condense the narrative. Later, he goes on to acknowledge that he will shorten his trip dramatically, but he makes those admissions only after asserting a bold and comprehensive summary judgment of the greatness of America. As above in the passage that argues for an impressionistic road experience, the following passage demonstrates Steinbeck's undeniable skill. He begins by implying failure in his "search of America" and notes that "it would be pleasant to be able to say of my travels with Charley, 'I went out to find the truth about my country, and I found it.'"[29] Steinbeck, it seems, has found the nation too complicated and his chosen task too daunting. Yet, in the same segment, he boasts that he could have overcome such challenges rhetorically and, after doing so, "lean back comfortably with a fine sense of having discovered truths and taught them to my readers." He claims that he chose not to perform such trickery.

This commentary is interesting in that Steinbeck affirms the limitations of his perceptions and thus narrows the narrative experience to a more honest engagement with the road. That is fair. Any writer should feel free to make such a choice. However, he follows with bombast, noting, "From start to finish, I found no strangers. If I had, I might be able to report them more objectively. But these are my people and this is my country."[30] This comment shows a writer at work, but it is well-crafted balderdash more reflective of ego than engagement. He goes on to note the greatness of the nation, and he stamps this appraisal with, "This is not patriotic whoop-de-do; it is carefully observed fact."[31] To be sure, "this" is most certainly "whoop-de-do," and the problem is not the patronizing calculation of the statement but the fact that it is rhetorical cover for a narrative choice revealed in the next paragraph: "Starting on my return journey, I realized by now that I could not see everything. My impressionable gelatin plate was getting muddled. I determined to inspect two more sections and then call it a day—Texas and a sampling of the Deep South."[32] Weary of the journey, he bails out halfway through. I wish he would have said as much rather than including this disingenuous sleight of hand. It was his trip. He was free to make any adjustments he wanted to, and readers would have indulged him without hesitation. It seems that he did not trust that option.

What follows Steinbeck's pronouncement is generic material meeting a minimum word count. He offers a glimpse of Texas via one extended experience on a ranch, then takes a cursory look at "the South" before heading quickly home to New York City. The segment in New Orleans—"the Deep South"—is gripping even though we must recognize that it is a pastiche of genuine travel writing, the work of a master author who is also a weary traveler. He does what he needs to do rhetorically to create content, mainly by giving rides to others in need and establishing the dialogue as authentic experience. To believe that he reports the specific encounters of riders is a stretch. Yet he ensures that the package of "the Deep South" is presented true to form with all the expected components nicely represented straight out of central casting. Steinbeck makes two key mistakes for travel writing. On one hand, his process is pretentious—the grand old master of letters takes to the open road in a traveling home, a camper, to be among the people like Henry V. On the other hand, he sets himself up as a dispassionate observer. The inherent contradiction is unworkable. He tries to blend the tough task of reportage with an individualized heroic quest. Unfortunately, he had neither the energy for the quest nor the actual democratic road experience he had envisioned. In the supposed second half of the journey, *Travels with Charley* lacks substantive interaction between self and place, and it therefore lacks threshold moments as catalysts for any awakening for an alert, engaged traveler.

Travels with Charley therefore skirts the essential exploration of liminality, the central tenet of the road narrative. Steinbeck finishes his trip by offering a brief and rushed ending that matches the narrator's exhaustion. Despite the promising departure, there have been few collisions (none of transformative power) and thus no genuine awakening, other than his becoming aware of the fact that an aging man of significant economic means is willing to tolerate only so much discomfort. Yet, true to Steinbeck's skill, the ending is rhetorically fitting and rewarding.

Desirous of being done with it. Steinbeck writes a stark but still effective conclusion. He has returned and sits "lost" a few miles from the safety of his home. As he moves toward Manhattan, he gets caught up in the cacophony of automotive congestion: "The increasing river of traffic for New York carried me along." After exiting from the Hoboken ferry, he is flummoxed by the crush of downtown traffic during rush hour: "I made a turn and then another, entered a one-way street the wrong way and had to back out, got boxed in the middle of a crossing by a swirling rapids of turning people." He manages, as he reports, to get out of the flow and park the car, and he begins laughing, "shaking with road jitters."[33] This is a great moment of humility and humor that is wonderfully appealing. It follows the theme of being overwhelmed by the entirety of the journey. The closing sequence indeed shows Steinbeck caught in a "rush" of energy, and he is terrified. Unable to maintain his place within the "swirling rapids" of snarling traffic, he parks Rocinante.

Despite the complaints I have about the foreshortening of the narrative, this moment is one of the best revelations of the complexities of mobility we could find. Its irony is charming, and, whether or not it is true to Steinbeck's actual experience, it rings valid within the narrative. Steinbeck, having driven around the country, gets lost a few miles from home. This moment remarks on Steinbeck's age and increasing immobility. He is profoundly happy to be close to home and thus relieved of the pressures of driving. Despite any hopes he may have had to scratch a subversive itch at the beginning of the narrative, Steinbeck's travels are firmly within a stable mode. The journey, having been endured more than embraced, is over. Readers can easily infer with confidence an implicit but undeniable thought in Steinbeck's mind: there's no place like home.

William Least Heat-Moon is one of America's most successful and capable travel writers. Unlike the other writers of seminal works discussed in this chapter, he is, indeed, a professional travel writer, and he has put together a remarkably successful career, all made possible by his astounding first effort, *Blue Highways*. His works have steadily demonstrated a fully charged imagination that is both literary and epic while also being methodical and grounded in day-to-day life. Those books are also defined by beautiful prose, line by line, mile by mile. He has had great ideas, and fruitful travel writing often hinges on framing. He has built road narratives based on a circular journey around the United States on "blue" highways, a "deep map" exploration into Kansas, a journey by water across the country, and a "mosey" around the edges of normalcy on American back roads, among other nonfictional works.[34]

Great writers have found the most success by tapping into the mood of the nation's readership, and of all Heat-Moon's books, it is *Blue Highways* that had the most perfect vision and timing. It caught fire in the public, spending forty-two weeks on the *New York Times* bestseller list in 1982 and 1983. Heat-Moon successfully employs the narrative framing at the heart of romantic open-road mythology: a man down on his luck gets in a vehicle and drives. Reestablishing the power of the road narrative after the malaise of the late 1970s, his trip occurred thirty years after those early trips taken by Jack Kerouac.[35] His marketplace success illustrates the ongoing power of the road narrative well into the 1980s, and the content of *Blue Highways* consistently aligns with the perennial struggle to find balance in subversive and stable modes of travel.

Heat-Moon pairs well with Steinbeck, both writers drawing on substantive literary skills. Fully engaged throughout his journey, Heat-Moon taps into the emotional appeal of the open road as a place of both discovery and mystery, the unknown evoked by the alluring but also foreboding blue-hewn roadways of rural America. The epigraph explains the logic behind the use of the term "blue highways" as a poetic distinction but also a practical one, since the color is representative both of the inherent liminality of travel but also of the actual colors used on Rand McNally maps to indicate older national, state, and county highways as distinct from the interstates in red. More importantly, this imagery sets up the overarching focus on the shifting self that the narrative is equally concerned with, wherein "blue" highways represent mood and desire as well and can beckon a man to "lose himself." Implicit in the poetry of this epigraph is that the road always offers opportunity to be lost and found at the same time. Heat-Moon's ability to capture this liminal tone from the outset is the key to the formidable reach of *Blue Highways*.

He builds on this mood in the opening lines of chapter 1: "Beware thoughts that come in the night. They aren't tuned properly. They come in askew, free of sense and restriction, deriving from the most remote of sources."[36] Few works of literature have stronger opening lines. In short, his disordered thoughts in the night result from his loss of stability. In this sense, his position parallels that of Sal Paradise in *On the Road*. Heat-Moon's predicament, however, catches him in middle age, and the blow strikes comprehensively. His job has gone away, his wife has gone away; what is left for him to do? The answer is this: "A man who couldn't make things go right could at least go." Heat-Moon chooses the subversive mode not from youthful energy but, more poignantly, from middle-aged desperation.[37]

Ironically, he infers that the choice will force him to face the "real jeopardy of circumstance" definitive of subversion, yet his heretofore assumed stability had already revealed plenty of jeopardy, leaving him in dire circumstances indeed. But the stable mode—as always—will nonetheless figure into Heat-Moon's journey. His plan, concocted in the night, makes this point clear: "Following a circle would give a purpose—to come around again—where taking a straight line would not." This statement reflects more than just symbolic convenience or basic geographical practicality. Tracing the round assumes a "purpose" affirmed by a return home, even when that home must be rebuilt. Implicit in Heat-Moon's desire for stability is the vehicle that he chooses, a van that he converts into a mobile home of sorts, a 1975 Ford Econoline that was "self-contained but not self-containing."[38] He transforms the van from a "clangy tin box into a place at once a six-by-ten bedroom, kitchen, bathroom, parlor." Of course, although he is traveling in a vehicle lacking in many of the typical comforts of a home, he nonetheless carries that home symbolically with him. Heat-Moon's plan for his road journey, then, is built on stability, the organic wholeness of the circle itself made manifest in the mode of travel, a home on wheels that parallels his desire to put his sense of self back together.

Heat-Moon creates his version of the heroic quest by weaving in thoughtful engagements with people and their struggles to add texture to his own story. The people he talks to in his first five days on the road offer a strong indication of a theme: men restoring a log cabin in Shelbyville, Kentucky; an aging couple in the middle of a six-year process of renovating a houseboat in Brooklyn Bridge, Kentucky; a family barely making ends meet running a general merchandise store in Nameless, Tennessee. The stories indicate underlying desires for stability, all moving in one way or another toward idiosyncratic but nonetheless universal dreams.

Encounters with locals do not always have a positive impact, however. As he waits for a rainstorm to subside in Louisiana, Heat-Moon provides a strong meditation on his experiences thus far (still in the first quarter of the trip) and his struggle to find order. He writes, "Reading my notes of the trip—images, bits of conversation, ideas—I hunted a structure in the events, but randomness was the rule. Outside, sheltered by a live oak, a spider spun a web. Can an orb weaver perceive the design in its work, the pattern of concentric circles lying atop radiating lines?"[39] Drawn to the symbolic order implied by a circle, Heat-Moon craves a structure to clarify his purpose, but he has yet to be on the road long enough to fashion fragments into meaning. The downpour continues the entire day, trapping him inside the humid vehicle. At sunset, it stops, and Heat-Moon walks around to get air before retiring for the day, which had been unproductive. He shares a simple but provocative encounter. He watches a man stand over a barbecue grill, "his belly a drooping bag, his face slack." Heat-Moon recoils, writing, "The man's numb stasis disturbed me. Got to get moving, I thought, and hurried to my rig and drove."[40] In this moment, Heat-Moon unfairly castigates this man, but he sees a version of himself. The use of "stasis" is telling here, in that Heat-Moon's response to this man directly follows being hampered by the weather. The mundanity of the man at his grill, in that moment, unnerves Heat-Moon, who seeks separation so as not to be implicated by the stagnation he sees. He moves.

The man does not simply represent a lack of mobility; rather, he shows a lack of imagination. By distancing himself from this particular man lording it over a grill, Heat-Moon reveals his inner disquiet. This reaction is an important if fleeting moment because he continues to develop this pattern of juxtaposing his fears of stasis with perceived failures in other men he encounters. The quick observation and dismissal of this man at the grill sets up a sustained consideration later as Heat-Moon engages at length with another man. Having moved into the American Southwest, Heat-Moon emphasizes the uncertainty of the desert landscape itself: "There's something about the desert that doesn't like a man, something that mocks his nesting instinct and makes his constructions look feeble and temporary."[41] This line is reminiscent of the opening of Robert Frost's "Mending Wall"—"Something there is that doesn't love a wall"—and the isolation it explores. The line also draws on the deep, comprehensive fears suggested in another of Frost's poems, "Desert Places," which focuses on an empty, indifferent, and overwhelmingly lonely landscape "with no expression, nothing to express."[42] The pivotal idea here is the tenuousness of man's "constructions," which can apply to physical walls as well as emotional ones. In all of these references, the key is the vulnerability of a self defined by uncertainty. He is in a liminal state of mind.

At the end of a grueling day wherein Heat-Moon crosses the Continental Divide four times, he stumbles on a pleasant natural scene in the Chiricahua Mountains of Arizona. He finds himself in a bower of sorts that provides a lovely place for him to make camp along Cave Creek. The setting is ideal. Its peacefulness promises to counter the negative images of the desert. He writes, "I was in one of the strangest pieces of topography I'd ever seen, a place, until now, completely beyond my imaginings. What is it in a man that for a long while lies unknown and unseen only one day to emerge and push him into a new land of the eye, a new region of the mind, a place he has never dreamed of? Maybe it's like the force in spores lying quietly under the asphalt until the day they push a soft, bulbous mushroom head right through the pavement. There's nothing you can do to stop it."[43] This evocative passage builds on the underlying sense of liminality and implies a more optimistic tone for this restful moment on the road. He ties the landscape directly to his state of mind on the verge of a shift in sensibility, "a new land of the eye," that promises to burst through his consciousness (his construction of self) like a "mushroom . . . through the pavement." Into this setting, however, with "a sudden movement in the darkness," a man enters and asks, "Writing a book?"

The "Boss of the Plains," as Heat-Moon defines him, the name deriving from his Stetson hat, serves as a doppelgänger of sorts for Heat-Moon, and this encounter is a fleshing out of the underlying antagonism of the earlier reaction to the staid man hunching over a charcoal grill. After listening to Heat-Moon's summary of his journey to the banks of Cave Creek, the Boss makes a provocative point: "Your little spree sounds nice until you go back." He implies in this short statement the troubling doubt Heat-Moon carries, his uncertainty as to the ultimate success of his plan, what the Boss calls a "little spree." The conversation continues:

> "Don't have to go back who I was."
> "Can you get out of it?"
> "I'll find out. Maybe experience is like a globe—you can't go the wrong way if you travel far enough."
> "You'll end up where you started."
> "I'm working on who. Where can take care of himself."[44]

Heat-Moon reaffirms the purpose of his quest, to remake himself on the road. He defends himself to a skeptical audience, a man who harbors similar frustrations but lacks the gumption to risk his complacency. This is the same stagnation that Heat-Moon inferred from the grilling man and feared in himself. With the Boss, the same conflict appears but is rendered this time as a fully-formed antagonist imposing on an otherwise peaceful setting. Heat-Moon cannot simply drive away.

As the Boss recounts his persistent troubles, his "ten thousand mistakes," he makes Heat-Moon weary, but we should see that fatigue as self-referential. As the two men converse and drink bourbon around the campfire, Heat-Moon adds this imagery: "Occasionally, when the fire ignited a drop of resin, our twin shadows, absurdly big, would stretch to the edge of night, then shrink back with the dying flame." More than a simple bit of texture for the conversation, this image asserts the "twin" relationship between the men in Heat-Moon's mind. In that context, his response to the Boss shows his growing confidence: "I wanted to slap him around, wake him up. He had the capacity to see but not the guts; he mucked in the drivel of his life afraid to go into the subterranean currents that dragged him about. A man concealed in his own life, scared to move, holding himself too close, petting himself too much."[45] This is a harsh appraisal of the Boss, but Heat-Moon fears that he sees too much of himself in his "twin," so there is no space for ambivalence when judging him. The Boss is "scared to move," lulled into stasis by the warm glow of the flames. This segment is a collision, but it is one that also immediately suggests a liminal awakening solidifying Heat-Moon in his quest. Its depth fortifies his journey forward.

In the end, *Blue Highways* completes the geographic circle with a pleasant and evocative blending of stable and subversive ideals throughout, wherein he maintains a steady commitment to mobility as personal growth. Heat-Moon returns to his starting point, not a conquering hero but a man who has, all in all, achieved his stable goal by being open to subversive whims along the road. Unlike the Boss or the grilling man, Heat-Moon moves, and that makes all the difference. That holistic approach definitive of the open road assures the ultimate success of his quest. The underlying fact revealed in the beginning of the narrative is that his home had been erased, so he never really has a specific home with familiar facets of stability to return to. However, the broader goal of his circular journey is to leave the wreckage of a previous life and build a new one with a home that is self-contained but not self-containing.

Blue Highways closes with a seemingly incidental encounter as the narrator is nearing completion of his circle. As with Steinbeck's narrative, which is also built around a search for America on a circular path, *Blue Highways* ends with Heat-Moon in conversation with a local man who is simply doing his job. Steinbeck encounters a policeman to whom he confesses that he is hopelessly lost, a mere few miles from his home. The closing is pleasant and offers a bit of self-deprecating humor, showing that Steinbeck is vulnerable. In a similar fashion, Heat-Moon stops to fill the gas tank for the last push homeward to Missouri. His brief discussion at the pump likewise allows him to close out the narrative with a bit of levity while also continuing to be on the move. However, unlike Steinbeck's flourish, Heat-Moon's closing image comes across as organically tied to his aspirations throughout because we know that his vulnerability has been authentic. It rings true page after page. He writes, "I filled the gas tank—enough for the last leg. From the station I could see the blue highway curving golden into the western afternoon. I'd make Columbia by nightfall. The circle almost complete, the truck ran the road like the old horse that knows the way. If the circle had come full turn, I hadn't. I can't say, over the miles, that I had learned what I had wanted to know because I hadn't known what I wanted to know. But I *did* learn what I didn't know I wanted to know."[46]

By reasserting the circle, Heat-Moon affirms his completed purpose while also reminding readers of the nature of mobility. By claiming that his growth is still a work in progress, he insists that the travels are ongoing, even if the narrative has ended. The attendant asks, "Where you coming from . . . ?" Heat-Moon replies rather obliquely, "Where I've been."[47] The answer, perhaps annoyingly cryptic to the gas station attendant, strikes readers as apt in its ambiguity as well as in its humility. A narrative that begins with uncertainty—"who knows?"—has never promised to provide absolute answers and certainly not absolution. It has, however, realized the core promise of the open road by engaging fully with the ever-present potential for change. Heat-Moon takes the chance to discover the unknown with a steadfast conviction that finding a way back home is possible with every tank of gas.

EASY RIDER AND *ZEN AND THE ART OF MOTORCYCLE MAINTENANCE*

As discussed earlier, the motorcycle stands apart from four-wheeled vehicles in its capacity to evoke powerful emotional responses in the American imagination from both those who ride them and those who refuse to. Holding handles rather than a steering wheel creates a decidedly different road experience. It should come as no surprise, then, that two of the most provocative road narratives feature motorcycles. Both narratives explore significant splits in American culture by using motorcycles as wedges to delve into the zeitgeist. Asserting ambitions to investigate "America" similar to those expressed in *Travels with Charley* and *Blue Highways*, each seeks a cohesive version of the national consciousness as perceived from the road. These two motorcycle journeys, however, draw decidedly different conclusions.

For many people, *Easy Rider* is the go-to American road movie. It has entered the American grain as an essential cultural document revealing the tumult of the late 1960s. A definitive tier 1 narrative, *Easy Rider* is also on par with *On the Road* as a first-order text of record when we think of subversion. Just five years after *Easy Rider*, another blockbuster caught fire with American audiences. Though it has retreated in reader consciousness over the years, Robert Pirsig's *Zen and the Art of Motorcycle Maintenance* was a sensation.[48] Taken together, the two works are equally adept at expressing the social turmoil of the late 1960s and early 1970s, arguably a time of transition from open-road confidence to trepidation.

The motorcycle has no competitor in its status as the ideal vehicle for the American open road, yet it is also plagued by a persistent popular image of outlaw behavior. The nature of media coverage created a lurid narrative that played well in the quickly developing Cold War culture of fear.[49] It is the inescapable nature of the machine itself that makes the motorcycle and its rider forever outliers to respectability. No matter the good-hearted interests of most of its owners, the motorcycle—whether or not it suffered from the bad behaviors of a small number of riders—has been destined from the beginning to be a symbol of nonconformity at best and anarchy at worst. The motorcycle came of age in uncomfortable juxtaposition to the family sedan—the former perfectly suited to the iconoclastic thinking, the latter perfectly suited to domestic thinking. A motorcycle can never match the multilevel functions performed by the sedan, a vehicle perfectly matched to the nuclear family, which a nation in transition could embrace without fear. Therefore, troubling events became media fodder because the die was already cast. This context serves as the essential backdrop for *Easy Rider* and *Zen and the Art of Motorcycle Maintenance*.

Easy Rider, the low-budget film directed by Dennis Hopper and written by Hopper with Peter Fonda and Terry Southern, is second only to *On the Road* in its appeal among audiences passionate for tales along subversive roads. It enjoyed a greater-than-expected initial marketplace success, and its iconic status has expanded over the years. *Easy Rider* has thereby become arguably the most resonant of road narratives of the 1960s. The key element for our consideration is the overt split between the two protagonists of the film: Wyatt, or "Captain America" (Peter Fonda), and Billy, or "Billy the Kid" (Dennis Hopper). Despite the basic assumption that Wyatt and Billy are both in sync as to their modes of mobility, the values implied by each character suggest a more nuanced divide in American culture than the overarching conservative-liberal political wrangling that earns the most attention. Though the two countercultural friends ostensibly seem congruent, they are contrasting figures. Wyatt represents a much stronger appreciation of stable road ideals as evidenced by how he relates to others, but he also remains consistently open to experience as a true subversive. Billy, on the other hand, is distrustful of others and lacks interest in novel encounters. He is more eager to complete the journey than to gain varied experiences. *Easy Rider*, though positioned in our cultural imagination as a recalcitrant subversive statement, offers a much more complicated interplay between the two modes of road mobility.

Acknowledging the differences between the two characters reveals how the film exploits cultural schisms. Wyatt and Billy are criminals. Their trip across America is set up by an illicit drug deal that occurs in the pre-credit opening sequence. The result is that the two gain a significant wad of cash as well as two new motorcycles. Their plan is to drive across the nation, reversing the direction of frontier mythology, to make it to New Orleans for Mardi Gras for a subversive celebration. This fact is complicated by Billy's revelation near the end of the film that their ultimate goal is to retire in Florida, a decidedly mainstream, even clichéd, aspiration.

Two key homeplaces demonstrate the core split between the two men. The focus is primarily on Wyatt's roadview, with Billy's ethos revealing itself more through his indifference. Wyatt and Billy visit counterbalancing homesteads during the first part of their journey, the portion of the film that is most celebratory of open-road ideals. The first is a segment titled "Rancher Hospitality."[50] The bikers stop to repair a flat tire and encounter a rancher and his large family. The scene gives viewers an appealing juxtaposition of road modes initiated when the bikers stop for help. In a particularly compelling shot, we see both parties working on their mobility, the subversive bikers fixing a motorcycle and the stable rancher shoeing a horse. This moment is a conscious directorial choice to evoke two distinct but related time frames, the traditional Western mythology built around the steadfast dependence on horses and the updated version focused on the motorcycles as a workhorse for a contemporary counterculture.

The family shares a meal with the bikers, and there is mutual respect around the table. This scene is especially important in contrast with the horrors that Wyatt and Billy will face as they move into the South. More importantly for our purposes here, we can see Wyatt's stable perspective regarding place and personal roads. Whereas the rancher indicates that his own mobility had stopped due to domestic responsibilities, Wyatt admires the beauty of the ranch and respects what it represents. The episode concludes with Wyatt stating, "You do your own thing in your own time. You should be proud." Wyatt's point implies that there is no conflict between the two parties, one travels around his home on horseback, the other travels across America on a motorcycle. Billy, on the other hand, shows little interest in the stable life around him. He is destination focused, and his position from the outset is to keep moving. He sees the challenge of needing to fix a flat tire purely as an inconvenience rather than an opportunity for a side-window excursion into the surrounding landscape. This contrasting sensibility is continued in the next homestead visit.

The two bikers pick up a hitchhiker, "Jesus," who directs them to a commune populated by a group of hippies with decidedly different values than those of the rancher family but who nonetheless represent a similar goal of stability. Viewers witness an ostensibly different version of the American dream in this scene, but the contrasts are more tied to style than substance. Both homesteads embrace a stable roadview, with each home populated by people who took to the road in search of a place to put down roots, their subsequent mobility tied to the practical needs of survival. The scene further illustrates Wyatt's and Billy's divergent road assumptions, with Wyatt yet again inclined to respect the homesteading dream.

When asked to give a ride to others "across the canyon," Wyatt agrees without hesitation, but Billy, in an aside to Wyatt, states, "Hey, man, we're not no traveling bureau. Let them get their own ride." This is a striking rebuke of road ethics, especially among countercultural youth. Billy had been hesitant to offer Jesus a ride in the beginning, and he is steadfast in this attitude. Again, Wyatt's wish prevails as he notes, "We're eating their food." They stay longer than Billy wishes, but he reasserts later the need to get back on the road, telling Wyatt to "get it together." Billy is motivated by an overarching desire to complete the journey to Florida (though viewers are yet to learn of that goal). He is wary of any variation to the original plan, which is a strikingly stable attitude. His concerns are unfounded; when Wyatt is asked to stay at the commune, he replies with the subversive mantra: "I just gotta go." His choice to keep moving is by no means a rebuke of the stable desires of those at the commune. Wyatt's interactions with everyone he meets reveal a steady appreciation for stability, but Billy need not worry. Wyatt, at this point, sees no reason for such a transition. His moment will come later, after much turmoil and pain. Nonetheless, Wyatt's belief system provides a consistent openness to multiple modes of travel philosophy. He fully embraces the open-road mythology and avoids being trapped by simple assumptions. In the commune sequence, as with the rancher homestead, he asserts a genuine inclusivity reflective of his ways of seeing the road throughout the journey.

The tone of *Easy Rider* as celebration of the open road and its varied applications shifts, however, as the two bikers move into the American South, which becomes the setting for an aggressive and even vicious response to the supposed threats of subversive strangers. When Wyatt and Billy enter the small-town roads in Texas and then Louisiana, they face formidable collisions and are seen as threats to local stability. We witness the direct collisions between the countercultural bikers and mainstream America reminiscent of the conflicts typical in films like *The Wild One*. The bikers are intruders intent on causing trouble as defined by the local point of view. They insert themselves rather obnoxiously into one of the most common and symbolic acts of stable mobility—a small-town parade—and are put in jail. Later, they stop at a café for food but are not served, a collision that directly leads to the savage response by locals who attack the bikers at their campsite. This act of violence results in the death of George Hanson (Jack Nicholson), the disaffected young lawyer who had joined the two bikers after their night in jail. These examples, along with the often bizarre and always discomfiting acid trip scene in New Orleans, together erode the tone of shared road experiences encouraged by Wyatt in the first half of the film.

As they depart New Orleans, heading eastward, we seem to be witnessing a now-familiar progression, a day of varied scenes along the road followed by introspective discussions around a campfire. In the penultimate scene, the final campfire discussion, the tone is much more contentious between the two protagonists, and they seem no longer to share any practical compatibility. Viewers learn, at long last, of the ironic context for the entire journey as Billy vocalizes for the first time the overarching dream of the cross-country trek. As Wyatt gazes into the fire, Billy becomes celebratory, stating, "We've done it. We've done it. We're rich, Wyatt." He continues with some repetition, then adds, "We're retired in Florida, mister." It is a curious revelation in that it undermines any broader countercultural philosophy rejecting such materialistic dreams. What is more mainstream than retiring to Florida?

Wyatt responds with the provocative, ambiguous statement, "We blew it." Billy objects by noting, "That's what it's all about. You go for the big money, then you're free." Wyatt sticks with his observation and makes his final break with Billy's mercenary embrace of materialism and stasis. He states again, "We blew it" and turns over to go to sleep, the American flag again foregrounded in the frame. We can argue about what the pronoun "we" implies here. Does he mean the two bikers, youth counterculture, and/or American culture at large? I prefer the more focused personal interpretation, the one that emphasizes an awakening for Wyatt on the road. The moment is liminal, as Wyatt's rejection of Billy's dream suggests. Far removed from the drug dealer that began the journey, Wyatt is no longer compatible with Billy. He awakens to the underlying corruption of their journey, which began as the ostentatious follow up to a drug deal on motorcycles purchased from its proceeds. The cash was stuffed into the gas tank painted as an American flag. They traveled the open road not in search of a lost America but in celebration of a get-rich-quick scheme moving two young men to an old retirement in one sweeping, fraudulent gesture of greed. They betrayed both stable and subversive roads. They blew it. Wyatt's journey is completed because he has awakened to the inherent contradictions of their quest, and he opts out. The following morning is defined by tragedy, with one last collision pathetically initiated by a belligerent man in a pick-up truck who points a shotgun at Billy.

Confused, back-and-forth movements define the chaotic scene. The men in the pick-up truck (driver and passenger) challenge Billy's right to the road and shoot him in a perverse side-window encounter. Then, with malice aforethought, they turn around to murder Wyatt. The chaotic violence defines the tragedy, but the odd characteristics of the mobility reflect the anarchic awfulness of the collision. Consider a retracing of the basic movements: a pick-up truck pulls alongside motorcycle one, and a shotgun blast blows the motorcycle off the road; the truck continues forward; motorcycle two stops and turns around to retrace the road; the truck continues forward and passes that motorcycle; motorcycle two pulls to the side of the road at the crash site of motorcycle one; the truck likewise turns around to retrace the road; motorcycle two returns to the road and moves forward to seek help; the returning truck meets motorcycle two again—another blast from the shotgun; and motorcycle two, engulfed in flames, flies off the roadway.

As the final extended aerial shot pulls back, the truck is gone, and the two motorcycles are off the road. The only movement is the rising smoke from Wyatt's motorcycle, and the muddy waters of the ever-flowing river. The cross-country odyssey is over, all those open-road miles from earlier in the film contrasting sharply with the final quarter mile being traced and retraced in violent absurdity. Whereas the final shot shifts emphasis to the river and thus offers a more hopeful tone of movement, the fact remains that the two protagonists are dead at the side of the road, a corrupted heroic quest ended.

Robert Pirsig's *Zen and the Art of Motorcycle Maintenance* is a more ambitious effort to assess just how "we" have blown it. In many ways, Pirsig responds to *Easy Rider* and seeks a corrective for the tragic ending of that film. Using genre-bending prose, he builds his "inquiry into values" around a motorcycle journey and pursues rather boldly a rhetorical and practical revision for what he sees as the sorry state of affairs in the 1970s. American culture was facing a dead end. As the narrative develops, Pirsig shows that the motorcycle may be the symbol for unity rather than division, for true freedom rather than isolation. Pirsig's heroic quest is to refigure the American open road by establishing a practical and romantic unification of seemingly disparate roads.

Zen and the Art of Motorcycle Maintenance (*ZAMM*) has sold millions of copies and has been translated into more than twenty-five languages. However, Pirsig's successful book has received relatively little critical attention from readers interested in travel.[51] This is partly because the book is typically placed with philosophical, religious, and/or inspirational texts in bookstores. HarperCollins Publishers agrees with such placement, categorizing the book formally on its cover as "philosophy." This is not an incidental choice. As Pirsig notes in his introduction, *ZAMM* has been referred to as "the most widely read philosophy book, ever."[52] As its subtitle, "An Inquiry into Values," suggests, it undoubtedly offers a remarkably readable dissertation on complicated intellectual issues, and much of its content explores philosophical debates carried out by Aristotle and Plato, Hegel and Nietzsche, among others. The key to the success of Pirsig's narrative, however, derives not from its philosophical content but from its adherence to the promise of the open road.

Pirsig defines his work wholly in terms of the American open road, creating a narrative journey at once physical—a record of a seventeen-day trip from Minnesota to California—and symbolic—a heroic quest of introspection and social commentary, what has been called a "yearning toward synthesis."[53] Pirsig's narrative is vitally dependent on travel for its energy, its emotional power, and its form and content. Therefore, it is most certainly a travel book, and a very good one at that. Yet Pirsig skillfully blends fictional elements into the ostensibly nonfictional genre. A prose work built on the ideals of the heroic quest, it is persistently dependent on liminal transitions, the essential element of the road narrative.

Steady movement along the road is the structural essence of *ZAMM*, and it frames the philosophical analysis, giving otherwise staid content an energy that readers have clearly appreciated. In short, Pirsig allows readers to immerse themselves into complicated intellectual material while also providing them with a pleasurable ride along the backroads of the American northern plains. Though many of the narrator's observations and confessions are decidedly interior moments of self-discovery, they are carefully couched in the physicality of motorcycle travel. Rather than assuming the road content of *ZAMM* serves simply as metaphor or even as narrative convenience, readers may benefit from considering how the American road mythology determines and frames Pirsig's journey into the heart of American cultural schizophrenia, which can be demonstrated via the ever-present tensions between stability and subversion.[54] *ZAMM* asserts a unity of mind and spirit as a model for healing a culture exhausted from divisiveness, which by the early 1970s threatened to tear the nation apart. The popular success of the book indicates that many people were ready for that road trip.

On the practical level, that Pirsig chose to make his trip across the northern plains on two wheels was simply tied to his personal life. He was already an avid motorcyclist, despite his humorous disclaimer at the beginning in the "Author's Note" wherein he warns that the book is not very factual regarding Zen Buddhist practice and then adds, "It's not very factual on motorcycles either."[55] This statement is meant to be self-deprecating; Pirsig is knowledgeable on both counts. His mode of transportation, moreover, is crucial to the narrative. *ZAMM* is layered with multiple rhetorical goals. The key, however, is the consciousness of an unstable narrator who grips the handlebars of his motorcycle as his troubled son, and passenger, holds him around the waist. The narrator, a current identity, struggles to avoid his former self, whom he calls "Phaedrus," a man who suffered a complete mental breakdown and went through shock therapy. Pirsig presents readers with a split identity, and both protagonists are on the threshold of change. The narrator is a mind divided, and his division parallels, as Pirsig sees it, the split in American culture. The trauma of the insanity has also formed a chasm between the narrator and his son, Chris, who is eleven years old at the time of the trip. Chris is troubled because he no longer knows his father. The narrative arc uses the journey across the northern plains as movement toward a reunion of Pirsig's selves, a reunion of father and son, and a symbolic reunion of a divided American culture. It provides a roadmap, so to speak, for that cultural quest.

A true experience on the road demands an open vehicle in addition to an open mind. Early in the narrative, as Pirsig argues for a revision of popular notions of the motorcycle, he makes the obvious point about the value of such travel in practical terms: "You see things vacationing on a motorcycle in a way that is completely different from any other. In a car you're always in a compartment, and because you're used to it you don't realize that through that car window everything you see is just more TV. You're a passive observer and it is all moving by you boringly in a frame."[56] Pirsig makes a significant point here, emphasizing a core conceit of motorcycle travel: it is open and thus closer to the real world. It is therefore more authentic. Also, as a celebrant of open-road ideals, he represents fully mainstream values by seeking stability, but he does so by embracing the key value of the subversive mode: full acceptance of the ever-present moment. The motorcycle in this manner accentuates the core road experience, making it visceral.

The narrative is, after all, the story of a father "vacationing" with his son. In its essential character, it reclaims the motorcycle from subversion and positions the power of an oft-distrusted machine in service to a mainstream activity. He accomplishes this task by celebrating the essential qualities of movement within an idealized landscape. Pirsig writes, "On a cycle the frame is gone. You're completely in contact with it all. You're *in* the scene, not just watching it anymore, and the sense of presence is overwhelming. That concrete whizzing by five inches below your foot is the real thing, the same stuff you walk on, it's right there, so blurred you can't focus on it, yet you can put your foot down and touch it anytime, and the whole thing, the whole experience, is never removed from immediate consciousness."[57] In a narrative that tries to destroy dualistic thought patterns that divide people and culture—classical or romantic; hip or square; normal or deviant; sane or insane; good or bad; or, for that matter, stable or subversive—Pirsig pays special attention to sensorial responses to movement and landscape. He travels "*in* the scene," not as passive observer but fully engaged in the place and in movement itself. The road is always inches below his feet: "You can touch it anytime." The key phrase that ties the practicalities of motorcycle travel with the emotional and intellectual journey is "immediate consciousness." The man, the machine, the road—all reinforce cohesion. All is now.

The text offers many examples in support of this basic point that the motorcycle—unlike any other machine—allows the traveler to experience immediacy. This is a vital point, not only to the mythology of the open road but to Pirsig's effort to unite a fragmented American culture. As the riders move through the northern plains, Pirsig notes, "We are following a creek to its source. It contains water that was probably snow less than an hour ago. The stream and the road pass through green and stony fields each a little higher than before. Everything is so intense in this sunlight. Dark shadows, bright light. Dark blue sky. The sun is bright and hot when we're in it, but when we pass under trees along the road, it's suddenly cold."[58] As the road follows the creek, Pirsig expresses sensorial responses to the ever-changing landscape, all tied to physical interaction. The passage offers classical components and romantic appeal. Pirsig asserts the experience in terms of being "in" the landscape; sun equals heat, and shadow equals cold.

This passage contrasts with the opening of the book, which introduces a narrator who is anything but "in" the moment: "I can see by my watch, without taking my hand from the left grip of the cycle, that it is eight-thirty in the morning. The wind, even at sixty miles an hour, is warm and humid. When it's this hot and muggy at eight-thirty, I'm wondering what it's going to be like in the afternoon."[59] Although a seemingly straightforward description in a classical mode, this passage is more accurately an essential illustration of the personal and cultural conflict the narrative will explore. The narrator reveals the physical reality of the traveling moment as he responds to the air that is "warm and humid." The implications of this observation, however, are couched not in the moment but in the future. The narrator focuses on how much hotter the day will become as it progresses. In this opening, "immediate consciousness" holds no real value. The issue, rather, is time—that classical regimentation of the movement of the sun. This first image readers encounter is of the narrator who, while looking ahead, is seeing nothing of the landscape imaginary that surrounds him. He is not part of the road, nor is he immersed in the joy of movement. His experience exists only in terms of the ticking of his watch.

By the end of the journey, the narrator has awakened to the limitations of such a road experience and equates such traveling with the inherent flaws of the culture built around suburban dreams of prosperity: "There's this primary America of freeways and jet flights and TV and movie spectaculars. And people caught up in this primary America seem to go through huge portions of their lives without much consciousness of what's immediately around them. The media have convinced them that what's right around them is unimportant. And that's why they're lonely."[60] The motorcycle for Pirsig is the machine that can allow mainstream America to escape that trap as he discovers in his own journey. Controlling a motorcycle requires full engagement of the senses and the mind. Pirsig argues that the world is best perceived via our "immediate consciousness," wherein we can intuit its value, what he calls "Quality," free of restrictive frames (like windows). The quality of life, then, can be elicited by engaging our perception of the road. For the narrator, the apprehension of quality has the potential to awaken a unified worldview, which can be illustrated by consciousness of our immediate roadview.

The awakening potential is best illustrated by how Pirsig describes his son's first genuine encounter with the open road. In the concluding scene of the narrative, Pirsig asserts unity by emphasizing his son's travel experience.

For the first time in the seventeen-day journey, the son, Chris, who has been feeling increasingly estranged from his father, enjoys mobility. Up until this moment, Chris has not understood fully the stimulating power of the motorcycle on the move. As a passenger, and a small one at that, he sits behind his father and is thus denied an unfettered view of the road ahead. His sense of the horizon via a windshield roadview, that crucial and conventional element of any aspirational road experience, has been blocked all along by his father's torso. In the following passage, we see a vital transition as Chris physically alters the dynamic and, in doing so, crosses his own threshold: "More trees and shrubs and groves. It's getting warmer. Chris hangs onto my shoulders now and I turn a little and see that he stands up on the foot pegs."[61] Through this self-assertive act of standing, Chris, for the first time, can see over his father's shoulders and into the road on his own terms. Chris feels the road and responds to the beauty of the scenery and the pleasure of movement with brief, excited comments: "Oh," "Ah," and "Wow," words of childlike wonder. When the father asks him to explain his ejaculations of joy, Chris claims, "It is so different." In answer to his father's request for clarification of "it," Chris simply responds with, "Everything."[62]

ZAMM is an ambitious redefining of "everything" via a journey into American road mythology. Pirsig frames the vital awakening in Chris with a closing reaffirmation of the road experience: "The sunlight makes strange and beautiful designs through the tree branches on the road. It flits light and dark into my eyes. We swing into a curve and then up into the open sunlight."[63] This image is classical ideology at work, as the two—father and son—are reunited as they move into the American sunset, always a road image of hope. To reassert the cultural implication of the personal and familial reunification, Pirsig also incorporates direct references to the culture at large. He writes, "The engine which has carried us halfway across a continent drones on and on in its continuing oblivion to everything but its own internal forces. We pass through Asti and Santa Rosa, and Petaluma and Novato, on the freeway that grows wider and fuller now, swelling with cars and trucks and buses full of people, and soon by the road are houses and boats and the water of the Bay."[64] Pirsig brings the solitary bike into the public spaces—wider roads filled with cars and buses, houses and boats—wherein people are not separate from each other, nor are they in opposition. The vehicles simply represent a busy and complicated world in motion. He and his son ride into the sunlight as an assertion of shared experience on a shared road, and a shared hope for a unified future.

For Pirsig the trip recaptures a lost American landscape, one directly linked to American theoretical ideals. This optimism has always been tied to American road sensibilities. The key symbolic cohesion within the narrative thus depends on Pirsig's capacity to make that landscape mesh with the motorcycle itself. As Nancy Corson Carter notes in one of the earliest and most astute readings of *ZAMM*, the narrator retraces the travels of his former self (Phaedrus) to "re-establish his connection with the land and to recreate living metaphors rooted in his knowledge of it."[65] That journey is both personal and political. The narrator's effort toward unity through his interaction with the open road and natural landscape mirrors the cultural effort to regain the unity of the American promise interwoven in the landscape and the road. The narrator's journey is by extension the journey of American culture in crisis, both "yearning to find unity beyond division."[66]

The cultural schizophrenia, which hit crisis levels in the late 1960s and early 1970s, is the primary target of Pirsig's metaphysical journey as he seeks to reunite a split sensibility. The maintenance he performs on his motorcycle, then, places the vehicle at the crux of a cultural dilemma, and, in the end, he demonstrates the value of the motorcycle as an ideal mode of transportation to celebrate the open road and an ideal metaphor for personal growth and social cohesion. Everything needs maintenance. Full awareness of this value derives from being encouraged to seek sensory awareness of "immediate consciousness," which allows for a reformation of a shattered self. Pirsig unifies the stable and subversive modes of travel by insisting on the unity of the human mind, body, and spirit.

Zen and the Art of Motorcycle Maintenance forges a comprehensive statement of road mythology that eludes *Easy Rider*, as well as *On the Road* and *Travels with Charley*, and it does so at a time when many bemoaned the loss of the open-road ideals in the doldrums of the 1970s. It is thus a holistic rendering of the American open road celebrated without misgivings. The motorcycle may not be the only way to travel, but Pirsig makes it a compelling symbol for the only way to live. It is Zen; it is art; it is maintenance. It is available to all who are open to feeling the road just beneath their feet and who are willing to embrace the desire to touch it.

* * *

The epic tier 1 road narratives examined in this chapter present the complexity of narratives that define the American open road and further illustrate useful patterns and conventions discussed in the previous chapters. These works, prose and film, are wholly immersed in the mythology of the open road and demonstrate its potential to explore liminality with myriad opportunities for an evolving sense of selfhood. Taken together and via logical but overlooked pairings, these road stories demonstrate the core function of the road narrative on the whole: to explore the constant interplay between self, place, and mobility. The narratives do so by adhering to pervasive motifs of the genre and by capturing the persistent tensions between stable and subversive modes of travel. The narratives covered in this chapter are seminal works, and they suggest the broad reach of open-road ideals. In some ways, however, they are the resulting stories of the free-roaming capacity of their authors, all enjoying freedoms not available to everyone. Several significant cultural challenges to such aspirations will be the focus of the remaining chapters, which consider essential themes tied to race and gender to demonstrate how the open road can be adapted and expanded to broader horizons.[67]

Part III

Blurred Lines along Divided Roads

6

Claiming Mobility

African Americans and Civil Rights

Travelers are strangers anytime they venture beyond their home circle. This condition applies to all journeys, but it is especially important to consider how open-road experiences reflect the extent to which travelers can feel welcomed on the road. The road is rife with barriers, real and imagined, physical and emotional, that can be daunting. For Americans who have endured political and cultural pressures that have persisted throughout the automotive age, the traveler's status as outsider carries an additional profound and comprehensive weight. The challenges arising from such burdens derive from pervasive limitations to mobility that are anything but accidental or incidental.

The rhetorical and implicitly celebratory question prominent in Kerouac's *On the Road*—"What's your road, man?"—is one proffered from a place not only of sincerity but also of privilege. Underlying Kerouac's question is the unfettered assumption that the primary obstacle to a life on the road is found within individual choice. The question assumes without hesitation that there is a "road" for "your" desire. As geographer Edward Relph notes, "It is not just the identity of a place that is important, but also the identity that a person or group has with that place, in particular whether they are experiencing it as an insider or as an outsider."[1] Negotiating open-road dreams from outside the paradigm of mainstream America is a persistent challenge to those who pursue happiness along the open road. If they are by social and political definition outside of established power structures, especially as tied to racial identity, their roads may be far from open. At this point it is crucial to make this complementary point: whereas males of European ancestry have enjoyed the most consistent opportunity to take to the open road, they have never held a monopoly on the desire to do so.

In this chapter, I focus on the challenges facing Americans of African heritage as they have sought to realize that desire for mobility along often unfriendly and, indeed, closed roads. The pursuit of happiness has never offered equal access to mobility, and as an obvious result, the history of American road narratives must be informed by recognizing that reality. Kris Lackey makes a useful point along these lines, asserting the crucial connection to personal identity central to all road experiences: "Consider that staple road book prerogative, a new identity. Many white highway writers, perhaps drawing upon both the Romantic idea of plastic subjectivity and the picaresque emphasis on disguise, assume that distance untethers their identity: the farther you go from home and work, the more freedom you have to adopt a new self . . ." Lackey then follows with the contrasting context, noting that "Black road writers . . . have found no such solace in American space. Wherever they go, they find . . . that their identity, insofar as it is determined by others, is fixed."[2] Applying the word "solace" to the implicit confidence granted by such privilege is especially apt. Open-road mythology is built around the self not being "fixed," to repeat Lackey's term, and thereby being open to liminal opportunities.

The heroic quest so crucial to road narratives depends on a fluid identity, a capacity for expansion in response to interactions between self and place. Americans of European heritage have been largely free of constant pressure to view themselves as "other" while on the road, a convenience largely unavailable to minority travelers. As Lackey notes, "White writers may pick up alienation as a theme, as a feature of their projected discontent or their dissatisfaction with American culture, but they may also lay it down again."[3] For the unique historical context for African Americans, such liminality is compromised by overarching power structures benefitting the majority population. Any individual sharing of perceived whiteness enjoys the solace of anonymity, which makes such a transition readily available. When we also add to that demographic fact a complicated and often harsh racial history antagonistic to Black mobility, then the severe challenge encountered by African Americans is clear.

However, critics should not go so far as to remove all agency from such travelers for the sake of asserting cultural realities. Claiming without qualification that African American identity is "fixed" risks condescension by erasing any self-determining power. Such racial fixity may also imply that any identity can, really, be defined only by others. Making such points without elaborating on self-definition—even under horrific conditions—confines resulting narratives to a string of encounters with victimhood. Whereas no softening of the very real historic context should be indulged, it is long past time to recognize a more complex relationship with the American open road for minority writers, one that is often complicated by racial bigotry.

Explorations of the challenges to mobility for African Americans have long focused on diasporic movements, and rightly so, but more attention in recent years has been placed on automobility, especially how African Americans worked to claim their own rights to the open road. Gretchen Sorin's *Driving While Black: African American Travel and the Road to Civil Rights* combines a range of political and cultural resources with nuanced retellings of personal stories to explore this complicated relationship to mobility. Sorin makes a crucial point regarding the American open road as emblem for idealized potential. Recounting her personal history, she notes that "each car trip could be fraught with anxiety, and it required special preparations and careful planning to ensure success."[4] The chronic "anxiety" demanding "careful planning" is antagonistic to the open-road ideal. The centrality of spontaneity for the subversive mode as expressed by Kerouac is simply made impossible for any rational mind with the restrictive history that Sorin explores. Therefore, the comment above simply asserts a basic apprehension undergirding any movement for African Americans, which undermines the core conceit of the open road. The symbolic question used in earlier chapters—"why go?"—in no way considers this complication. Therefore, in this situation, such a question must be paired with another question that all minority travelers must consider: Is it safe to go?

We all move in and out of modes of discovery and meld a more complicated road narrative than we often imagine. The stable and subversive modes thus exist not as a dichotomy but as an uneasy symbiosis wherein cultural conflicts are in a constant push-and-pull battle for common ground and distinction. The implications are equally restrictive for any travel in the stable mode because any family travel planning is made much more complicated and thus potentially immobilizing. In effect, the road and the home are both rendered insecure. Sorin effectively illustrates this tension by focusing on the remarkable series of publications put forward by Victor H. Green, *The Negro Travelers' Green Book*, which, beginning in 1936, supported African American road travel for thirty years by providing state-by-state and city-by-city listings of friendly overnight accommodations.[5]

The 1957 edition, for example, features on its cover an aerial image of an interstate interchange appropriately enough and includes a variation on the common statements made in the *Green Book* foreword: "The White traveler has had no difficulty in getting accommodations, but with the Negro it has been different."[6] This line shows remarkable restraint with its understated "difficulty" facing African American drivers. As with the passage taken from

Sorin above, its simplicity is the point. I have already discussed how careful planning ruins the first day on the road for Sal Paradise in *On the Road* and how Steinbeck and so many others decry the implicit limitations on the spirit of the road caused by programmed, overly planned travel. For Steinbeck and company—sharing the privilege of whiteness—the risks of under-planning are meager when compared with the hazards facing African Americans, whose vulnerability is much more evident. The inevitable result is that there are two roads just as there are two Americas, and the open road must be considered in that context. However, a vital point remains and will be the focus of the rest of this chapter: in resistance to the seemingly overwhelming historical limitations, African Americans have been persistently mobile.

The American open road is a national story, but it plays out in variations over time, among overlapping constituencies, with varying sets of desires, and, most certainly, through multiple geographical regions. For the African American road narrative, however, it is in the South that the volatile elements of the open road most often collide. The civil rights movement gained energy in the 1950s and 1960s, coinciding with the national push toward automobility, and this intersection is not incidental. The monumental political successes of the struggle took place most significantly along Southern roads. Whereas the practical and tactical reasons for the Montgomery bus boycott, the Freedom Rides, and the marches from Selma to Montgomery are clear, the metaphorical power suggested by these events demonstrates the centrality of mobility—the right to move freely on open roads as inextricably tied to the right to pursue happiness.

The civil rights movement provides the most compelling and instructive application of open-road mythology. In his "Letter from Birmingham Jail," Martin Luther King Jr. opens with a logical clause: "While confined here in the Birmingham city jail." This is a simple statement of fact, yet it carries metaphorical weight, as King was "confined" in innumerable ways by law and by custom. This introductory clause King employs does more than serve as clarifying context; it also sets the letter in direct relation to his lack of mobility as a citizen of the United States. King's purpose in the letter has a specific context but also addresses the broad conditions that the civil rights movement writ large was seeking to redress.[7]

He composed the letter as a formal response to the condescending call from moderate religious leaders for King to be more patient, to wait—to be still. In offering a list of frustrations that make clear that waiting was an absurd proposition, he includes the following clause: "When you take a cross country drive and find it necessary to sleep night after night in the uncomfortable corners of your automobile because no motel will accept you."[8] This point strikes directly at the heart of the stable mode of the open road. Here

King notes a cornerstone of all the promises of the new mobility celebrated by the automobile industry, government entities, tourism boosters, and so on. In revealing the core fact facing African Americans within the broad cultural myth of mobility, King notes that he has no option to embrace the stable mode of the open road in a segregated South. His racial identity forces him to be subversive, not by choice but by existence, ever-viewed as a challenge to the status quo even when desiring simply to move along the open road. Motels are not open to him, and so the road is not open. Therefore, King directly connects mobility to civil rights. The movement itself, broadly envisioned, was defined by nonviolent "direct action." That meant taking to Southern roads.

The Montgomery bus boycott confronted confinement in Montgomery, Alabama. It sought to ensure freedom of movement, to allow African Americans to go about their daily lives with mobility equal to that of whites, who move from home to work to shopping unfettered by restrictions and indignities. Rosa Parks claimed a right to a seat on a city bus on the move. The crux of this encounter is not a seat on a bus but a seat on a bus in motion. The metaphor becomes powerful when that bus stops, and she is removed. Likewise, the Freedom Rides were an audacious but simple challenge to segregation affecting interstate travel throughout the South. The metaphor is powerful in its joyful subversive expression but made politically influential as well when the buses were stopped with violence. And again, when marchers took to the road in Selma as they headed to Montgomery, they performed direct action in celebration of mobility along a public roadway. Yet again that expression became most dramatic when the movement was stopped violently by Alabama state troopers at the Edmund Pettus Bridge. The eventual success of the march on the third try became more compelling still as Americans—joining the protesters from all over the nation—took to the highway to express freedom of movement in direct support of the freedom to vote. Mobility is all. These vital victories in the civil rights movement drew from and exploited marvelously the dream of the American open road. They serve as political backdrop to other efforts by African Americans to participate in open-road mythology via more personal road narratives. The discussion below seeks to explore several provocative narratives that work fully within this basic context of confinement in reference to mobility. These capture very different roads from those explored thus far.

BLACK LIKE ME

Racial conditions in the United States have created many absurdities in our cultural imagination. It should come as no surprise, then, that one of the most important and early road narratives focusing on the African American experience on the open road was penned by a European American posing as an African American. John Howard Griffin's *Black Like Me* cannot be ignored.[9] It is an important document, and its reach into the cultural imagination was significant. As Robert Bonazzi notes, the book sold "more than twelve million copies" and has been translated into at least sixteen languages.[10] The book was turned into a film in 1964 directed by Carl Lerner and starring James Whitmore.[11] Although the film was met with uneven reviews and a small box office, it nonetheless furthered *Black Like Me* and its premise in the public's eye in the midst of the tumultuous 1960s. I will focus solely on the book.

Black Like Me is a crucial and problematic part of that political push represented by the Montgomery bus boycott, the Freedom Rides, and the marches from Selma. Griffin's moral goals in his travels into the South were clear, and he considered his effort necessary and, for that matter, logical. His willingness to carry through with the experiment—his road journey—should not be regarded as heroic, but it was laudable, and his ethical position was sound. Griffin shows himself to be intuitive, and his narrative proves to be committed to attacking the Jim Crow South. Griffin alters his appearance enough to be "Black" by those invested in strict color lines, no matter the inherent absurdity of such an act. He is never an African American, and he is never, in that sense, doing anything other than playing with racial identity as a tourist of sorts. That point should not be glossed over, yet he reports an astounding experience to Euro-American readers, and that is the reality that makes Griffin's narrative not only provocative but necessary. Americans who enjoyed white status were the audience and the target of his exposé. It was their complacency and moral dismissiveness of the challenges facing African Americans seeking the full privileges of citizenship that needed to be eradicated.

Black Like Me is an astounding text that forces a reconception not only of race in America in the early 1960s but also of the American road narrative. Its scope is larger than the open road, but mobility is a core concern throughout. Therefore, as a tier 2 road narrative, *Black Like Me* puts the basic assumptions of open-road ideals into question and, in the end, puts to rout any notion that those terms carry universal applications across color lines. The rationale offered by Griffin in the preface is crucial. By historical necessity, the travels on the open road by Americans of African heritage must be rendered to audiences via a thesis, an argument that must assert the full right to enjoy American mobility and its benefits or, indeed, to be first-class citizens. John Steinbeck's *Travels with Charley* is the most applicable corollary here. Even though he demonstrates and often acknowledges his disengagement with the America of the early 1960s, and even though he is often befuddled by the world he encounters on the road, he never questions whether it is *his* country. This is the core privilege shared by males of European heritage who also have economic means. He enjoys the assumption of belonging in any given place. He is therefore never under any pressure to prove to readers why or how he travels through America. He is implicitly and explicitly free to roam.

Griffin set up an experiment that tested the universality of such assumptions by removing the inherent confidence and thus comfort of the narrative "I." Griffin, posing as a "Black" man, stood in stark contrast with that innate comfort zone shared by Steinbeck, Kerouac, and others. As a result, his self is altered, and that inevitably alters the experience of place. Griffin approached his experiment with such a thesis-driven goal—to explore and expose the racial injustice that permeates Southern culture. To do this he employed America's greatest and most enduring mythos, the open road. Griffin states in the preface that he had begun his project as "scientific research" but "fled the data" and instead focused on his "experiences living as a Negro" on the road in the Deep South and on the streets of its urban centers.

Of course, Griffin, the man, tours with a borrowed and temporary perspective. He also must assert an adopted point of view that forces an inescapable inner split in his sense of self. In this way, the liminality so crucial to travel is caught up in a provocative anthropological investigation. Griffin's narrative "I" is a lie known to the reader but not those he encounters on the road. The alias is genuine in that all travelers are strangers to those they encounter. All can assume false pretenses, so the only thing that matters in this context is the narrator's perception on the threshold of revelatory experience within that mobility. Griffin's perspective emphasizes the obvious and crucial weakness of his work, in that his identity is temporary. Not only will he one day stop taking the medication and return to his actual racial identity, but he knows this all along. But Griffin's effort is nonetheless a genuine, immersive social challenge to a cultural lie. His narrative is an effective exploration of road liminality with an especially complex interaction between self and place.

His text bears out the basic premise of his road journey, and several key passages illustrate his overall political and anthropological mission. His self-definition is essential. Griffin vows never to change his behavior or identity otherwise, meaning he uses his name, and if people ask him about who he is, he will be honest. "I would merely change my pigmentation and allow people to draw their own conclusions."[12] This is a perfect approach that demonstrates the thesis that racism depends on the cultural assumptions that lead people to "draw their own conclusions," which are not, in the end, their own at all. They, moreover, are not even conclusions emanating from any rational process. On the contrary, racism depends on performative reactions to learned stimuli. Griffin demonstrates in simple terms that his *self*, his inner identity, does not matter. Pigment is all.

Griffin understands this from the beginning. He is not embarking on an intellectual quest of discovery. The grace and power of *Black Like Me* is in its emotional shock, which is apprehended via intellectual empathy but demonstrated by direct action. His physical movement is thus intended to show his road experiences as evidence that in any given moment, at any given place, his mobility is bounded by societal adherence to the color line. Despite the crucial qualifications to his sense of self, the frame essential to road narratives remains active. Griffin embarks on a heroic quest defined by ongoing liminality. His awakening is emotionally transformative for the narrator and riveting for readers.

Griffin writes a dramatic introduction. He looks into a mirror for the first time transformed and writes, "In the flood of light against white tile, the face and shoulders of a stranger—a fierce, bald, very dark Negro—glared at me from the glass. He in no way resembled me."[13] This is a challenging introduction. Griffin's response emphasizes the conversion—one that we must believe in as readers—but also the entrenched, if unconscious, white revulsion. The word choice betrays the racism of the moment: the reflection is "fierce," "glare[s]," and is "a stranger." In short, Griffin sees the racial other in the mirror as threatening. Such a response should put readers on edge. The ethical backing for the journey itself is built on absolute rejection of any substantive difference between the races, but this moment implies otherwise. If the narrative is built around letting people "draw their own conclusions" as to who he is, then this is the first test.

The superficial change affects the narrator in a profound and thus disconcerting way. Griffin continues, "The transformation was total and shocking. I had expected to see myself disguised, but this was something else. I was imprisoned in the flesh of an utter stranger, an unsympathetic one with whom I felt no kinship."[14] From the beginning, readers are asked to confront a racial way of looking at and defining the world and themselves that runs deeper than pigment. As he grapples with the shock of recognition—on both levels—we are to do the same, and in resolving to move forward, he must "walk through a land hostile to my color, hostile to my skin."[15] His isolation is legitimate for a man trapped on the color line. Despite his progressive morality, he cannot escape his own assumptions and visceral reactions. In blackface, though most assuredly with none of the mockery implied by that term, he feels "hostile" toward his skin. In other words, the "skin" that bears the hostility is at times ambiguous, and at the core of his confusion is the angst of humanity itself.

This moment also captures his peculiar multiple perspective, a layered existence that allows him a point of view that can be both nuanced and also limited by the temporality of his experiences. Mobility for Griffin is physical and emotional movement, both drawing from a constant uncertainty born of the persistent racial inequalities along the road. He is a traveler moving through space and as a confused self with alternating identities. His outward appearance defines his identity for a world mad with racial obsessions, but his inner self is always conflicted and off-balance as well. He is thus like everyone on the road, forever in a state of liminality, but his outward identity is steadily rendered even more challenging due to the unbearable lie at its core. The steady pressure caused by his restricted mobility becomes the key theme throughout, and he learns that every movement must come with cautious planning in a way that he has never experienced.

Whenever Griffin tries to move, he faces collisions, to use the term as applied to road narrative conventions discussed in previous chapters. He offers a wealth of dispiriting examples with varying modes of mobility—being trapped on a bus with no opportunity for a bathroom break; arriving in town (Biloxi, Mississippi), unable to find accommodations and being forced to sleep in a shed; hitchhiking out of desperation and being propositioned sexually. He faces exhaustion as his mobility is perpetually challenged. He writes, "I walked what—ten, fifteen miles? I walked because one does not just simply sit down in the middle of a highway, because there was nothing to do but walk."[16] In such passages we find the strength of the text—its understanding of whiteness and the inherent necessity for white people to perpetuate their willful blindness. He writes, "I concluded that, as in everything else, the atmosphere of a place is entirely different for Negro and white. The Negro sees and reacts differently not because he is Negro, but because he is suppressed. Fear dims even the sunlight."[17] We can see it most clearly on the road, the stress compounding with each encounter, with each challenge, with each step. Exhausted, Griffin shares with readers one of his most instructive and humane experiences. Desperate for a ride, he takes a chance. Griffin writes, "I turned to see a yellow glow on the road's horizon. It grew stronger and headlights appeared. Though I dreaded riding with another white man, I dreaded more staying on the road all night. Stepping out into full view, I waved my arms. An ancient car braked to a halt and I hurried to it. To my great relief, the reflections from the dash light showed me the face of a young Negro man."[18] There is profound relief in finding a ride that provides mobility without degradation. What follows is one of the most poignant, if sentimental, segments in the narrative wherein he is wholly welcomed into a modest homestead.

The experience parallels the stated value of guides like *The Green Book*, to help the weary traveler move safely and without humiliation, a frustratingly formidable task. Weary and weakened, Griffin finds comfort in the kindness of a stranger who is kin as determined by the codes of the color line. In a landscape dominated by Jim Crow laws and customs, finding support outside of the harsh glare of whiteness provides the only true solace. The peace he finds in this brief stay at a home in a swamp helped Griffin affirm his overarching thesis: "When all the talk, all the propaganda has been cut away, the criterion is nothing but the color of skin. My experience proved that. They [whites] judged me by no other quality. . . . I had spent a day without food and water for no other reason than that my skin was black. I was sitting on a tub in the swamp for no other reason."[19] Griffin's whiteness helps to provide the power of this segment. He acknowledges above this passage his efforts to provide a more nuanced conclusion, to give white folks as much benefit of doubt as possible, but he cannot find a legitimate way to forge a more forgiving conclusion. Skin color is all. The last sentence in the passage above shows him immobile, symbolically and practically trapped: "Sitting on a tub in the swamp."

Under this pressure, after this segment, Griffin takes advantage of his touristic status and returns to the comforts of whiteness. This becomes the dominant theme of the last quarter of the narrative. It is vital to note that he has been on the road for only *three weeks*. Griffin, in one of the most astounding ironies one could imagine, begins "passing" back into whiteness in a desperate effort to lessen his burden. Simply functioning moment to moment has become too unpleasant, and he demurs under the relentless torment of small and large collisions. He first finds succor by hiding away in the restroom: "Here, with a latch on the door, I was isolated from the hate stares, the contempt." In the solitude of the restroom, he builds on this observation, noting that the darkness of night also offers respite from the constant pressure of "hate stares."[20] The nighttime provides a symbol of nature itself affirming the humanity of Blackness too often lost in the glare of daylight and seemingly omnipresent whiteness. In Montgomery, Alabama, he returns to the comfort of whiteness, a desperate act of escape, but this sequence provides another illustration of the absurdities defining the system of segregation. His period of "zigzagging back and forth" alters his basic plan.[21] While it allows for a stronger and more direct exploitation of the color-line madness, it also betrays his commitment to his developing emotional self, which peaks during his night with the family in the swamp. He moves back to the more analytical traveler, bouncing between racial identities to build more depth into the core conclusions he has known all along. His thesis has been proven within the narrative, but the solace he takes by leaving Blackness becomes the most aggressive illustration of the point. The narrative power of this sequence is palpable, as he offers a fast-paced, episodic look at the tortured behaviors deriving from a comprehensive racial absurdity, all seen in the numerous encounters with actors wholly invested in their assigned racial roles.

Not long after this series in Montgomery, Griffin returns to his normal self for good. The entire experience has lasted five weeks. His short passage dated "Dec. 14th" is concise and demands some critical scrutiny: "Finally the photos were taken, the project concluded, and I resumed for the final time my white identity. I felt strangely sad to leave the world of the Negro after having shared it so long—almost as though I were fleeing my share of his pain and heartache."[22] This passage is preposterous, the rhetorical flourish patronizing and patently untrue. We can all be sure—because the narrative has proven it without doubt—that Griffin is in no way "sad to leave the world of the Negro." That road is too hard, and no white man could have been prepared for its comprehensive and insidious attack on his psyche. But for the temporary nature of the entire experiment, Griffin's sense of self would be in shambles, a man symbolically trapped in a swamp with no view of a horizon to grant a dream of escape. His statement of sadness is rhetorically expedient, yet Griffin has proven nonetheless his deeper point. The fact that his travels were relatively short ironically supports and deepens his revelations regarding the heavy burdens placed on African American mobility, year after year, generation after generation. It bears repeating: Griffin's journey lasted only five weeks.

The final section of the book focuses on the initial reactions to the publicity his experiment receives via interviews in print, radio, and television. The closing twenty pages, therefore, serve as an epilogue after the road experience has been completed, and this section focuses wholly on the political discussions in the public sphere. For those readers interested in the open road, the journey is over with Griffin's return home, his oasis of racial stability. The heavy burdens confining his mobility during his experiment in Blackness proved far more daunting than he had expected and more than he could handle.

THIS IS MY COUNTRY TOO

In the late summer of 1963, following King's "Letter from Birmingham Jail," John A. Williams began his own road journey, seeking to affirm the necessity of direct action in reference to racial strife, and his experiences provide a necessary, individualized expression of the open-road ideals to complement the broader movement. On assignment for *Holiday* magazine, Williams traveled American roads to find out just how challenging it could be. The resulting narrative first appeared serialized in *Holiday* in 1964 and then in book form as *This Is My Country Too*.

A significant portion of travel narratives to the South have been thesis-driven in one way or another, as discussed above with *Black Like Me*, but rarely is the argument so directly stated in the title. In making this choice, however, the editors of *Holiday* followed the implied assertions of the civil rights struggle: that individuals must claim *my* bus seat, *my* lunch counter, *my* road, and, of course, *my* country. Williams also echoes John Steinbeck's *Travels with Charley*, the best-selling road book that appeared a year earlier. As already noted, Steinbeck claims that even though he was exhausted by traveling, he remained confident that "this is my country."[23] Williams's narrative should be encountered in direct reference to Steinbeck's complacent full membership in all things implied by being an American. For Williams, however, claiming such belonging cannot be assumed; it must be demanded. For the mass of mainstream American readers, the title of Williams's narrative is a provocation and his act of taking to the "open" road a challenge to the status quo.

Along with the title itself, the publishers of Williams's narrative also placed on the front cover of the paperback issue a compelling question: "What is it like for a Negro with a fistful of credit cards driving a shiny new car across White America???" Indeed. This inflammatory question implies the dream of automobility so enmeshed in postwar America—"credit cards" and a "shiny new car." As Ann Brigham notes, the presentation on the book cover "juxtaposes and collapses the language of mass consumption with that of a militant black civil rights movement, thus producing an agitated vision of black spatial and social mobility in 'White America.'"[24] Even without the challenge to expectations accentuated in the marketing approach, when Williams took to the open road, his mobility "agitated" racial notions of stability in the mainstream. Williams has all he needs to enjoy postwar prosperity according to all the rules of the generic American dream in a consumerist Cold War culture—except for his race. That is the ironic position presented by the claims on the cover. What happens when a Black man tries to participate in America's greatest metaphorical pursuit of happiness? Trouble. To drive a new car asserts not only personal power on the road but also economic power. The cover art and its messages reveal and, to a degree, exploit the core fact that Williams is forced to travel, no matter his inclinations, as a subversive.

Given the carefully presented political context for *This Is My Country Too*, the encounters that Williams shares within the narrative carry significant weight beyond the typical exploration of self and place intrinsic to road narratives, and we need to read them within that highly charged context. I explore crucial passages while also respecting the text for its universal aspirations. Williams, while examining an open road that exists in stark and often horrific contrast with the road writers like Kerouac and Steinbeck traveled, also confirms the overall appeal and potential of the open road as an ideal worth claiming. Williams travels all around the nation and encounters a range of experiences. The narrative sometimes reveals a very different America, but it also astutely employs and celebrates road-narrative conventions.

A few examples from his narrative may help show his complicated encounters with automobility. In describing his thoughts as he drives toward Nashville, Tennessee, his first direct foray into the South, Williams writes, "Ominously all directions to Nashville were via the Dixie Highway. Where did it end, the Dixie Highway—in a cotton patch surmounted by a Confederate flag and an *a cappella* choir of White Citizen Council members singing *Dixie*? I thought then of how all travel into the South must dull the hearts of all Americans. If we do not know the South firsthand, we know it through its history, and the reportage from it. We know almost completely the attitudes of its people. We do not have to go there to know that, on the whole, it is not a good place to visit. It is not altogether a sense of fear, but a greater one of shame and of helplessness."[25] How many narratives of the South contain words like "ominously"? Williams plays on stereotypes here, which is not surprising, but his choice is also justified given the context within which he is moving.

A common, even essential, trope for any travel narrative is to employ the surroundings as impressionistic emblems of mood and emotion, all influenced by shared notions of the landscape imaginary. He adds, "The very roads seemed downhill . . . "[26] For Williams, the political and social history tied to place cannot be divorced from the landscape or from the road itself. As he drives toward Nashville, the roads move "downhill." He reflects in his movement his trepidation and writes, "I felt something close in around me and wished I had not come. This land is death to me." He continues, "Down went the roads, down, then up, sweeping around mountains and great masses of pines stumbling up the hills. There was in the air that morning a certain stillness, a waiting. It is me, I thought; it must be me. Somewhere between Louisville and Nashville, I lost the sense of ownership that I had thought seven generations in this land had brought me. At the moment I did not feel fear, just uneasiness from being acutely aware that I might run into trouble and not be able to emerge without great difficulty."[27] The ease of the open road, promised to middle America, is not available to Williams, and his awareness of his lack of a "sense of ownership" is not only of the land but also of the road.

This compelling segment reminds readers that his thoughts are presented as he drives through this landscape but also denied any welcoming connection to it. At each moment, his mobility might be halted, no matter the implied power of his credit cards and his new car or, for that matter, the strength of his will. His descriptions of landscape, which are infrequent and often brief, nonetheless incorporate the political struggles that have marred the South throughout its history. This, to no reader's surprise, follows the specific context and purpose of his movement, which is defined by the historical moment as well as his unease.

Later, his exit from the South provides a rhetorical bookend to this moment and confirms the ongoing struggle. Williams writes, "The drone of the car was making me sleepy and I lowered the rear window. Cold air came snapping into the car, whipped at my ears, numbed my nose. I should stop now, I told myself, for I was driving with my left foot on the gas, my right knee had almost locked on me and I had it stretched out toward the right-side door. There was no place along my route where I could stop in safety. And the rule among Negroes who travel in the South is: don't sleep in your car. I had now reached the stage where the headlights of oncoming cars and the lights of towns blinded me for a second, and I knew that soon I'd have to stop." At this point, Williams captures his desperation as the building stress of fatigue and growing pain in his leg represent the overarching fear dominating his travels in the South. Mobility grants him some protection of anonymity in a white car. Stopping for needed rest, however, risks revealing his racial identity to potentially unfriendly locals. He continues, "Where was I? Tennessee, Tennessee, Kentucky! Kentucky, Kentucky, Illinois. Finally, Illinois. Let it have changed in this section, let it have changed."[28] This anticlimactic ending to his sojourn in the South (not the end of the narrative) again makes the inextricable connection between the practical and the symbolic that defines road narratives on the whole. It also matches the same go-stop, go-stop pattern of mobility, wherein the stops help define the movement. However, as is the case with civil rights movements, the stopping represents the assertion of the Jim Crow South, the power of mainstream, stable expectations.

As King, Griffin, and Williams, among others, demonstrate, the road that offers no comfort or rest for the weary is not open and therefore is not a symbol of freedom. Williams cannot stop at night as he moves through Tennessee and through Kentucky because stopping represents danger. He does not stop; he drives on and on, "foot on the gas," until he extricates himself from a landscape of despair. Although his movement through the South serves as the key for the thesis of his narrative, it by no means provides the only proof of the challenges he faces. Williams travels over fifteen thousand miles, by his estimation, which is equivalent to the travels of Steinbeck and Heat-Moon, and he finds a complicated road experience everywhere. Williams provides a complete narrative in that context, and the following passages reveal his capacity to fully realize the promise of the open road even with its daunting political roadblocks.

Perhaps, other than the South, the most instructive segment of *This Is My*

Country Too occurs along the northern Great Plains. What is especially important is that this sequence reveals an impressive range of road encounters. The uncertainty of the open road that affects all travelers creates the steady presence of liminality for Williams as well. He negotiates a mobility that is always, by definition, personal and, by cultural reality, political. That context does not remove the more universal context of mobility itself. Thesis-driven narratives, as Williams shows, can also tap into the broader open-road mythology, and his narrative merits attention for that content as well. Let's begin with an unswerving declaration of the joy of the open road, as he notes, "It felt good to be on the open road once again." Moving westward from Chicago and into Wisconsin, Williams continues, "I let the car out and it jumped ahead, moving clearly and easily, and the joy of having so much power at toe tip filled me completely. Here it was, the ground-level height of Everyman's automated existence. Open the doors, press a button and lower the window, turn the key, set the gear and mash down. Beneath the hood, currents surged like flashes of lightning, and hundreds of horses snorted, kicked, and began to gallop. Two and a half tons of brightly burnished metal, resting on rubber hoofs, bucked for one second, then soared ahead."[29] No passage in Kerouac's *On the Road* shows a stronger or more vibrant expression of open-road excitement. Williams's description captures the positive power the road represents, a celebration of automobility with all the obligatory praise for horsepower and individualism. This passage is a riveting expression of road joy. Williams embraces the power of the mobile moment without hesitation. The racial politics that define his mission are gone, and his enjoyment is pure and unfiltered. This passage captures a wonderful sense of pleasure afforded by the open-road dream, and Williams's unrestrained celebration of the moment bears witness to his desire.

The practicality underlying this passage is also compelling, as he asserts the experience as true to the "ground-level height of Everyman's automated existence," which is followed by simple, declarative statements of the interactions between human and machine—"open the doors, press a button . . . " In continuing his thoughts, he refers back to his discomfort along Southern roads as they complicated an otherwise pleasant interaction with the car and road. Though the car was always a "vault of safety" for him as long as he kept moving in the South, he notes that elsewhere he can enjoy this perfect open-road moment unencumbered by the overwhelming fears. In this contrasting experience, he wants to remain in the car "because of the sense of power it gave me; power to move rapidly, for miles, at so little cost of energy to myself."[30] In her appraisal of this sequence, Brigham notes that "the expression of power . . . defines the road's freedom."[31] Readers must enjoy this as well in that it captures a core belief: it feels "good to be on the open road."

Every moment on the road, however, is transitory. For Williams, the racial perils lurk forever around the next bend. Anonymity behind the wheel of a car is never assured, and Williams reports the intrusion of the politics of the early 1960s into the "vault of safety" with a simple observation just a few pages after the passage discussed above. He provides an instructive testimony to his very existence on the road as a provocation to any sense of "normalcy" for most Americans—demographically "white." He is being watched. In Grand Forks, North Dakota, he shares the following encounter: "One man, his car filled with children, turned to grin and point at me. His car suddenly spurted dust as it veered off the narrow road. I watched him in the rearview mirror as he skidded back on the highway, and I felt nothing for him or the kids, not hate, not joy."[32] This is a concise and compelling scene, a psychic collision wherein mobility is momentarily on the verge of disaster. A wreck is narrowly averted by chance, as two men/two cars meet on the highway and race rocks the normal movement of two vehicles from different worlds.

This scene provides a quick reminder of Williams's stress as he travels the American open road. His vulnerability is forever palpable. As indicated earlier, Brigham provides a strong reading of Williams's narrative, but I must diverge from her interpretation of this moment.[33] She argues that this encounter immobilizes Williams, an interpretation that goes too far in insisting on his victimization at the expense of recognizing his power. Williams carefully uses this encounter to show two things: first, that white America, especially in the northern plains, finds the novelty of a Black man on the road amusing, and second, that such an obsession undermines the power and control of white America. The dimwitted father in the other vehicle nearly wrecks his car in a clumsy effort to point out Williams's Blackness to his children. Williams, to the contrary, has full control of his own movement, and it never falters. Ironically, the shock to the sense of normalcy given to the other driver lays bare his limited view of the open road so much so that he loses control of his vehicle, veering onto the shoulder of the road in a blast of dust. Williams keeps moving without distraction. I take him at his word, and this passage reads as power. The capacity to drive a car is always an expression of control, and Williams in this moment, despite the unpleasant reminder of social context, is in charge of his mobility.

The key to understanding Williams's reason for being on the road depends on acknowledgment by Euro-American readers of the oppressiveness of the cultural matrix that makes the open road not-so-open for African Americans. However, the recognition of this crucial context must also be balanced by awareness of the capacity of African Americans to claim the road nonetheless. Toward that purpose, the assertions of power and joy that Williams also provides are equally important. To continue this point, I need to jump back to a scene that appears earlier, when Williams is still in the South.

In a compelling example of road ownership, Williams meticulously reports of a tense moment at an intersection. While traveling through Alabama, he notes how the Confederate battle flag was placed atop official roadside signs. During this reminiscence, Williams indeed loses his focus and screeches to a halt as he almost runs through a red light. In contrast with the scene above wherein he maintains control when forced to reckon with his racial vulnerability, here he loses composure and comes to a stop under duress. The danger is that his anonymity is at risk because his screeching stop draws too much attention.

He is trying to be hypervigilant to avoid unwanted scrutiny from local police. As he "cringed" at the intersection, worried over his mistake, he thinks back to a waking dream he had as a child: "After every reported lynching I saw myself in a specially made car, heading South. Built into the front of the car were three machine guns, two .30 caliber and one .50. The two .30s could track 90 degrees to the side. The car, of course, was bulletproof, and being especially built, the engine was supercharged; nothing on the road could catch us."[34] The paragraph ends without further comment, and in the next paragraph he simply states, "The light changed and I continued on through Alabama." The old dream—still current for Williams—is one of revenge in response to the long legacy of racial oppression, but it is perfectly presented wholly within road mythology, a "specially made car" designed to fight back against the all-too-common lynchings in the South.

Brigham notes Williams's "profound uneasiness" in this moment and refers to Kris Lackey's use of the phrase "*defensive* fantasy" to characterize this passage. She goes on to conclude that the car is defined by its capacity for escaping danger, noting that "victory comes with outpacing any pursuers."[35] I must disagree with any interpretive reduction of Williams's imagery here as placing him in a cowering posture. The core purpose of the dream is one that rejects victimhood, and as such the dream Williams shares expresses unadulterated and unqualified power. The assumption that the potential speed of the dream car is to allow for an escape from inferred white pursuers misses two key points: first, the dream is of *killing* any would-be pursuers, and second, speed itself is power. The dream car, indeed, cannot be caught on the road, but that is not the reason for the "supercharged" engine. To be sure, a street racer would brag that a car could not be caught to emphasize its speed for *leading*, not *escaping*. As a young boy, Williams dreamed of winning, not running away. Moreover, the guns Williams imagines are placed on the "front of the car" to be used in pursuing and overtaking. And killing. This dream does not display a defensive posture.

Williams, though stopped for a moment, invokes aspirations to speed down the road in absolute control of his mobility: the car, the road, his eyes, his weapons all pointing toward the road ahead. The reverie is framed by his present momentary stop in Alabama, wherein Williams knows quite well that he has no power and that his road is far from fully open. Idling in the car, his mind and rage are fully engaged in sharing with readers an alternate reality. By bringing the childhood memory into the present moment, Williams makes it emotionally liminal, an opportunity for transition in sharp rejection of his anxiety while stopped at a crossroads. He shifts his mindset from defense to offense. Looking through the windshield, he is an avenger, destroyer of injustice set on bringing death to white supremacists. He rightfully claims an unbounded horizon.

Williams challenges the open road by revealing the cultural realities that render the assumptive adjective "open" as false, but he also celebrates it by taking advantage, when possible, of opportunities to assert power and joy on the road. Both facets of his narrative are essential in the African American road experience. *This Is My Country Too* captures the inherent challenges in a racialized America that steadily diminishes such unbridled enthusiasm. Williams is true to both components of the open-road mythology for an American of African heritage, exploring the underlying deception of the American dream fused with the undeniable desire to assert that dream nonetheless. In the closing segment of *This Is My Country Too*, Williams reaffirms the American dream of mobility. He writes, "I had fear and anger and loneliness in my travels, but, the paradox that is America, there was much love too and goodwill. Perhaps the time will come when in parts of this nation I will not have to fear for my life. When that time comes, a white will not have to fear for his either. We are that intertwined here and now. The challenge is to really look and see how much. And the land still stretches vast and bold."[36]

Williams closes with a vision of road stability, sharing a more nuanced road. As with all narratives, the secret is in the play of language and image, of expectation and desire, of memory and meaning. The inevitable tensions between stable and subversive modes are perverted by the racialized historical context that haunts the open road, yet the core and universal desire for an open road persists, as Williams affirms throughout his narrative. What remains as he closes his personal journey is for America to "live up to the challenge of it, and what we have wanted it to be."[37] For African Americans, open mobility can never be assumed. The road remains too often unsafe. The fight for mobility is therefore persistently a heroic quest for belonging and a persistent fight for domestic tranquility. The search for the horizon is forever a search for home in a nation that is "vast and bold," yet desperately lacking a truly open road.

SOUTH OF HAUNTED DREAMS

Roughly thirty years after Williams's road trip, another African American man embarked on a similar journey, testing a similar thesis, this time with the logical follow-up question in mind: Have things changed? Whereas Williams consciously asserted his broad thesis directly in his title, Eddy Harris in *South of Haunted Dreams* conjures a more nuanced and metaphorical tone as he takes to the open road in the American South. He looks backward to the personal and political history so that he can successfully look forward along the road to his horizons.

Eddy Harris by 1993 had already established himself as a compelling travel writer. His biggest success was with his first narrative, *Mississippi Solo*, covering a trip down the fabled river by canoe. He followed that up with *Native Stranger*, a journey to Africa.[38] *Mississippi Solo* provides the most applicable complementary text to *South of Haunted Dreams*. It is decidedly not a road narrative, but it covers Harris's journey—physical and emotional—into the heart of darkness of the South via the Mississippi river, so firmly entrenched in the national psyche. Vulnerable and highly conscious of the complexity of his undertaking, Harris produced a formidable narrative in *Mississippi Solo*, a study of self and place that makes for first-rate travel writing. With *South of Haunted Dreams*, Harris reengages with the idea of immersion into the American South by considering his relationship with its complicated past and its ongoing struggles. He does so not in a canoe, however, but on a motorcycle. This time, he takes to the open road.

The subtitle, "A Ride through Slavery's Old Backyard," implies Harris's intention to test the question of his place along Southern roads. His journey is an essential complementary text to Williams's. He sets out with much more confidence in his power as a traveler and as a "Blackamerican" (the self-identifying term he prefers) than Williams could have claimed. He nonetheless is well aware of the history and the ongoing legacy of slavery and segregation. As with Williams, a crucial moment is marked by the physical entry into the South, that practical and symbolic threshold-crossing into the intimidating unknown. In the opening segment, he crosses the Ohio River and moves into Kentucky, then observes a roadside sign that reads "Daviess County Coon Hunters' Club," which to him implies the use of "coon" as a racial epithet and thus a reference to the long, horrific legacy of lynching in the South. He writes, "Instinctively my hand locks tighter around the grip of my motorcycle and twists open the throttle. The engine roars. The bike—a blue BMW—quickens. I hold on tight. I crouch forward on the bike and hurry past the sign, hurry past the evil spirits that hold the thing upright and steady. These many years later, the South still owns my nightmares and haunts my memory."[39]

Several elements of this passage demand attention. First, rhetorically, he sets up the core tension of the narrative that will directly engage with a place that haunts his sense of belonging. Harris deftly, with simple declarative sentences, also firmly couches his notions of the South in his mobility.

The stimulus and response pairing is succinct: he crosses the river and sees the sign; he tightens his grip on the handlebar and "twists" the throttle, increasing his speed. This moment harkens back to Williams's comments about using speed as a talisman against evil. We may also see the twist of the throttle as power. Though chastened by the almost immediate encounter with the dark spirits of the South, his speed is also an assertion of his capacity to move through the challenge on his own terms. This is fight, not flight. He does not stop, and he does not turn around. His response also indicates anxiety as he seeks to move past the sign and its "evil spirits."

Harris follows this scene with a substantive discussion of the historical nightmare that his journey intends to awaken from. He recounts representative stories of lynching and Jim Crow laws maniacally devoted to preserving the color line. He also includes his own family struggles under the daunting political and social systems of segregation. With the memories of his father's ordeals replaying in his narrative consciousness, Harris asserts his thesis: "I travel to the South to confront the source of my anger. I am half hoping to hurt someone. At the same time I am longing to find a new South, a new America, hoping with heart and soul that all is not hopelessness and despair."[40] This passage provides the essential optimism so crucial to the open road, the desire for change, but that optimism is defined first by his anger. He enters the South not simply desiring a different road but demanding a better one.

Referring back to the "Coon Hunters' Club" sign, he writes, "The sign helps to awaken me. The sign helps me remember. I am black, and being black matters. I turn the bike around and go back—slowly this time—back to the sign and to the arrow pointing down a narrow lane that disappears around a sharp bend."[41] The physical loop here—turning around and retracing his movement to reread the sign—gives him direction. He follows the arrow painted on the sign to the uncertain road ahead. Harris finds the club house, a forlorn structure, but cannot find anyone to provide him with more information. However, the episode provides a useful rhetorical framing—a circular returning to places and to history—that illustrates his complex expectations of his upcoming journey into a South that blurs time distinctions more so than any other region of the country. As he moves back to the main road, he finds what he thinks will be the standard conflict that the "Coon Hunters' Club" represents for his journey.

With a purpose so intrinsically tied to the past and with an implicit expectation of the future, the ever-present moment so central to road narratives is perpetually expressive of liminality. Harris, keenly aware of this threshold state of travel, delves into his uncertain place along the road. The South is a mysterious place that offers the potential for insight to his selfhood. Harris has embarked on a heroic quest. In the opening of the following chapter, he stops to look behind him on the road, thus creating, in effect, a conventional mirror-roadview moment: "The road behind bent in the distance and disappeared in the trees; ahead it ran straight like a time-line into the haze of future. It ran to the horizon and got lost in the glare, shrank near the faraway limits of my sight and was gone. I faced forward on the machine, toward tomorrow, toward the unknown. I put the bike in gear. Spurning the fear and apprehension that vibrated through me, I rode on, into the labyrinth of time."[42] Harris consciously creates a conventional road moment of looking into the future—the road ahead—while also considering the past—the road behind. Yet the future in this instance is "straight" like a "time-line" while also being in a "haze." He ties his own fears to the vibrations caused by the movement itself. His rhetoric emphasizes liminality as Harris stands between two worlds, taking the time to look in both directions. Moreover, when his gaze turns "forward," as if using a windshield roadview, he sees the future as he simultaneously invokes "the labyrinth of time." The threshold moment ends, and he moves forward.

Soon after the passage above, Harris makes clear his mindset for his journey, which firmly places him within the larger narrative of mobility for African Americans. He writes, "I would travel this country for the first time in my life as a racist, with color and race always on my mind."[43] This expression—defining himself as "a racist"—is not a confession of bias or an implicit admission of seeking conflict as a way of satisfying self-fulfilling prophesies. Rather, this is a necessary acknowledgement of a reality that forces an ever-present consciousness of such challenges to the open road. The place, to Harris's manner of thinking, demands foregrounding awareness of the overarching racial legacies that built the road he is taking.

The narrative tension between past and future pivoting on the road present is an essential element of travel writing, but Harris also uses this context to set up the predominant racial challenge of the American South, which places his movement in an uneasy state of liminality. The African American road narrative in response to systematic and incidental challenges to mobility is forced to reckon with instability. In this context the South provides a provocative challenge since it serves as a place of both foundation for African American identity and proving ground for self-expression. Harris captures this paradox: "I did not travel across Africa to find my roots. I traveled the South to find them. For the South, not Africa, is home to Blackamericans, and Blackamericans as a race are essentially southerners. Only in the South could I discover where my beginnings as a Blackamerican have gone. Without realizing it at the time, I was going home."[44] The repetition of "Blackamericans" defines his racial identity in his own terms, but it is also tied to his sense of self when reckoning with place. He travels to confront an antagonistic past while also retrieving a lost sense of home. In this context, moving forward demands a repairing of a broken past, and in that journey the only healing search is for the stability of a home, a point of reference that can serve a sense of self rather than deny it. In other words, Harris is trying to travel in the stable mode.

In Hartford, Kentucky, Harris reports his first encounter wherein the past and present collide in his mind as he stops to "stretch his legs, to cool off, to clear my head." As he sees a police officer move toward him, he prepares himself "for trouble," and he makes the historical connection blurring time. The officer "is the spitting image of Bull Connor to me."[45] Harris then recounts his unpleasant personal history of such encounters, but this specific moment runs counter to his expectations. No trouble occurs as the two men connect via a shared love of the open road and fast motorcycles. After Harris tells the officer that his travel plans are open—"I'm just going"—the officer responds, "Living every man's dream. . . . Ooo-wee! That's just about heaven."[46] The friendly exchange carries no conflict, unlike others Harris has experienced. The moment simply celebrates the joy of the open road. After noting the beauty and power of his motorcycle and thus refocusing reader attention, Harris returns to the road, matching the optimism of the encounter: "I put the bike in gear. In half a moment I was gone. I forgot all about Bull Connor and the hateful past, forgot I was in the South. And for the moment I was back to my old self, a tall man with a beard, now with a hot-looking motorcycle. I was king of the world again. Being black hardly mattered."[47] This is a stunning passage, not because it shocks his expectations but because it effectively captures the liminality of the road. Harris does not forget the horrors of the past nor neglect the thesis of his narrative. Rather, he is demonstrating the power of the road and the centrality of expressing the value of the ever-present moment. His identity has not been erased by the historical context or by an abusive voice of white authority, and "*for the moment*" (italics added), no memories of the past or ambitions for the future intrude. There is only a man, a motorcycle, a road. All three components cohere to make Harris a "king."

All moments pass on the road, and the congenial interaction with the police officer serves as one of a wide range of encounters that form Harris's narrative and push and pull his sense of self like curves on a highway. Throughout the journey, however, he maintains an openness to experiences while keeping true to his intentions to move, always conscious of racial influences at any given moment. The thematic push is to find a confidence in thinking of the South as home to his racial identity and earning some peace within the inherent paradoxes. He repeatedly comes back to this thought. Moving further into the South, he increasingly tries to balance the obscenities of the past with a desire for connection to his ancestry that is affirming. As he rides, he notes, “Their voices whisper in my ear.” He continues, “This land is home to me, bought and paid for with the sweat, anguish, and joy of those who went before me and willed it to me. This air is familiar to me. This land is familiar to me.” That awakening to the South as “familiar” makes it possible for Harris to declare the South as home: “This land is mine. I have come to reclaim it.”[48]

In a collision similar to the one that opens the journey (the “Coon Hunters’ Club” sign), Harris recounts seeing an eighteen-wheeler truck with a large confederate flag emblazoned across its grill soon after expressing his reclamation purpose quoted above. Harris notes, “To be black is to always be reminded that you are a stranger in your native land. To be black is to be surrounded by those who would remind you. To be black is having to be ever vigilant, never completely at ease.”[49] Harris has a strong reaction to the trucker and expresses his desire to confront him. He steps into the road to force the driver to “take notice.” He then gets back on his bike and chases the truck, but to no avail. Once Harris realizes that he cannot catch up to the offending truck, he “slowed down and laughed” at himself. He ponders his reaction and the impact of seeing the flag. He brings back into our awareness the problem of time on the road in the South and wishes for a revision of sorts. He writes, “What a miracle if we could somehow erase time, retrace our steps to where we went wrong, start all over again.” Then he provides a revised version of the unpleasant encounter, building on the idea of starting over: “If we could do that, I would come back one of these days to the rise in this road. No, farther back to when the truck with the rebel flag painted on it came racing over the hill and spoiled my morning. I would go back to the dawn, back to the lake, and start this day once more. I would not look up when I heard the truck coming this time. I would not allow him to harm the peace.”[50] This is a fanciful dream of time travel. Harris cannot regain the beauty of a morning by the lake any more than he can expunge the horrors of the past that the truck represents. There is no escape. The incidental moments, however transitory and arbitrary, are nonetheless parts of the larger narrative of self and place. Harris’s escape here privileges the present—that universal dream experience on the road—and the joy implicit in the freedom of movement creates its own narrative and its own reason to continue.

As the narrative progresses, Harris expands on the themes already discussed and moves toward an optimistic future, just as Williams did thirty years previous. Having asserted the necessity of moving through the South to solidify and clarify his self-identity and having claimed the South as his home, Harris needs only to embrace that home and incorporate it fully into his sense of self if he hopes to move forward at peace with his road. In the final two chapters, he moves northward to complete the circle by traveling on the same roads on which he entered the South. He writes, “I knew I had come to the South to face my fears and to surrender them, to forget the many things it is best to forget, and to remember what is essential to remember. Until I did these, the South would own my anger and my sanity, my dignity, my pride, my sense of self."[51] Harris accomplishes his goals and completes his quest. A changed man, Harris has gained a stronger sense of self. The closing pages are carefully presented to affirm his conclusions.

Two clarifying scenes parallel earlier moments and therefore rhetorically close his circular journey. The first is an unpleasant encounter with an unswerving racist who confronts Harris. In the end, the scene becomes one of healing and power for Harris. He does not flinch, nor does he lose his composure. He controls every facet of the encounter, its roiling emotional tension and its underlying threat of violence. In the earlier near-confrontation with the truck driver displaying the confederate battle flag, Harris failed to stand his ground, being able only to step into the roadway anemically as the truck roars past. In this scene, however, Harris completes the necessary assertion of self in the face of hatred. Once he does so, he departs contented: "I hopped on the bike and didn't look back."[52] In the second scene, he returns to a restaurant near the Kentucky border wherein he could not get service at the beginning of his journey. Deducing at the time that the lack of service reflected malevolent intentions tied to race, he chooses to return to the site to recast his narrative. This time the experience is quite different, as he meets with courteous and friendly service, and it thus serves as a corrective to the earlier unpleasant stop.

The key again is Harris's state of mind. Harris controls the moment and is affirmed by his choices. On the road, Harris moves with purpose and confidence made stronger by the varied experiences had during the preceding miles. As he once again finds himself on the same roadway, he notes, "I was led no longer by the voice of addiction nor by the soft whispering voices of travel muses or the ghosts of those who had gone before, but this time by my own volition and desire."[53] In the liminal moments that directly speak to the racial collisions on the road, Harris consistently and intently emphasizes willful choices tied to but not bound by the past. Confronting a painful history, as well as the ongoing challenges to mobility, he finds a way to define a home. Harris completes a circular tour of the American South. In the process, he transforms the place and his identity, a man moving along a road fully of his choosing.

"REPLAY"

John Howard Griffin's *Black Like Me* captured his experiences posing as a Black man on the road in the late 1950s. He found trouble. John Williams in the early 1960s and then Eddy Harris in the early 1990s both embraced more nuanced experiences but most certainly also found trouble. And others found themselves on the road and encountered similar experiences, some captured in narrative and many never told beyond circles of family and friends. They found trouble. The weight of repetition year after year, road after road hangs heavy. Similar encounters replayed, revised, replayed, revised, replayed.

In 2019, Jordan Peele took the lead in rebooting the remarkably provocative and substantive television series *The Twilight Zone*, originated by Rod Serling in 1959.[54] The original version ran for five seasons and still holds a formidable grip on the American imagination well into the twenty-first century. There have been two other revivals of the show and there has been a film version, all demonstrating the series' cultural authority.[55] Peele's version is the strongest of the reincarnations and the most representative of the heft of Serling's original. The third episode of the first season merits attention as an excellent tier 1 road narrative exploring the ongoing challenges to African American mobility. Written by Selwyn Seyfu Hinds and directed by Gerard McMurray, "Replay" is a powerful work of cinematic art firmly rooted in open-road mythology.[56] It demonstrates the universal attractions of the open road while also showing in methodical and maddening repetition the challenges to an open-road ideal for African Americans. The plot frame is simple: a mother is driving with her son to begin his college career, a cherished ritual of the stable road that takes place annually for myriad families. Such road trips always evoke liminality as parents and children are on the thresholds of change. The mother, Nina (Sanaa Lathan), and the son, Dorian (Damson Idris), clearly share a close bond, and the drive carries with it all the optimism expected of the moment. However, they do not travel in a vacuum. As they move from home to college, they encounter a menacing police officer who seeks to thwart their mobility.

This story, as with others we have seen, cannot simply be a personal journey of transition, because the road is political and laid out along clear color lines. This mother and son are taking "a fateful drive through the perilous highways of the twilight zone," as the narrator (Jordan Peele) explains. The depth of "Replay" derives from the juxtaposition of a surreal interplay between the magical realism of the show and the horrifyingly familiar historical reality that informs every moment on the road. The essential appeal of *The Twilight Zone* has been its effective use of extra-normal phenomena to force viewers to encounter the truths of the world and of the human heart. The strongest episodes have always played with fluid realities and the fine, often misleading, distinctions we make between "light and shadow," as the introductory comments explain. And "Replay" is no exception.

The title itself is both practically minded and metaphysical. The term "replay" refers to the manipulation of time within the story made possible by an old family camcorder. Nina, in a moment of high stress, discovers that pushing "rewind" not only rewinds the videotape but also rewinds time, thus allowing her to "replay" and thus *revise* the ongoing present. The trauma of the narrative is that she is forced over and over again, out of desperation, to use the machine to alter the time sequence. Yet she cannot avoid trauma. This is a compelling and well-worn plot device for science fiction and is perfectly suited to *The Twilight Zone*. What makes the time travel in "Replay" so stirring, however, is the increasing anguish in the moments that lead up to Nina's pushing of the "rewind" button. The pressure ratchets up as the narrative progresses maddeningly toward a familiar but increasingly violent and devastating result with each revision.

After the initial use of the rewind function, stumbled on accidentally, Nina begins to use the camcorder as a resource to shape the road journey, to make it safe and stable. This strategy is her first grasp at power. In each subnarrative, she is steadily harassed by the persistent and pernicious efforts of a police officer who moves in methodical and unswerving dedication toward one goal: stop the mobility of the two African American protagonists. The episode is a finely crafted metaphor for "driving while Black," with each encounter precisely resonant of the struggle for the open road. In a simple plotline moving main characters from point A to point B, the narrative pivots on the question of mobility. An antagonist stands determined to stop the protagonists, and, as such, the story is a heroic quest to claim the open road by slaying the dragon of intransigent systemic racism. The exhaustion evoked by the narrative framing creates a near-constant and uneasy liminality as the characters teeter on the verge of disaster with each encounter. Rewind, replay; rewind, replay; rewind, replay.

The narrative begins with Nina and Dorian enjoying a meal in a diner. In this opening sequence, the specter of police harassment enters the frame in the background haze as mother and son talk about the future. Through the window of the diner, viewers see a police cruiser park and an officer exit the car and move toward the building. We never see his face, only his legs and torso. As he opens the diner door, his gun (or taser) is centered. The police officer, once inside, takes a seat at the counter and orders lunch. All seems well. As the mother and son enjoy the quiet moments in the diner, Dorian curses playfully when he accidentally sprays ketchup onto his white T-shirt, and the officer takes notice. This incidental moment locks the two parties—mother/son and police officer—into repeated sequences all leading to violence.

After leaving the diner, Nina and Dorian get back on the road, only to be pulled over by the officer, the first of many confrontations. As this becomes a repeated pattern, each potential revision initiated by Nina to avoid violence inevitably ends with increasingly tragic results. The racial overtones of the police officer's actions worsen as well, beginning with clear but subtle racist remarks and ending with violence toward Dorian. This surreal journey reflects American racial inequalities and police harassment and brutality, and the key frustration for Nina becomes the fact that no matter what she does to revise the narrative by altering her and Dorian's behaviors, the result is the same. She cannot avoid the tragedy because the pressure placed on them by the officer's systematic attacks on their mobility allows for no corrective action on her part. The officer will never *not* accost them. As Nina understands, "He's always on the verge of killing Dorian."

The initial encounter is represented by the screenshot below (fig. 6.1). The scene represented employs a side-window view to emphasize contrasting, even combative, roadview perspectives. As the focus changes from figure to figure (from the officer to Darian) during the encounter, viewers witness not just a practical filmic technique but also a symbolic performance of selfhood as both characters play a perverse role of racialized repetitive behaviors. The foregrounding techniques to direct audiences toward the speaker of the moment create a substantive symbolic representation of the erasing of the figures who are trapped in a long-standing, oft-repeated power dynamic between white authority and Black mobility. The individual faces, as well as actions, are indeed largely irrelevant in this historical context. Their individual features are inconsequential. Skin tone defines the interaction.

Fig. 6.1. *Twilight Zone*, "Replay," side-window blur. CBS Always, 2019, Blu-ray. Author's screenshot.

The only way out of the cycle for the family is to seek help and to subvert the dominance that the police officer holds on their mobility. They go underground, an homage to the movements of escaping slaves in the Underground Railroad in the mid-nineteenth century, and Nina begins drawing on support beyond the "replay" function on the camcorder. In the last push of the rewind button, Nina finds a way to make it to Tennyson College, but she does so only by reasserting her connections to her family, from which she has been estranged since her own escape from her hometown, the location of the college. Here the personal story expands and therefore provides the only way out of the repeating legacy of racialized violence at the hand of white authority: the reconnecting to home. She, indeed, is not alone, and with the help of her brother and others in the community she can get Dorian to the safety of campus and be surrounded by other African Americans who bear witness and provide support, helping to break the cycle and change the narrative. But that, in the end, can be done only through confrontation and a refusal to appease a corrupt police officer and a corrupt system. As with Williams and Harris, Nina and Dorian must claim their place on the road without apology and without deference.

The closing scene of the episode becomes much more straightforward as the final confrontation plays out, and it makes clear the direct references to the broader struggle for civil rights. The key to diminishing the power of the police officer and what he represents is the broad exposure provided by the camera itself. As the officer once again seeks to stop the movement onto campus—home and safety—Nina stands in the officer's way and refuses to move. She is no longer dependent on the rewind button because she is no longer alone and, equally important, no longer trying to appease the officer. By regaining her connection to her home and family and broader community, Nina is reminded of her strength and thus better recognizes the inherent weakness of the officer: "You're the one who's really afraid." She goes on to assert that "we're all witnesses," and the camera slowly pans around dozens of African Americans with cameras filming the scene. With that broader threat of exposure, the officer and his backup retreat. They no longer control *this* road.

The episode then includes a flash-forward sequence, ten years later, as the mother visits her son and her granddaughter in a scene of stable, domestic contentment. Dorian leaves his home to go out for ice cream. As he walks out the door, a flashing light, seemingly from a police cruiser, startles Nina. It is not an assertion of impending tragedy necessarily, but a reminder that the threat persists. The teleplay ends, per *Twilight Zone* formula, with these closing remarks from the narrator: "The future remains uncertain, even here in the twilight zone." This a poignant but ironic reminder of the context for the entire episode. "Replay" is not about the twilight zone; it is about the United States of America.

***

Americans will always be on the move as long as popular imagination celebrates mobility as a cultural birthright. To claim that birthright has been heartbreakingly difficult for African Americans. The fight for civil rights along the open road has been especially arduous, and although the long story is marked by vigilance and dignity for African Americans, it has also been marred by setbacks and tragedy. Prominent road narratives deriving from these challenging roads have demonstrated the oppressive weight of racialized power. No pursuit of happiness can sustain itself within a system that limits access to the open road. The African American road narrative has nonetheless required a belief in the possibilities implied by the national ideals, even when they have fallen far short in the practical realities of day-to-day life. The road is a symbol for cultural vitality and a reproach against stasis. It requires that we hold steadfast to the belief that it must, in the end, belong to anyone willing to look ahead and dream of what is just around the corner. And then to claim it.

7
Grabbing the Wheel

Women and Power

THE OPEN ROAD historically has privileged a male sensibility and, furthermore, a masculine freedom delineated by racial and class distinctions. The word "open" can always carry a footnote no matter who is doing the driving; however, a man of economic means and racial privilege has had the road laid out for him in a way that is as open as it gets. That does not mean that travelers with that privilege do not face obstacles or hardships, or that they do not fail. They do fail, and often. But they move with a confidence and expectation of the dawn that can be considered both annoyingly persistent and worthy of envy. Women travel different roads.

I wish to return to automobile advertisements as a shorthand for illustrating the pervasiveness and depth of the gendered expectations and codes of behavior that have defined our sense of automobility since the late 1940s.[1] Print advertisements of the 1950s are especially instructive cultural documents that capture core assumptions of American desires and behaviors. To be sure, these ads are designed to sell cars, but marketing in its many forms exploits our consumerist desire for happiness as determined within a materialistic culture often intertwined with social values.[2] Advertisers try to sell products by promoting ideas emmeshed with personal identities. Omnipresent in the periodic press, car ads appeared in local newspapers nationwide and popular magazines like *Life*, *Collier's*, *Saturday Evening Post*, and *Newsweek*, among many others. Twenty-first-century readers will no doubt find some amusement in the copy of such ads, but, if they choose to be honest, they may also find much that is familiar. Gendered assumptions persist, and they inform the multifarious road narratives that have emerged in response.

A Ford print ad from the early spring of 1947, for example, evokes the basic assumptions tied to women as revealed in its pitch (fig. 7.1). This ad is from the wildly successful advertising campaign for Ford created by the J. Walter Thompson agency and built around the phrase "There's a Ford in your future." This example, which carries a tagline "Ford's out front from a woman's angle," is a clear effort to address female consumers.[3] This ad appeared in *Ladies' Home Journal, McCall's, Woman's Home Companion, Good Housekeeping*, and *Household* magazines, which boasted a total readership of over sixteen million. The messaging regarding gendered expectations is not subtle. In full-color drawings, it shows four young, smartly dressed women surrounding a Ford sedan, seemingly thrilled by its features. The copy has six numbered captions presented as excerpts from their supposed conversation and complemented by smaller images of the vehicle and the women.

Fig. 7.1. Woman's angle. The Benson Ford Research Center, Dearborn, Michigan. Accession 19, box 28.

One example should provide the gist of the ad: "My husband says the brakes are self-centering and hydraulic—whatever that means! All I know is they're so easy that I can taxi the children all day without tiring out!" This passage captures two key overarching ideas regarding the mainstream expectations of the female consumer: a woman is ignorant of and cares little about the technical specifications of automobiles, and a woman desires a car that helps her serve family needs. The playful, self-deprecating "whatever that means!" is helpful in discussions of power behind the wheel in that such power depends on the capacity to control a vehicle and keep it running. Ignorance is dependence. Most car consumers are astoundingly unaware of how cars work, but only men are required to feel guilty about that. For women, that ignorance is strength, it seems, as the copy assumes that trying to master the mechanics of automobility would be wasted time.

The second point emphasizes the expectation that women drive in support of domesticity. The imaginary woman voicing the statement upholds the idea that she is a "taxi" service for her children. The other supposed conversations highlight features of the automobile while also sustaining the basic assumptions of the "woman's angle." In short, women appreciate sleek styling and plush comfort and little else. More important is the fact the ad contains no hint of desire for autonomous mobility, or even a nod to the inherent joy of driving. In other words, this ad sells mainstream domestic comfort tied to the car as materialistic marker. Though simplistic, as most ads are, it illustrates succinctly the pervasive challenges facing women drivers. When women grab the wheel, they do so within a complicated cultural framework that is doggedly antagonistic to their mobility.

Road narratives arise from challenges that spark and engage the human spirit, so when anyone takes to the open road, they encounter myriad chances for joy and anguish, and those stories often are profoundly informed by cultural realities. This chapter examines narratives defined by complicated and restrictive codes of behavior for women. The intricacies of stable and subversive modes are prominent in all narratives in one way or another, but how the mobility manifests itself for travelers in a highly charged, gendered culture demands ongoing attention. The underlying desire for home within a road mythology haunts both male and female protagonists, but the road that has provided the escape crucial to men has not been as open for women. Nonetheless, as the narratives reveal, liminality defines the experience.

Yet women have always taken to the open road, they have always driven, and they have always embraced a desire to do so on their own terms. The central critical framework for understanding road narratives featuring female travel is the subversion implicit in any act from a woman that runs counter to domesticity. When men leave home, they can do so for many reasons, most of which fall firmly within gendered expectations of behavior that support a heroic, self-affirming ideal. When women leave home, their actions thus inevitably threaten domestic order. The question "Mom, where are you going?" implies a sense of danger to familial tranquility not found in "When is Dad coming home?"

Whereas noting power limitations and thus emphasizing the stringent restrictions forced by gendered norms correctly establishes the historic context for women's mobility, it also tends to render what self-assertive power they demonstrate as too often desperate or even negligible in reference to dominant social forces. Balance is elusive. The close readings that follow address women protagonists struggling to shield their desires for autonomous mobility against the cultural norms pressuring them to remain in the domestic sphere. As with all road narratives, protagonists make choices and respond to the world around them in ever-present moments of liminality. Eager for such change, women behind the wheel embrace new horizons of possibility.

PLAY IT AS IT LAYS

Joan Didion's *Play It as It Lays* employs key conventions of mobility in the development of its main character, Maria Wyeth, and her struggles with self-definition.[4] As a tier 3 road narrative, it depends on multiple conventions in significant portions of the novel. The moments during which she asserts the most control take place when she is behind the wheel of her Corvette on the freeway, so aptly named not so much for the absence of tolls (free-way versus toll-way) but for its symbolic promise of an open road—free.

Didion takes full advantage of this symbol, explaining that when Maria's life seems to be unravelling (which it is), she seeks solace in mobility: "Maria drove the freeway."[5] She creates a ritual wherein she dresses each morning "with a greater sense of purpose," that "purpose" being simply to drive on the freeway, nothing else. She also consciously begins her ritual by ten o'clock in the morning to ensure the proper rhythm of her movement, what she thinks of as "its precariously imposed momentum." The summary description of this ongoing performance by Maria represents a substantive exploration of the power of automobility. It involves a complex relationship between self and place as Maria moves around the sprawling Los Angeles metropolitan area within its matrix of limited-access highways. Using phrasing common in reference to many of the roadways, she names highways not by their number or direction but for destinations ("the Santa Ana," "the Pasadena," "the Hollywood," etc.). Roads not only suggest places but become places, and Maria's driving demonstrates mastery of her car and the expanded environs of her homeplace:

> Once she was on the freeway and had maneuvered her way to a fast lane she turned on the radio at high volume and she drove. She drove the San Diego to the Harbor, the Harbor up to the Hollywood, the Hollywood to the Golden State, the Santa Monica, the Santa Ana, the Pasadena, the Ventura. She drove it as a riverman runs a river, every day more attuned to its currents, its deceptions, and just as a riverman feels the pull of the rapids in the lull between sleeping and waking, so Maria lay at night in the still of Beverly Hills and saw the great signs soar overhead at seventy miles an hour, *Normandie ¼ Vermont ¾ Harbor Fwy 1.* Again and again she returned to an intricate stretch just south of the interchange where successful passage from the Hollywood onto the Harbor required a diagonal move across four lanes of traffic. On the afternoon she finally did it without once braking or once losing the beat on the radio she was exhilarated, and that night slept dreamlessly.[6]

This is a beautiful expression of the joy implicit of driving with skill and control and, most importantly, autonomy, the core thrill of automobility. Coming early in the novel, its importance to her sense of self becomes more resonant as other components of her life fall apart.

Maria expands her sense of power through the self-conscious act of driving the complicated and crowded freeway system of greater Los Angeles. Didion makes an astute connection in this sequence, comparing the maneuvering along asphalt to the grace of a nineteenth-century steamboat moving along a flowing river, an iconic image captured so eloquently by Mark Twain a century earlier.[7] Updating mainstream mobility from riverboat to automobile, Didion celebrates the thrill of mastering the organic flow of traffic. Maria is "attuned to its currents" and "feels the pull of the rapids." Just as Twain had expressed the contradicting ways of seeing the river (romantic and realistic), Didion demonstrates how the freeway functions in a similar way as Maria balances the practical notations of names and signs ("the Hollywood to the Golden State" and "*Harbor Fwy 1*") with the poetic "intricate stretch" wherein she successfully conducts a "diagonal move across four lanes of traffic," like crossing a river with its treacherous snags and sandbars. She recognizes the pragmatic challenges to movement while also feeling the pleasant rhythms of the open road. Maria is "exhilarated." At the end of the day, she sleeps "dreamlessly," free of her haunting pain, a peace of mind directly emanating from her morning road ritual. The passage affirms her power.

Didion continues with this imagery, defining the freeway as Maria's source of solace. There are, however, times when she meanders through small road systems wherein the road rhythms are disrupted, creating a wholly different tone. When she is not on the freeway, her mobility becomes compromised and more tenuous: "Sometimes the freeway ran out, in a scrap metal yard in San Pedro or on the main street of Palmdale or out somewhere no place at all where the flawless burning concrete just stopped, turned into common road, abandoned construction sheds rusting beside it. When that happened she would keep careful control, portage skillfully back, feel for the first time the heavy weight of the becalmed car beneath her and try to keep her eyes on the mainstream, the great pilings, the Cyclone fencing, the deadly oleander, the luminous signs, the organism which absorbed all her reflexes, all her attention." Didion provides a keen contrast between the interstate system and urban America. Once Maria runs out of freeway, she encounters a significant stoppage to her therapeutic, high-speed mobility. Her movements seem no longer free. Though she maintains "careful control," she is tentative and anxiety-ridden, and she "feels" not the thrill of the freeway but the "heavy weight of the becalmed car beneath her." In short, she is no longer in unison with the car or the road. She experiences the doldrums and can find peace only by making her way back to the freeway and its brisk mobility, the "organism that absorb[s] all her reflexes, all her attention."[8]

The chapter wherein these passages occur closes by reasserting the centrality of Maria's mobility in relation to her well-being. During the summer when her marriage falls apart, "Maria put seven thousand miles on the Corvette." Being behind the wheel is the only emotional expression that Maria can control. Those seven thousand miles do not mark substantive physical progress along a straight line from point A to point B. Rather, the progress is better measured by time, not distance. As she moves in the Corvette, a muscle car, she gains power via her control of the machine and her eager distancing from the domestic sphere and the stasis it implies. The last reference reiterates this crucial component of her struggles and her ownership of open-road space. Didion writes, "Sometimes at night the dread would overtake her," but "she never thought about that on the freeway."[9]

The gendered dynamics that define the balance of the novel as Maria fights for some level of autonomy in a celebrity culture wherein men dominate are not present when she drives. It is the road that stands as the escape for her, which is wholly in line with the subversive dream characterizing male assumptions of power behind the wheel. Moreover, the Corvette, as an idealized muscle car, has long been associated with hyper-masculinity, so Maria's mode of transport claims the power implicit in the vehicle as well. She asserts control of her sense of self as surely as she controls the horsepower under the hood. This is the portion of her life in which she can enjoy absolute mastery via subversive mobility. And she does so without hesitation.

In addition to capturing the joy Maria gains from her driving, Didion effectively employs the tattered promise of the postwar dream of automobility as defined in reference to interstate highways. By the late 1960s, the remarkably complex system in Los Angeles had become both a prime example of its value to a vast metropolitan area and a measure of the system's dysfunction. Maria travels vast spaces but intentionally goes nowhere, a symbol of her emotional stasis. Maria is a woman in crisis, and her assertions of power behind the wheel offer sharp contrast to other facets of her life. A once semi-famous actress desperate for some level of celebrity, or at least some sense of self to hold on to, Maria is lost, and her mind is muddled by the perversities of LA culture and the self-destructiveness of drug and alcohol abuse. She has a shallow craving for applause that leads her to madness, an escape defined not by the road promise of a horizon but by a trap of self-delusion.

The closing segment is telling. On a movie set filming on location in the Mojave Desert, she moves only from hotel to town to desert. The overarching mood is one of stagnation, the emphasis relentlessly on the lack of movement. Though earlier in the narrative two prominent men, Carter and BZ, had provided some avenue for professional mobility, these poisonous relationships had long since grown confining. Didion methodically foregrounds this immobility by repeated references to her gazing into the desert: "Maria stared out the window into the dry wash behind the motel"; and "she would not take her eyes from the dry wash."[10] Maria willfully focuses on symbolically dead space, choosing to fixate on it rather than the dominating men around her. Her escapes from the stress of her life are no longer aspirational, and the concluding segments of the novel provide no affirmation.

Maria's last movements stand as a foil to the empowerment she had earlier found on the freeway. With ten days left on the film shoot, Carter tries to get Maria to join him on site, but she refuses. What she does that day is telling: "Instead she sat in the motel office and studied the deputy sheriff's framed photographs of highway accidents, imagined the moment of impact, tasted blood in her own dry mouth and searched the grain of the photographs with a magnifying glass for details not immediately apparent. . . . The next day she borrowed a gun from a stunt man and drove out to the highway and shot at road signs."[11] Though couched in road imagery, her actions defy mobility rather than celebrate it. She obsesses on images of death on the highway and then destroys symbols of mobility—highway signs—with a borrowed gun. These are not acts of assertive rebellion. To the contrary, they embrace lifelessness. Her movements are minimal and grant no comfort and, more importantly, no power.

Again, she refuses to join Carter on the set and chooses to stay in town. She talks to a woman who invites Maria to come to her home. Maria agrees. Didion captures an overarching plight facing the two representative women, both struggling with their pursuits of happiness: "The House was on the edge of the town, a trailer set on a concrete foundation. In place of a lawn there was a neat expanse of concrete, bordered by a split-rail fence, and beyond the fence lay a hundred miles of drifting sand."[12] This homestead description emphasizes stasis. A trailer, implying at least the promise of mobility, is mired in concrete, and the only movement evident is the "drifting sand." Unlike an idealized landscape suggesting potential for stability, the desert is steadily encroaching on the house: "The sand was blowing through the rail fence onto the concrete, drifting around the posts, coating a straight-backed chair with pale film." The woman sweeps the sand, trying to keep the desert at bay, but "new sand blew in as she swept."[13] Maria weeps at the scene as it represents her own feelings of desperation, as sand buries the space around her.

Maria is inert. The underlying desire that unites all people behind the wheel in the end can be unveiled by the fragmented question implied in liminal moments on the road: Moving or not moving? If a character is moving toward a horizon—a vision of stability in mainstream culture or a vision of subversion in counterculture, or a fusing of both—there is life. If, however, a character is not moving toward a horizon, there is death. Maria finds profound pleasure on the road, but she cannot sustain its power off the road. As a result, the narrative leads to tragedy. The title of the novel gives away the conclusion within a road sensibility in that it asserts an acceptance of stasis, of playing the hand that is dealt, the hand that just lies there. For anyone, but especially for a woman seeking power and autonomy, that hand carries few options and few escapes. Maria, who has bought into the illusions of selfhood promised by the Hollywood image machine, can find no way out of the inevitable stasis. Her only escape is into her own mind and its disengagement with the surrounding world and whatever limited horizons it may offer.

IN COUNTRY

Bobbie Ann Mason's *In Country* is a tier 2 road narrative that has earned a solid critical and popular success. It spawned a film version that expanded its reach, though the film failed to achieve a wide audience.[14] The novel takes its framing from a road trip from Kentucky to Washington, DC, but the story also depends on automobility in defining the growing power of the lead female character, Samantha Hughes ("Sam"). The novel is divided into three parts, with one and three containing the trip to Washington, and two providing the local narrative, the bulk of the content overall. In all sections, however, Sam's mobility is the primary focus, and her struggle for agency is expressed via her fight for power behind the wheel. The presentation of the open road is crucial to understanding how Sam sees her future and her awakening to the impact of gendered restrictions on her horizons.

Mason evokes the stable dream of mobility in the post–Vietnam War era in the 1970s and early 1980s, a climate with far less optimism than the World War II boom. The trip to Washington, DC, from Kentucky, however, is made feasible by the interstate system that arose from that earlier time; moreover, Sam's conception of the American landscape derives from her sense of the national identity organized by interstate highways. The novel opens with Sam, along with her uncle Emmett and her paternal grandmother, "Mamaw," on I-64 headed eastward. The narrative voice offers Sam's perspective from the third person and reveals her comfort on the interstate, which is "easy." Sam thinks that she "could glide like this all the way across America."[15] This is a succinct expression of the dream as established in the 1950s, and it affirms its ongoing resonance into the early 1980s, no matter the decline of American automobility during the challenges of the 1970s. In this context, Mason uses the dream of mobility as a foil against stasis and despair.

The novel examines the effects of the Vietnam War on American culture via its devastation of the Hughes family. Therefore, Sam's growing awareness of that legacy of pain—her father dies in the war before her birth—parallels the nation's struggles to understand the implications of the war. Sam's mobility plays out along this emotional fault line. Sam later notes that "you can't get lost in the United States," which affirms its road systems, in her mind, but she goes on to say, "I wish I could, though. I wish I'd wake up and not know where I was."[16] Her confidence in the open road is carefully paired with her own emotional turmoil, and her wish implies a liminality that places her on the threshold of change typical of any road narrative. Sam's survival depends on her capacity to move and, more importantly, her willingness to grab power behind the wheel.

The middle portion of the novel is defined largely by Sam's struggle against stasis. She has yet to purchase a car as the narrative jumps back to the months preceding the trip to Washington. The gendered context for Sam's mobility is clear throughout the novel, but perhaps the best and most concise indication of its centrality comes from Sam's pithy assessment of typical high school graduation gifts. She notes that "boys got cars for graduation, but girls usually had to buy their own cars because they were expected to get married—to guys with cars."[17] Her mother gives her a *Collegiate Dictionary* for her graduation, "a hint that she should go to college." At this point, Sam is well aware of the freedoms provided by a car but is yet to comprehend that her mother is trying to advance her long-term mobility as well via a college education. Sam nonetheless reflects subversive inclinations. As a girl from small-town America, she recognizes that stable mobility is placed in deference to male authority—as head of household and as driver. About that social mainstay Sam is skeptical.

Not yet a car owner, she moves around town in two main ways: as a passenger in her boyfriend's truck and as a runner using the power of her own legs. Only one of these modes of transport builds her strength, and she is fully cognizant of its importance. "When she ran, she felt free, as if she could do anything."[18] Mason employs her running on the streets of Hopewell to reflect the oppressive gender norms Sam faces. She feels "free" because she is in control, but, even so, she is often challenged by men. She receives sexualized yells from construction workers, and she encounters a man who "exposed himself" and another man who frightens her by "following her."[19] Such incidents serve as conventional collisions in the narrative as they effectively thwart her desires. Her running builds her physical power while also forcing her to face the ever-present potential of being accosted by men. Yet she persists.

Sam's mother, Irene, provides a useful corollary for mobility challenges. She has managed to assert some independence by escaping the strictures of Hopewell. The relationship between mother and daughter has been strained, however, because Irene has remarried and moved away to Lexington. Sam refused to go with her, but these tensions do not dull Sam's enthusiasm for her mother's mobility. We can see how she serves as a model for Sam in her capacity to control a vehicle. This key awareness is thus crucial for Sam's own eventual desire to grab the wheel. Irene's power, as Sam understands it, is clear: "Irene drove her Trans Am through Paducah like a goddess driving a chariot. She whipped across railroad tracks. She made left turns at busy intersections without hesitation." As Sam sits in the cramped back seat, she "wished she could drive the car."[20] Irene has two markers of power in this passage. The first is the vehicle itself, the Pontiac Trans Am (Firebird), a muscle car most often associated with young male drivers attracted to its horsepower and aggressive race-car styling. The second is her comfort controlling that muscle. Sam wants both. Irene's ability to escape the restrictions of Hopewell, despite the discomfort her departure causes Sam, nonetheless affords Sam a model of female mobility worthy of respect.

Eventually, Sam parleys Irene's wish for Sam to leave Hopewell and go to college into her own car. Irene helps her buy a 1973 Volkswagen Beetle, a vehicle with substantially less power than the Trans Am but one that offered mobility nonetheless. Sam understands from the beginning what that means: "Owning a car gave her power."[21] She experiences a "strange exhilaration" that confirms her feeling that she is "free to do anything that she wanted to do."[22] The Beetle has limitations mechanically. Its transmission is barely holding on, but it represents her capacity to move and, more importantly, her growing desire to do so on her own terms and not in reference, or deference, to a man. Sam has grown tired of being a passenger. Her awakening to full mobility matches her growth into adulthood.

Sam's narrative arc is toward a positive mobility that asserts her subversive and stable desires. She rejects the gendered restrictiveness of her hometown, but she also seeks to reaffirm and strengthen her family and her connections to her dead father. Her changing sense of self draws from both impulses. Within the action of the novel, she secures her own mobility and saves her uncle Emmett's self-destructive stasis. As they complete the journey to Washington on a pilgrimage to visit the Vietnam Veterans Memorial, Sam finalizes symbolically her connection to her long-gone father as she touches his name on the reflective wall of the memorial. It is only part of her awakening. During the entire factual and emotional journey that made the framing road trip to Washington possible, Sam also regains a sense of her inherent power. She reengages with her wanderlust and returns to running, both tied to self-determined mobility, and "she remembered that she wanted to see the world."[23] Sam Hughes is ready to move. Readers do not know where she will go as the novel ends. The choice, though, will be hers and hers alone.

ANYWHERE BUT HERE

Mona Simpson's best-selling novel *Anywhere but Here* is another tier 3 road narrative that explores the strained relationship between mother and daughter.[24] Simpson makes keen use of the road in defining her characters and in demonstrating their struggles to find expressions of self from behind the wheel. The road narrative context is, all in all, rather thin in that there is one major journey—from Wisconsin to California—that represents the search for a better life central to the road narrative writ large. That journey takes very little textual space and exists almost exclusively as a defining element to explore tensions between two parts of familial identity. However, other road components within the novel are vital and worth exploration. Simpson methodically exploits crucial elements of automobility. The characters are intricately tied to the social and psychological facets of car culture, and the mobility for the characters within their Southern Californian life exists to define their overall emotional transformations.

The title, *Anywhere but Here*, asserts the inevitable tension between mobility and stasis by implying desire for movement toward "anywhere" while also inferring the oppressive containment represented by any assumed home. Anyone wishing for a horizon does so from being in a place—here—and imagining another place—not here ("but here").[25] In this context, a horizon is simply elsewhere. The novel is structured around segments keyed to character's individual vignettes, and it opens with one titled "Anywhere." The first voice we encounter is that of the daughter, Ann. She establishes the overarching theme of mobility and recaps the primary journey from Wisconsin to California from a child's perspective. This opening section provides the only detail concerning that key road trip, though it is often referred to in abstraction. Ann's summary of the initial journey sets up the overriding tension in the novel between mother and daughter. The first two words are instructive: "We fought." This simple provocative statement is followed by the specific context for that crucial road journey of escape: "When my mother and I crossed state lines in the stolen car, I'd sit against the window and wouldn't talk. I wouldn't even look at her."[26] Though Ann does not refer to the surrounding landscape in the statement, the use of a side-window roadview is implied here—the young girl pressed against the window and purposefully not looking at her mother in the driver's seat. Ann, likely looking out of the window, thus draws on the landscape to emphasize isolation. This separation between the two becomes more dramatic as Ann is forced to get out of the car.

A defining road moment occurs as the child (Ann) is left on the side of the road—lost and bewildered—as a form of punishment applied by the mother (Adele), who speeds off in her car. Ann reports the moment: "I got out. It was always a shock the first minutes because nothing outside was bad. The fields were bright. It never happened on a bad day. The western sky went on forever, there were a few clouds. A warm breeze came up and tangled around my legs. The road was dull as a nickel. I stood there at first amazed that there was nothing horrible in the landscape." Ann is abruptly forced to exit the car on the side of the road, and her first act is to explore the landscape imaginary and remark on the implied vastness. She is ambivalent, but this is a liminal moment. She is shocked back to awareness of the car: "But then the wheels of the familiar white Continental turned, a spit of gravel hit my shoes and my mother's car drove away."[27] The argument preceding this scene, one that Ann reports as having happened more than once, derives from Ann's disappointment along the road. Adele's promises of touristic scenes of interest to appease her daughter do not pan out for the little girl. The landscape imaginary in this passage is instructive for Ann's road sensibility as Simpson gives her an awareness of place far deeper than the childish argument that precedes her being left at the side of the road. Ann invokes the horizon, noting that the "western sky went on forever." She embraces the place immediately as a "warm breeze" tangles around her legs, and she notes "nothing horrible in the landscape." But that implicit comfort is torn away as her mother drives away, the breeze supplanted by "gravel" that hits her. She notes that "my mother's car" leaves, acknowledging the power that Adele has as its driver in juxtaposition to Ann's very evident immobility.

This tumultuous emotional dynamic between Adele and Ann plays out in various ways throughout the novel, but this sequence best captures the central framing of mobility. The ability or inability to move drives self-identity.

Simpson demonstrates the allure of the idealized open road in the context of much smaller movements by juxtaposing expectations of passivity and stasis with dreams of assertiveness and mobility. She writes, "My mother and I should have both been girls who stayed out on the porch a little longer than the rest, girls who strained to hear the long-distance trucks on the highway and who listened to them, not the nearer crickets." She goes on to assert that they were "girls who looked at the sky and wanted to go away."[28] Ann shows her inclination to listen to the hum of "long-distance trucks" rather than that of "crickets," and that such a tendency synchronizes with her mother's. She continues, though, and acknowledges that such dreams of escape (to Ann Arbor, Chicago, Cheyenne, etc.) are balanced with the pull of home and resignation: "We would have been the kind of girls who thought we, more than other people, saw the sadness of things, the poignance of lush darkness around stars, but who finally sighed and, calling the dog with a mixture of reluctance and relief, shut the door and went in home."[29] Simpson acknowledges that these "kind of girls" choose to go back inside—"in home"—with conflicting feelings, the subversive that stays at home with "reluctance" and the stable that does so with "relief." Simpson thus uses the porch as transition in modes of mobility, a liminal threshold between opposing forces of desire, a stage for aspirations.

The mainstream safety of mobility in a family context is also crucial to the novel. The car represents an extension of home, not simply a separation from it. The car in motion holds the family, and Ann holds on to memories of family cohesion: "We kept driving in the dark but it was different. I watched the red disks throb on stakes by the side of the road. I looked for the skeletal antennas of the radio stations out in the fields, in the country, broadcasting through the night. We felt safe together in Ted's car, we could feel ourselves moving."[30] Simpson captures a crucial facet of mobility in that she describes it in terms of "safety." The vehicle suggests the former togetherness of the family, and, for Ann, it still offers stability. The two, mother and daughter, are at great risk as they travel from the familiar to the unknown along lonely roadways. The darkness accentuates the unknown world that surrounds them, but the vehicle serves as womb of reminiscent certainty, which is comforting as they move in "Ted's car," a nod to the man who had been associated with the home but now is only a vague owner. A transition is in process: "We could feel ourselves moving."

Simpson exploits the implicit power evident in someone who drives with skill and authority. The more a driver claims a selfhood separate from others and escapes the mundane, the more the skills behind the wheel become evident. In short, a stronger person becomes a stronger driver. In one of the few moments wherein Ann is willing to acknowledge any grit in her mother, she does so in direct reference to Adele's driving skill. Handling a car well is evidence of competence in a car culture, a sign of capacity to thrive despite all other circumstances, and it earns the daughter's respect: "Sometimes, I really liked my mother. She drove easily, with one hand, as she pumped the gas with the toe of her high-heeled shoe. We looped on the freeway ramps smoothly. She talked to me and drove almost unconsciously on the six-lane highway with a freedom and confidence anyone at home in Bay City would have admired if they could have seen her." She goes on to remember how afraid her mother had been when they first arrived in Los Angeles. As the passage above indicates, Adele had gained power, and Ann reveals that "there were things to be proud of my mother for. I doubt she ever thought about it, how she'd learned to drive here."[31]

In a narrative deeply cognizant of the failures of the mother to provide proper modeling behavior for her daughter, this passage embraces the opportunity for the daughter to acknowledge her mother's strength. Adele's transition is marked by her awakening behind the wheel. In contrast to her initial efforts to survive on the roadways of Southern California, where she moved wholly terrified, she had transformed. She became a driver in full. Simpson defines strength in terms of driving skill and illustrates a core open-road fact: a woman driving is a woman asserting power. Adele, by grabbing the wheel, claims the horizon.

THE BEAN TREES

Barbara Kingsolver's *The Bean Trees*, a tier 2 narrative, is framed by crucial elements of road conventions. Two distinct journeys, in particular, exploit liminality with precision as characters experience an evolving sense of selfhood via mobility. Kingsolver situates *The Bean Trees* within the transitional power of the open road.[32] The novel has multiple narrative voices, but the main character, Missy (also referred to as Marietta and later as Taylor), is the primary traveler, and her desire for mobility carries the novel.

As in the other examples discussed above, the purchasing of an automobile signifies aspirations for power in women characters. Acquiring a vehicle to make mobility practically possible, in such cases, subverts patriarchal assumptions. As Missy recounts the restrictiveness of her high school experiences, she says, "But I had a plan." That plan, one she characterizes as indicative of "serious intentions," is to get out of town: "I bought a car, a '55 Volkswagen bug with no windows to speak of, and no back seat and no starter. But it was easy to push start without help once you got the hang of it, the wrong foot on the clutch and the other leg out the door, especially if you parked on a hill, which in that part of Kentucky you could hardly do anything but. In this car I intended to drive out of Pittman County one day and never look back, except maybe for Mama."[33] This crucial passage illustrates two things about Missy: first, her belief that mobility was key to her pursuit of happiness and, second, her belief that any car would suffice because it, by definition and imagination, allows for freedom. The 1955 Volkswagen she buys is barely mobile, requiring her own leg power often to get it moving, but there is no indication in her comments that this represents a challenge to her goals. If it runs, *she* can run. As Missy brings the car home to show to her mother, the implications are clear: "The day I brought it home, she knew I was going to get away."[34] Her mother does not stand in opposition. To the contrary, she forces Missy to learn basic mechanical skills, thereby ensuring that her daughter can take to the road with autonomy.

Kingsolver ties Missy's developing identity to the liminality of the open road. As she leaves her home on a subversive journey, she also intends to alter her sense of self to match the new mobility. Tying her transitional selfhood directly to movement, Missy opts to change her name: "I decided to let the gas tank decide. Wherever it ran out, I'd look for a sign."[35] Deciding on a new name based on how far she can go on a tank of gas has a nice irony to it. She will have to stop moving to fill the gas tank, but the place where this practical act occurs will also determine *who* (via a new name) will move forward. Her threshold to begin a new life with a new identity, as her intentions imply, will be grounded at a gas station.

Her road narrative, initiated with her purchase of a car, has forced a genuine symbolic transformation to be marked by movement to a specific unknown place and tied to how far the car will go on a tank of gas. Although the passage below has a comic tone, it nonetheless represents an existential awakening for her. Kingsolver writes, "I came pretty close to being named after Homer, Illinois, but kept pushing it. I kept my fingers crossed through Sidney, Sadorus, Cerro Gordo, Decatur, and Blue Mound, and coasted into Taylorville on the fumes. And so I am Taylor Greer. I suppose you could say I had some part in choosing this name, but there was enough of destiny in it to satisfy me."[36] Though she rejects the first option, Homer, a name associated with one of the earliest heroic journeys, she is nonetheless performing an essential act of the open road. Upon establishing her new identity, Taylor begins her odyssey as a new self. She now must choose a way forward, equally relying on a mixture of choice and fate.

There is never a question in her mind as to direction; only the stopping point carries uncertainty. Kingsolver writes, "And so what I promised myself is that I would drive west until my car stopped running, and there I would stay." Again she combines the practicality of gas consumption or, more dramatically, the capacity of the car to run at all, gas or no gas—"until my car stopped running." She meets her first crisis in confidence on the plains of

Oklahoma, a place that makes her feel that "there was nothing left to hope for."[37] She faces mechanical trouble within the boundaries of the Cherokee Nation. Though she is able to have the car fixed, this stop becomes a conventional collision that alters her mobility and redefines her quest. This stop forces definitive change to the road ahead. What begins as a road narrative of self becomes an intensely complicated remaking of family as she is given a small child who has been abandoned. Taylor, formerly Missy, will no longer travel alone.

After a confused stay in Oklahoma, working at a motel, Taylor accepts the new dynamic and moves on with the child, a choice that establishes a tenuous family and an implicitly stable framing for her mobility. Yet her decision is also a subversive act as her movement has no tether to a homeplace. In this stage of her quest, she takes a more practical role in determining her destination, asserting, "Whether my car conked out or not, I made up my mind to live in Arizona."[38] At this point, the novel leaves the road as she tries to establish a new homeplace in Tucson. It only incidentally draws on mobility issues and does not return to the road until the final chapters, which serve to close out the road as frame. Eventually, Taylor must return to Oklahoma to legally and emotionally establish herself as the guardian of the child, which she has temporarily named "Turtle." Despite their time in Tucson, their identities are still in question, and the family remains tentative. The answers can only come from the journey back to Turtle's "home."

The drive to Oklahoma, the second of the framing journeys, brings the broader narrative together as Taylor completes the self-development quest she initiated in the first portion of the novel. The ostensible purpose is to return Turtle to her home so her identity can be legitimized. Her connection to Taylor, forged in the original journey, however, needs not only legal affirmation but also emotional affirmation, the road trip as an act of love. In addition, this journey back to the origination of this road family includes others seeking similar markers of stability on the road. Taylor is transporting Estevan and Esperanza, Guatemalan refugees who have entered the United States illegally. For all the characters, the unresolved question of how to define self in relation to place perpetuates uncertainty. As Estevan puts it, "What I really hate is not belonging in any place. To be unwanted everywhere."[39]

The overlapping doubts for all characters—Taylor of partial Cherokee heritage from Kentucky but having no real knowledge of the culture; Turtle, of Cherokee heritage but of unknown parentage; Estevan and Esperanza, of Mayan heritage and from Guatemala—capture both the transitory nature of road travel and the vagaries of identity in any place. All are displaced, and all are in motion and thus on the threshold of change. The Cherokee Nation provides the home place for all in this context. Such nuanced complications affect the road. Taylor admits, "Somehow I had been thinking that once we got back in the car and on the road again, everything would make sense and I would know what to do. I didn't. This time I didn't even know which way to head the car."[40] Whereas in the opening road segment of the novel, she is open to practical mechanical matters to determine her actions, here she struggles because she must make choices tied directly to formalizing her familial self and stabilizing identities forged on the road.

Though both journeys are linked to the establishment of a homeplace, this second journey carries much stronger implications for the stability she needs. She must act and thus extend the control she has behind the wheel outward to a complex world beyond the lines of the road. This second journey carries far more fear-inducing ambiguity than the first because a family unit is at stake. In a wonderfully apt choice, she reasserts confidence for her search by mimicking the core road-narrative structure of the stable mode: the family vacation. Her plan is simple: "We'll have a picnic by the lake, and stay in a cabin, and maybe find a boat somewhere and go out on the water. We'll have a vacation."[41] Such an assertion of normalcy, even while mired in a journey of desperation wherein such a thing seems forever out of reach, is crucial to the successful completion of the road journeys that define the novel. It signifies the long-term dream of stability.

Kingsolver encapsulates this desire for belonging enacted by mimicking the family vacation with an idealized landscape panorama, the perpetual but no-less-compelling icon of the American dream within road mythology. She writes, "The sun was setting behind us but it lit up the clouds in the east, making one of those wraparound sunsets. Reflections of pink clouds floated across the surface of the lake. It looked like a corny painting. If I didn't let my mind run too far ahead, I felt completely happy."[42] Although Taylor, in her typically snarky tone, notes that the image seems "corny," her reaction nonetheless acknowledges its power. The "wraparound" character of the sunset and the beautiful "reflections" on the water evoke vital emotion: "I felt completely happy." This liminal scene celebrates the beauty of an awakening of self on the open road.

The novel concludes with the travelers finding some level of certainty—direction—for the future, and all with a home of sorts. The closing moments foreground Taylor with her adopted child traveling westward, this time as a family headed not toward wherever the car breaks down but toward the already established home in Tucson, Arizona: "We had cleared Oklahoma City and were out on the plain before sundown. It felt like old times, heading into the low western horizon. I let Turtle see the adoption certificate and she looked at it for a very long time, considering that there were no pictures on it"[43] These two sentences combine the complementary identity issues tied to this journey home, Taylor's continuing growth and the formalizing of a new, sanctioned, mother-daughter relationship. First, the iconic western sunset prominent in open-road mythology indicates a promising future, and second, the specific official verification of that future provided by the birth certificate restates the fact that Taylor and Turtle are a viable stable unit. The emotional bond initiated in the original journey has been reaffirmed by law and love. Together they move toward the horizon, a family going home.

THELMA & LOUISE

The explorations of self along the American road so intrinsic to the novels discussed above found full cinematic attention in *Thelma & Louise*, the seminal narrative defining women grabbing the wheel. Firmly rooted in road mythology, the film, written by Callie Khouri and directed by Ridley Scott, was nominated for six Academy Awards. Khouri won the Oscar for Best Original Screenplay, and she earned the Golden Globe and the Writers Guild of America Award for best screenplay as well. *Thelma & Louise* garnered over $45 million at the box office, and its renown as an impactful cultural document continues to grow.[44] A tier 1 narrative and arguably the best overall American road film, *Thelma & Louise* makes a powerful cinematic and political statement that has received a wealth of substantive critical attention.[45] It holds up to scrutiny and has maintained an important place in the American cultural imagination well into the twenty-first century.

First, a clarification: Thelma (Geena Davis) and Louise (Susan Sarandon) are mobile at the end of the film and very much alive. The closing sequence has encouraged many arguments, and for good reason. We can all reasonably conclude that if a car takes to the air in the Grand Canyon, it will fall to the ground with catastrophic results for the vehicle and anyone who happens to be inside. We should also recognize that the film does not include such a scene. The frame freezes with the Thunderbird in flight. It is a perfect still shot. Then the screen fades to white as a sentimental montage of happy photographs of Thelma and Louise appear, a collection of images typical of a weekend vacation rather than a prelude to a suicidal jump into the void.

With the goal of working back to this dramatic ending, I must first focus on the domestic containment defined in the opening sequences of the film. After images of landscape in the opening credits, we meet Thelma and Louise firmly ensconced in domesticity—Louise in a diner, trying to please customers as a waitress, Thelma in a kitchen, trying to please her husband, Darryl (Christopher McDonald), as a housewife. In both scenes, the women are in service to others. Though Louise appears to have agency in her space despite its domestic restrictiveness, Thelma is anxious, steadily returning to the refrigerator for mini-bites of a candy bar, a guilt-ridden act of subversion. The scene, in addition to setting up their domesticity, establishes the stable mode of travel that the plot draws on. The two women intend to go on a simple weekend road trip, a circular journey that by design, if not true desire, requires a return to normalcy in the end. No substantive subversion underlies their plans, but the tumultuous events that follow explore the essential fact that women claiming a right to the road are inevitably confronted with patriarchal power rearing to impose itself.

Thelma and Louise become embroiled in the subversive mode, pushed toward rebellion by a series of collisions. The confinement of domesticity so evident in the opening scene quickly departs as the two women begin their mobility. They embrace the freedoms implied by being on the road, and the first hints of happiness portend nothing of impending trouble. As they move from Thelma's house and out of the city, the conventional display of joy is crucial. A turquoise 1966 Ford Thunderbird convertible, a perfect cinematic choice, emphasizes an openness to experience that both emanates from and influences the two protagonists (fig. 7.2). Thelma raises her arms in exultation and conjures the conventional hope of the open road.

Fig. 7.2. *Thelma & Louise*, joy. DVD, MGM Home Entertainment, 2004. Author's screenshot.

Despite the happiness shared by the two protagonists as they move along the open road, the film soon begins to reveal the persistent menace of confinement through its imagery and the behaviors of men. The predatory actions of Harlan (Timothy Carhart) are the most obvious, with a violent encounter leading to his death, which pushes Thelma and Louise into the subversive mode. However, he is merely the most egregious of the male figures, all of whom seek to control the movement of the two women and reassert masculine control of the open road. The film demonstrates the perils encountered by women who dare to move.

The sense of male ownership of the space, what Brigham terms "proprietary power," is the key to masculine control.[46] This context can be succinctly revealed via a series of images emphasizing the ever-present confinement of masculine framing on the road. Note the paired images below, the first showing the moments before Thelma and Louise turn into the Silver Bullet saloon, the second showing the moments after Louise kills Harlan and they speed away (figs. 7.3 and 7.4). As they arrive at the bar, there is no danger evident; however, the imagery signals a much different undercurrent. The Thunderbird looks small and vulnerable as the eighteen-wheeler trucks on both sides of the road lord over the convertible. The trucks facing the camera, along with the truck facing the car from the right, produce a tight frame, a suggestion that foreshadows the violent assertion of male power to follow.

The second image, this time with the Thunderbird moving away from the camera, bookends the earlier image but creates a more forbidding impression. The trucks, now in motion, actively serve as barriers to the Thunderbird. The women have moved out of prescribed lines of behavior, the car erratic in its movements during the escape from the Silver Bullet. These trucks squeeze the escape route as Thelma and Louise try to maneuver through the animated gauntlet. The foregrounded truck on the right of the frame is balanced by two lines of trucks in the middle and the left of the screen. Thelma, the driver, must negotiate a treacherous road. Following the violence in the Silver Bullet parking lot, masculine power seemingly inert in the earlier moment has awakened in response to the assault on Harlan. The struggle between a masculine road and the growing desire for autonomy within Thelma and Louise defines the remainder of the film. The weekend road trip has become a desperate flight.

Fig. 7.3. *Thelma & Louise*, confining road. DVD, MGM Home Entertainment, 2004. Author's screenshot.

Fig. 7.4. *Thelma & Louise*, moving trucks. DVD, MGM Home Entertainment, 2004. Author's screenshot.

The ever-present male menace reveals itself in several ways, but the repeated encounters with a specific trucker provide the best micronarrative progression to illustrate the changing dynamics of this battle for mobility. This sequence is one of the most often referred to in the film. Thelma and Louise encounter the trucker three times, but the first and last meetings are especially significant. In the first encounter, Scott uses a long establishing shot of the truck and the car, with the camera running along each, just above road level, and foregrounding the sides of both vehicles, with no images of the drivers or passengers at all. This is the road presented in its most primal and practical sense, emphasizing asphalt, rubber, and metal, the movement of machines. There is the difference in the size of the vehicles, but no other power dynamic is inferred, at least until the camera pans around and up to show the two vehicles from behind as the Thunderbird moves to overtake the trucker. At that point, Scott moves to a side shot of the car from the passenger side with Thelma and Louise (driving) in profile. This side-window roadview conveys confinement in an otherwise expansive moment as the Thunderbird passes the truck. Though they believe he is motioning them to pass out of a willingness to share the road, he reveals a much different motivation. The openness of the convertible renders the two women vulnerable to the ogling eyes of yet another predator. As the two slowly pull up alongside of the truck, the camera shoots under the truck and toward the Thunderbird, thus creating a much more restrictive framing of the car (fig. 7.5). Foregrounded is the chrome image of an idealized (cartoonish) female body lounging in profile, a mud-flap design popular among truck drivers in the 1990s. Thelma says, "I hate that." Though grotesque but familiar behavior intrudes on the mobility of the women as the trucker makes lewd comments, they pass by easily. They do not move, however, beyond the reach of the culture of harassment he represents.

Fig. 7.5. *Thelma & Louise*, trucker 1. DVD, MGM Home Entertainment, 2004. Author's screenshot.

Fig. 7.6. *Thelma & Louise*, trucker 2. DVD, MGM Home Entertainment, 2004. Author's screenshot.

In the final encounter, Thelma and Louise lure the trucker off the road and out of his cab. The framing reverses the confinement of the screenshot above. Thelma and Louise, large in the foreground, sit high in the frame, and the trucker—and indeed the truck itself—is rendered minuscule by comparison (fig. 7.6). Their bodies enclose the trucker. Though remaining defiant in the face of the challenge from the two women, the trucker is powerless as Thelma and Louise wholly control the interaction. They define the moment and complete the reversal with unhesitating violence, firing together on the tanker truck. When Thelma and Louise shoot the tanker loaded with fuel, setting off an explosion, they assert their gained power and rebuke everything that the trucker represents. The culminating violence of the scene celebrates the capacity of the two women to stifle male oppressiveness. The victory is brief. Other more dangerous forces are closing in. The massive smoke plume caused by the explosion provides the visual clue for the FBI and sets up an elaborate chase scene. The climactic moment of the film is impending, and the ultimate fight for mobility plays out on the rim of the Grand Canyon.

Before the closing moments, *Thelma & Louise* becomes a generic car-chase film with the excitement of such action paramount, plenty of crashes and impressive stunt work all around. This action comes to a full stop, however, on the edge of the Grand Canyon, that remarkable landscape phenomenon evoking the grandeur of the American West so vital to open-road mythology. As Thelma and Louise become trapped for the last time, the confine-escape narrative pattern that has driven the film climaxes in one of the most provocative endings of the American road film canon. As the chase sequence concludes, the seemingly endless line of police cruisers overwhelms the scene. The forces of male power stake out a line of defense for a final showdown straight out of a John Ford Western (fig. 7.7).

Fig. 7.7. *Thelma & Louise*, standoff. DVD, MGM Home Entertainment, 2004. Author's screenshot.

The image shows the line of defense with rifles at the ready. The overkill visual evokes the omnipresence of patriarchal power that has been working to stop the increasingly aggressive actions of Thelma and Louise. As the film has progressed, both women have adopted more typically masculine choice patterns. As Thelma and Louise have shifted the gendered codes of behavior and thus subverted masculine manners and clothing, the men in response have likewise adopted more feminized appearances of domesticity. The FBI, however, has shown no reluctance to unleash full-throttle violence. As the dust settles (literally), they face off. Thelma makes a simple, confounded observation: "All this for us?"

All parties are still. An officer on a megaphone demands that the two women raise their "hands in plain view." The following portion of his statement is especially significant in that it reveals the application not simply of police procedure but also of male power: "Any failure to meet that command will be regarded as an act of aggression against us." The bombastic pronouncement reflects a more basic cultural demand. Thelma and Louise, with their persistent desire to keep moving, have performed one "act of aggression" after another. In response, male authority figures demand one thing from them: be still.

Thelma and Louise reject the offer of continued confinement. Voicing their now-fully-formed mutual desire, Thelma states, "Let's keep goin'." What follows is a joyous and tragic gaze through the windshield roadview with all its evocations of the horizon, a longing for the American landscape of possibilities (fig. 7.8). Both women face forward and hold hands, Louise pushes the accelerator, and they move into the liminal air.

Fig. 7.8. *Thelma & Louise*, into the air. DVD, MGM Home Entertainment, 2004. Author's screenshot.

* * *

The navigation of the open road by women, as revealed by a range of narratives, exposes the severe limitations of gendered identities. The complex dynamics affecting the open-road experience for women have always been restrictive. This fact is made evident in many ways throughout popular culture, from specious jokes about women being lousy drivers to the still-very-common assumptions within many families that men should be the default drivers. The persistent message affirms the patriarchal assumption that men are more inclined and are more suited to all things mobile. This enduring context has discouraged women from getting behind the wheel. As a result, driving for women has often transgressed social norms, and women have therefore risked much when they have taken to the open road. Many have done so nonetheless and have fulfilled desires to define horizons of their own.

8
Releasing the Wheel

Men and Power

MEN HAVE ALWAYS enjoyed ostensibly unfettered access to the open road. How men have navigated their roads, however, demonstrates the range of experiences that complicates any notion of openness and its assumed synergy with freedom. The distinctions between men and women on the road arises from cultural norms that celebrate men as drivers. American culture has always affirmed a masculine right to the road, and, metaphorically, men in the twentieth century were born with the wheel in hand. There has never been a need, as is the case for women, for men to subversively grab the wheel. Still, the road is often hard, and men struggle to maintain control of their mobility. This chapter examines narratives tied to the complexities of male power behind the wheel. It continues with the basic argument of the previous chapter—that gendered dynamics of power on the road reflect a symbiotic intertwining of stable and subversive desires that affect men and women in profound ways. Road narratives demonstrate that no matter who is gripping the wheel, the inherent liminal experiences derive not only from how they imagine the road but also how they imagine the home, and their ever-changing dependence on both.

Although men have always been welcomed to the road, their experiences have most certainly not been free from travail. The standard assessment of masculinity on the road recognizes that men often revel in autonomy as a life goal. Men who take to the road stereotypically crave to be "unmediated."[1] To be sure, men have enjoyed the best chance to embrace mobility, but, despite the freedom from domestic restraints so alluring to men who chase the dream evoked by much of Kerouac's *On the Road*, the road most often revealed is one defined by a struggle not for unrestricted experience but for the stability of mainstream America.

On the Road has done much damage. The unfettered joy resonating in the pages of the novel is inextricably intertwined with a reckless abandon that is dismissive of and at times abusive toward women. The masculine wanderlust attracts most of the adoring attention, but few readers note the balance of the narrative or its conclusion wherein the havoc wrought from Dean Moriarty's hypermasculine consumption of cars and women is rejected. Sal Paradise still dreams of the open road, but in the end he does so from a position of domestic security claimed by a confident choice. A corrective is needed to balance readings of male power behind the wheel. Between 1947 and 1949, Kerouac made several cross-country road trips, gaining much of the experience that would later evolve into the tales of his fictional narrator, Sal Paradise. Concurrently, another fictional male figure crucial to open-road sensibilities was also taking form on the page and eventually the stage. Consider this: The first male protagonist essential to open-road mythology in American literary history following World War II is not Jack Kerouac's Sal Paradise. It is Willy Loman from Arthur Miller's *Death of a Salesman*.

DEATH OF A SALESMAN

Intrinsically intertwined with automobility and the postwar dream of prosperity, Arthur Miller's Pulitzer-prize-winning play, *Death of a Salesman*, features Willy Loman, the most well-known, if not well-liked, traveling salesman in American literary history.[2] The play is arguably the "most successful modern play ever published" and a testament to the compelling power implicit in any exploration of tragedy in middle America.[3] The core facts of the play rely on automobility: Willy is "a road man" in "a road business." An iconic common man struggling to make his way in an increasingly complicated world, Willy Loman demands more attention in direct reference to the open road. *Death of a Salesman* is crucial for approaching men's mobility because it provides a nuanced reading of masculinity and the interplay between stable and subversive modes of travel. The problem is that the play *invokes* the road and *refers* to the road, but audiences never encounter characters who are, indeed, *on* the road. All mobility is offstage for practical and staging reasons. Automobility is the linchpin for the story nonetheless, and Willy's ultimate choice to drive his car off the road to commit suicide presents a desperately assertive effort to follow the stable mode.

Death of a Salesman, a tier 3 road narrative, depends on a road ethos to frame its tragic story: Willy is a traveling salesman for most of his work-life; his father abandoned him, taking to the open road to escape domesticity; Ben, his older brother, leaves Willy, too, seeking his own fortunes, visiting on rare occasions during business road trips; and Biff, Willy's favored son, leaves the family and heads out West, the play's current action taking place during his return. All these road departures infer troubled male sensibilities. In contrast with his father and brother, in particular, Willy represents a full engagement with domesticity for over thirty years, and he likely covers more road miles than any of the men in his life. His failures and his mistakes are substantial, but unlike his male models, he remains devoted to a stable road to the end.

The play opens with Willy entering his home, holding his bags as his wife, Linda, calls out, uncertain as to who is at the door: "Willy?" He responds, "It's all right. I came back." According to Miller, these were the first two lines in his mind as he developed the idea for the play. Miller notes that Willy's first two statements reveal "'the whole disaster in a nutshell.'"[4] Miller understood from the beginning that his play would hinge on his protagonist's immobility, a "road man" who can no longer drive. He is a traveling salesman who cannot get past Yonkers on his way to his New England territory, a "disaster" with profound implications.

Willy Loman is never on the edge of the Grand Canyon, but his final act—much like the protagonists' final act in *Thelma & Louise*—is just as tied to gendered codes of behavior. Willy's last choice behind the wheel is a desperate attempt at self-determination. The ironic contrast, however, is that no symbolic representation of a promising horizon, no enfolding of the vehicle in filmic amber, can be offered to Willy. He has experienced minimal power behind the wheel, and his horizons are always confused and blurry. Yet he has one basic option as he understands it: drive off the road and into oblivion in service to his surviving family. The death act must be completed to fulfill a final assertion of self in supplication to the primary responsibility of the stable American male to provide for his family. Thelma and Louise live in that frozen movement in the open air of the Grand Canyon; Willy dies on the road, alone and in a fog of confused aspirations.

Willy's road to redemption, as configured in his delusional dream, can arise only from his movement away from his home one last time so that his family can stay in their home via the financial windfall provided by a life insurance policy payout. From all indications in the play, it is clear that the insurance is in arrears and that there will be no money for his beneficiaries. Nonetheless, in the closing of act 2, when Willy steps out of the house to grip the wheel of his car one last time, he does so certain that he is providing for his family. Though the action exists only via stage directions and the vocalized pleas from his family, we can safely envision that Willy drives with a determined look through the windshield roadview to a horizon of possibilities. As Miller notes in an interview, "He dies moving."[5] Sal Paradise and Dean Moriarty inform our overall notions of men on the road in the immediate postwar era, but American men are also profoundly haunted by Willy Loman, and in the discussions to follow, we will consider the tenuous power asserted by men forever gripping the wheel, dreaming of release more than unmediated experiences.

VANISHING POINT

The masculine road is often a fight for survival. Sometimes that survival is visceral and immersed in a world of violence, with mobility as the tool for manipulating how such confrontations are presented. More often, however, at least within substantive road narratives, power pivots on emotional struggles revealing masculinity as social performance. In most cases, the struggle for mobility becomes a desperate battle typical of heroic quests that often meet with failure. *Vanishing Point*, directed by Richard Sarafian from the screenplay written by Guillermo Cabrera Infante, provides an especially useful exploration of this roiling spectrum of masculine power along the open road.[6]

Vanishing Point is a ninety-minute chase scene, and the primary star is a white 1970 Dodge Challenger. This wildly popular muscle car was ideally suited to the narrative task: drive from Denver to San Francisco, a distance over 1,200 miles, in under fifteen hours. To clarify, meeting that timetable would require an average speed of eighty miles an hour. As a tier 1 road narrative, *Vanishing Point* offers more than an elaborate series of violent crashes and aerial stunts at high speeds. It is also a story of subversion on the open road as the protagonist, Kowalski (Barry Newman), is liminal, always on the verge of a tragic transition into oblivion. The film, as an action film, is defined most overtly by high-octane energy, but as a road narrative it also explores a more nuanced development of a man crushed by cultural manipulations and abuses of masculinity that have controlled his adult life. Kowalski, lost in a maze of delusions about his horizons, seeks solace behind the wheel defined solely by speed in a last-chance power drive of willful self-destruction.

Vanishing Point opens by blurring time. The first sequence suggests the last moments of the film as authority figures in an isolated town prepare to stop an outlaw driver. The first dominant image is of two Caterpillar bulldozers whose drivers lower their shovels to form a roadblock. The shot cuts to Kowalski in close-up, racing toward the encounter while hounded by a police helicopter. The landscape is open but desolate. At one point, Kowalski leaves the roadway, breaking through a barbed-wire fence, and moves into the landscape to evade the helicopter. Director Sarafian not only employs the bleak landscape in matching the driver's state of mind but also places junk cars as framing devices. Off road and temporarily away from police sightlines, Kowalski stops the Challenger between two decrepit vehicles. He walks between them, placing his hand on one of the rusting cars (fig. 8.1).

Fig. 8.1. *Vanishing Point*, junk cars. DVD, Twentieth Century Fox Home Entertainment, 2003. Author's screenshot.

The contrast of the Dodge Challenger and the dilapidated, moldering bodies of long-used-up cars abandoned in the desert captures the illusion of power on the road. This image provides a symbolic foreshadowing of the ultimate choice that Kowalski will make when faced with the obstacles to his mobility in the balance of the film. He is wholly committed to maintaining momentum and avoiding the decay represented by the derelict vehicles. He is desperate and has nowhere to go, a man who can no longer assert power along the open road.

This provocative opening sequence accentuates the liminality within the film. As Kowalski moves back to the highway, the film makes a time-shift to start the narrative from the beginning. After he passes over a railroad track, viewers see the police helicopter again in the middle distance, and this image is followed by Kowalski passing a stop sign and over flares scattered along the road, all indicating impending doom. The white Challenger, speeding down the open road from right to left, passes a black sedan moving from left to right. At the moment of passing, the image freezes. Kowalski is in two cars at once, a white muscle car moving westward and a black sedan moving eastward along the same stretch of road. Sarafian thus fuses time and emphasizes the search for self, implying repetitive movements hardly distinguishable but for the car. The white Challenger fades from the screen, and the black sedan reanimates, continuing its journey eastward. The text "two days earlier" appears on screen. We move into a nighttime scene at yet another railroad crossing, this time in Denver, Colorado. Kowalski delivers the sedan and picks up the Challenger set to return to California.

Kowalski is, like Willy Loman, doing a "road business." His speed glosses over a desire for mainstream normalcy, and it is clear from the beginning of this last fateful journey that his movements are always a buffer against failure. He delivers stolen cars for a living, and the faster he moves, the more money he makes. There is no sense of joy implicit in Kowalski's choices. He is on the job, a man working to make a living while also keeping his demons at bay. In this last journey, he garners too much attention from authorities, and they respond with force. Through the publicity created by a local radio DJ who follows the chase by listening to a police scanner, Kowalski becomes a folk hero. Super Soul (Cleavon Little), a radio personality who serves as a voice of the people, places the emerging narrative of Kowalski's drive in an American subversive ideal. He states, "And there goes the Challenger being chased by the blue, blue meanies on wheels. The vicious traffic squad cars are after our lone driver, the last American hero, the electric centaur, the demigod, the super driver of the Golden West." He goes on to assert that they will catch him and destroy him, "the last beautiful free soul on this planet."[7]

Although Kowalski becomes an antiestablishment hero by avoiding capture while speeding through Colorado, Nevada, and into California, his mobility is not intentionally subversive. As his backstory is filled in by incidental flashbacks, viewers discover that Kowalski has become a speed freak (drugs and horsepower) due to a series of disappointments that have undermined any hope for a horizon of possibilities. Unlike a standard heroic figure, Kowalski has no desire for liminal development. He sees nothing ahead but a dead end. A Vietnam War veteran honorably discharged, a decorated police officer who lost his career because he stood up to corruption, a man in love who lost his fiancée to a tragic accident, Kowalski is a man in ruins. Much like Willy Loman, he has failed. Whatever hopes he had for his own version of the American dream have been crushed, and his sense of normalcy has proven delusory. He uses speed to keep the pain symbolically in the mirror roadview.

He has many collisions on the road, and his encounters during occasional stops at the roadside often demonstrate his inner struggles. The one interaction that requires discussion at length is his substantive discussion with the old prospector (Dean Jagger) in the desert. The extended scene provides the most direct exploration of the ever-present tensions between stable and subversive modes. The old man convinces Kowalski to hide from the helicopter, that seemingly ever-present eye of authority. His undergirding assumptions, while effective in the moment, run counter to Kowalski's devotion to constant motion. The prospector has chosen a stable mode of travel built around circular movement in the desert. He advises Kowalski to hunker down. He states, "The best way, to my knowledge, to get away is to root right in where you are, just root right in." Kowalski has become aware that he is in trouble in the desert. He has crossed his own path again and again, creating a checkerboard of tire-tracks in the cracked soil, thus making his movements potentially easy to track from above (fig. 8.2). Kowalski chooses to hide, and the two men put brush over the car as camouflage. The ploy succeeds.

Fig. 8.2. *Vanishing, Point*, crossroads. DVD, Twentieth Century Fox Home Entertainment, 2003. Author's screenshot.

The symbolic implications are more difficult to pin down in that the old man argues for a stable road. He acknowledges a desire for movement but also an equally important capacity to know when *not* to move. In this case, the old man's advice is not against subversion itself; rather, it is for calculated movement, thoughtful mobility to maintain freedom of choice. His truck is seen by the officers in the helicopter, but they dismiss it as "derelict," having likely been in the desert "since the Depression." Its mobility is thus shielded from their awareness, hidden in plain sight. Covering the much more conspicuous Challenger accomplishes a similar task, but Kowalski cannot remain hidden for long. Once the helicopter has departed, he makes his way back to the road and inevitably reengages with the chase.

The narrative then catches up, so to speak, with the opening sequence of the film, and Kowalski moves intentionally to his death. The small space of light—a vanishing point—between the two bulldozer shovels is the threshold for that release. Sarafian notes that the placement of the bulldozers is intended not simply to form a barrier but to create a metaphorical "crack in the fence" that "our hero heads toward."[8] The crack is liminal space, and Kowalski moves not toward the bulldozers and death but toward the open space of light between them. He drives to reach the implied free space that he can access—metaphorically—via the increasing speed of the Challenger. The climactic scene is a precursor to the ending of *Thelma & Louise*. Unlike the choice made by Thelma and Louise, however, Kowalski acts in resignation rather than in defiance. Although Super Soul calls him "the last American hero for whom speed means freedom of the soul," Kowalski, in essence, tightly grips the wheel and quits a job that has provided no stability and no joy. Like Willy Loman, he is tired. The fiery crash and subsequent explosions complete the spectacle, and the film ends as first responders begin the cleanup and onlookers disperse. The camera pans away from the town and frames the natural surroundings to suggest, per convention, the openness of the American landscape and its implied horizon of possibilities.

DUEL

Steven Spielberg's *Duel* presents a decidedly different protagonist, David Mann (Dennis Weaver), who drives a 1970 red Plymouth Valiant, the perfect opposite to Kowalski's Dodge Challenger. The Valiant, despite its princely suggestion of masculine power, in practice offers none. The fact is that the Valiant was a modest sedan and thus an appropriate choice for Mr. Mann, a husband and father. A direct symbolic descendant of Willy Loman, he is a road man doing a road business. This journey of discovery is built around a simple trip for a business meeting that gets terribly complicated following a random encounter with a maniacal trucker. As the journey becomes archetypal, the core plot dynamic bears repeating: David Mann travels a stable road in full support of domesticity.[9]

The gendered dynamics of *Duel* are more foregrounded than in the other examples, and the marital tensions along with Mann's unease with masculinity provide the most dominating theme of the movie. On its surface, and in the original short story by screenwriter Richard Matheson, *Duel* is an updated Western film, a *duel* between a "bad guy" in a truck and an everyman "good guy" in a sedan who face off on the open road. Steven Spielberg creates a riveting tier 1 film with genuine moments of terror. The methodical opening sequence, added to the original television version for full cinematic release outside of the United States, demonstrates Spielberg's capacity to employ road tropes successfully. Domesticity defines the opening shot as viewers hear the starting of an engine while the screen remains black. Light enters the frame, and a point-of-view camera aligns audience perspective with the eyes of the driver, as yet unknown, to establish a windshield roadview. A suburban garage recedes as we pull out of the driveway and then turn to leave the neighborhood. This departure from home signals a stable mode that implies a regular road experience, which will be upturned as the day progresses.

Fig. 8.3. *Duel*, bumper. DVD, Universal, 2003. Author's screenshot.

Viewers quickly become immersed in the jostle of urban morning traffic in Los Angeles, at every moment competing for space and access to the road ahead. Spielberg at times also intersperses shots taken from the lower front bumper to complement the standard windshield roadview and enhance the aura of congestion and vulnerability. This is no open road, and confinement is the dominate impression (fig. 8.3). The car eventually enters Interstate 5, heading to Bakersfield. Traffic thins as we turn on to a two-lane state highway. At just under four minutes into the film, the point of view shifts, and we see the car, a red sedan in open country but significantly framed by barbed-wire fencing (fig. 8.4). The landscape has opened, but the suggestion of confinement persists.

The camera, at long last, shows our hero in the rearview mirror and then moves around to establish a looking-in windshield view. There he is: a middle-aged man with a mustache and sunglasses, dutifully looking at the road ahead, his hands gripping the wheel at the prescribed ten o'clock and two o'clock positions for safe driving (fig. 8.5). For the next few moments, we move to varying shots of the car and our hero. The framing of windows steadily emphasizes the enclosed sedan (though the driver's window is down). Is this a man *in* control or a man always *under* control? As he approaches a dirty, slow-moving truck, the camera runs along the side of

Fig. 8.4. *Duel*, barbed wire. DVD, Universal, 2003. Author's screenshot.

the car, our Man(n) on the open road is about to encounter a fire-breathing dragon, a Peterbilt beast with choking smoke bellowing from its exhaust pipes. Stability on the road is going to be tested.

Throughout this opening sequence, Mann is listening to the radio, often changing stations, moving from news to music, but once he makes his way onto seemingly open roads, he lingers on a talk show thoroughly couched in gendered power dynamics. A male caller seeking information on how to complete the United States census form seems befuddled as to how to define his role within the family. He states, "I'm really not the head of the family, and yet I'm the man of the family." He goes on to note that the "head" is most certainly his wife because she works, and he stays home raising the family, the traditional roles reversed. That is not the issue; rather, the problem comes from the fact that the caller is embarrassed by the situation. Mann makes an understated scoffing noise but does not otherwise respond; the audio nonetheless situates our understanding of Mann's uncertainty, which seems commiserate with that of the caller.

Mann is on the road to salvage his job and thus his dignity as a successful provider. The underlying stress of the journey is compounded by the fact that a major client is threatening to take his business away. The screenplay, according to writer Matheson, is meant to be a pure action-packed thriller,

Fig. 8.5. *Duel*, David Mann window. DVD, Universal, 2003. Author's screenshot.

an archetypal battle for survival.[10] Yet the full version released after the initial showing on television includes a more complicated context for the road narrative. The radio background and the roadview images set up a battle along the open road that has direct implications to Mann's ongoing struggles to meet popular demands on masculinity. Later, after his initial odd, but not yet threatening, interactions with the trucker, Mann stops for gas. Before entering the gas station, which also has a laundromat, Mann makes a telling comment to the gas station attendant, who suggests that Mann buy a new radiator hose. Skeptical, Mann declines, and the attendant responds with, "You're the boss." Mann comments to himself, "Not in my house I'm not."

Mann enters the building to call home, using the pay phone in the laundromat, and the conversation he has with his wife deepens the conflict. The ensuing scene is especially instructive for recognizing Mann's stable mode of travel as it reveals his angst regarding not just his professional life but his marital life as well. During the call, Spielberg again emphasizes Mann's confinement as he talks to his wife. A woman enters the scene, moves to the front of the frame and opens a washing machine door, and then departs to retrieve her clothes. The framing of Mann within the glass circle of the washing-machine door evokes a striking and unexpected image of domestic confinement (fig. 8.6).

Fig. 8.6. *Duel*, laundry. DVD, Universal, 2003. Author's screenshot.

In a shot filled with rectangular shapes, including the side window of the Valiant in the background, the foregrounded circle creates a new frame for Mann, one that indicates a traditional feminized sphere. As the scene progresses, the woman's arm, as she adds clothes to the washer, briefly but repeatedly intrudes on the view of Mann. The context for the phone call is crucial; he apologizes for failing to protect his wife's honor during the previous evening. It seems that a colleague named Steve Henderson made improper advances and that Mann did nothing in response. Mann notes that she seems to have wanted him to confront Henderson and "challenge him to a fist fight or something." She notes that he "could have at least said something to the man. He was practically trying to rape me in front of that whole party." This backstory transforms Matheson's original narrative of a "battle for survival" into a much more nuanced exploration of gender power structures on the open road. Mann's failure to act, to stand his ground, is an essential backdrop to the impending conflict on the road, which is indeed a duel to the death but one that also questions cultural assumptions defining masculinity. David Mann, in this reductive context, is an ineffectual prince driving an underpowered Valiant.

His wife quickly shifts the conversation back to work, but it is readily apparent that Mann is in the same weakened position on both issues. In response to her query as to whether he will be home by dinner time, Mann states, "If Forbes lets me go in time." Mann has no direct power over his actions. Meanwhile, a mad trucker lurks outside. The struggle for survival that will wholly occupy Mann's attention once he returns to the road is not a departure from his normal life but, more accurately, a symbolic extension of it. If he is to survive either collision, he must find a way, at long last, to act. He must assert power behind the wheel, which up to this point has been gripped with trepidation. The film becomes a steady ratcheting up of tension as Mann slowly recognizes his plight. Each collision pushes him further away from his passive tendencies and creates the liminal chance for awakening. In the end, Mann must slay the dragon.

To accomplish this task, he acts directly against his foe. Rather than continue his flight as prey, he turns to act as predator. He survives only because he shifts his tactics. In the liminal moments before the final showdown, Mann experiences a transition of self. Setting the car in motion, Mann wedges his briefcase between the floorboard and the accelerator to keep it fully engaged after he jumps free of the car at the last moment. The two vehicles collide, and both go careening over a cliff in a remarkable death roll for the Peterbilt truck and the Plymouth Valiant. Standing at the cliff's edge, Mann looks down on the wreckage and celebrates, a victor at long last. He chose to sacrifice his car and to separate his new self from his workaday self as symbolized by the briefcase, that mundane symbol of the company man.

He has survived the immediate challenge, but his life remains complicated. He has no car, he has missed his crucial business meeting, and he will not make it home for dinner. There is trouble ahead beyond finding his way back home, yet Mann remains in a stable mode. He will go home, but viewers can bet that sometime soon he will go looking for Steve Henderson. No longer the Man(n) who left his suburban home that morning, he is likely to claim more space on the road from now on. He has experienced a transition, a man who passed through a crucial liminal moment presented in the starkest terms of survival. The film closes with a romantic image emphasizing Mann's new self seated at the scene of the final collision, his torso in silhouette. Just off the main road but still tethered to it, Mann is bathed in the glow of light from a golden sunset, an end and a beginning.

NATIONAL LAMPOON'S VACATION

What if Willy Loman and Daffy Duck were combined into one suburban family man? Enter Clark W. Griswold (Chevy Chase) of *National Lampoon's Vacation*, arguably the most successful American road film of all time, grossing over $60 million from an estimated $15 million budget.[11] A parody of the ritualized American family vacation, the film presents a nostalgically driven homage to the dominant staple of the American open road. A tier 1 road narrative, *Vacation* has spawned a franchise of Griswold movies, all under the National Lampoon header: *European Vacation*, *Christmas Vacation*, and *Vegas Vacation*, and all built around the mobility of the Griswold family.

The publicity copy on the DVD version of the original film characterizes Griswold as "an Everyman eager to share the open road and the wonders of family togetherness with his wife and kids."[12] This is an apt description firmly placing the narrative in the stable mode, though it does so from a satirical perspective. Clark Griswold is a buffoon on a mission. The plan is to drive from Chicago to Los Angeles in a new station wagon, the "Family Truckster," and visit the Valhalla of American amusement parks, Wally World (read Disneyland—a moose instead of a mouse). It is the American family ritual writ large, wonderfully clichéd and comically tragic. As with the previous narratives featuring masculinity in crisis, *Vacation*, at its core, explores the fumbling efforts of a man with limited capacities to assert power behind the wheel. At every collision along the way in his misguided quest, Griswold seeks to grant his family a definitive stable road experience and thereby fulfill his patriarchal obligations. His efforts are increasingly erratic but (mostly) in service to a genuine desire to be a good husband and father. He is not highly skilled along these lines.

Griswold is not a very good driver either. The best way to work through this comic jaunt is to assess the failures of power behind the wheel that dominate the overall narrative. Director Harold Ramis makes substantive use of standard roadviews throughout the film. The two screenshots below show the family in these early moments on the road, the first capturing pure pleasure and the second hinting at mundane road challenges. As the family embarks on their epic journey, joy is evident. Via a looking-in side-window roadview, we witness a happy family. They focus on their shared quest by singing the Wally World theme song. The unified expression of happiness culminates with Clark's impression of Wally the Moose, closing out the song with "That's Me! Yuk, Yuk!" He is a happy man filled with optimism as leader, guide, visionary, and driver for the stable American road dream (fig. 8.7). The second image comes a bit later, as the mundane challenges typical of any road trip begin to assert themselves. The singing is long gone, and the path forward is already becoming muddled as family members recede inward. The looking-in windshield roadview of the second image hints at impending trouble as Griswold's control unravels in response to a steady barrage of challenges, mostly initiated or amplified by his incompetence. No one is focused on the road ahead, and even Griswold behind the wheel struggles with a roadmap, not an ideal driving posture. He seems unable to meet basic obligations as head of the family (driver) and often places everyone in precarious situations (fig. 8.8).

Fig. 8.7. *National Lampoon's Vacation*, singing. DVD, Warner Bros., 2003. Author's screenshot.

Fig. 8.8. *National Lampoon's Vacation*, map. DVD, Warner Bros., 2003. Author's screenshot.

This comedic film depends on the incongruities caused by his inadequacies regarding traditional masculinity. Griswold has spent fifteen years, as he later points out, making "new and better food additives," working to provide for his family. He seems to be a successful businessman, but this vacation reveals the uncertainty of his life journey. The road narrative puts everything to the test as he embarks on a romantic quest to prove, without qualification, that he is worthy of respect. He wants to be a beloved husband

and father essential to the well-being of his family and not just a generic "additive" forever pretending to be substantive. The stresses of his fifteen years preceding the vacation become more apparent via his moments of subversion. Griswold is a family man, but lurking in his psyche is an inner Dean Moriarty, a man craving the thrills of the open road unburdened by domestic pressures. Enter the "girl in the Ferrari" (Christie Brinkley). The temptations of the subversive road are all wrapped up in a clichéd package: a fast sports car driven by a supermodel who seems interested (inexplicably) in our hero.

Despite their predictability, the road sequences showing the interplay between Griswold and the "girl" illustrate the contrast between his stable and subversive road dreams. In the quiet moments when family members are asleep or otherwise distracted, his subversive self emerges. The side-window roadview is best used to suggest awareness of the surrounding landscape and, further, to elicit interactions with others on the road. In the screenshot (fig. 8.9), the framing is especially provocative in that the "girl in the Ferrari"—not the road ahead—becomes the center of his attention and thus fills the window of Griswold's imagination. She becomes the dream of the open road incarnate, carrying the promise of total affirmation for a simplistic man: she is beautiful and inviting, her car speaks of unrivaled speed, and as a convertible it is open symbolically to unfettered experience. And all is just out of reach, like the horizon.

Fig. 8.9. *National Lampoon's Vacation*, "girl". DVD, Warner Bros., 2003. Author's screenshot.

Griswold becomes wholly immersed in the ever-present promise of the subversive road. Is she *really* attainable? That hardly matters; the dream is all. The two thoroughly incompatible cars move in tandem down the road, a flirtatious interaction of carefree desire, until Ellen (Beverly D'Angelo) awakens to pull her husband back into the stable mode:

> "Clark, you're doing eighty miles an hour."
> "It doesn't seem like it, does it, honey?"
> "SLOW DOWN!"

He slows down. The red Ferrari pulls away toward the horizon, the dream deferred. The encounter is repeated, and the flirtation leads to a more treacherous moment on the road. The "girl in the Ferrari," as the idealized masculine road dream, stands in sharp contrast with the restrictiveness of the Truckster as symbol of mobile domesticity. These comic scenes caused by Griswold's incompetence behind the wheel serve as steady reminders of the subversive dream that complements his stable quest. Holding onto the wheel is a much tougher proposition than what is implied by the mythic simplicity of masculine power on the road.

The film is a persistent parody of the stable road and its most common showy application, the family vacation. The journey is liminal in that Griswold's quest is meant to affirm his status as a successful, capable head of household, a man able to carry his family across the country to the promised land of Wally World. He assumes all along that the trip will be transformative for his family, an act of participation in mainstream American culture designed to celebrate his rightful place within it. The screenshot below captures his most ostentatious failure as a driver, his bumbling incompetence with the family Truckster forcing a crisis moment. Though there are more failures to come, the wreck provides the best illustration of his inability to drive and thus his failure to meet the overriding challenge of his road quest. He is lost, and he has incapacitated the vehicle, rendering it and his family immobile. He stands on top of the car, looking desperately for a way out. Whereas climbing on top of the car may provide some extended view, it is an act of helplessness from a man trapped by self-inflicted stasis (fig. 8.10).

Earlier, in the opening scene of the film, Griswold pleads with Ellen to support the cross-country road trip to Walley World despite her assertions that it would make more sense to fly. He argues that the road trip would provide opportunities for quality time with his family before his kids grow up and leave home. The scene establishes the parameters of the quest, not just for fun but for family unity. He is fighting for his sense of self and domestic

Fig. 8.10. *National Lampoon's Vacation*, wreck. DVD, Warner Bros., 2003. Author's screenshot.

stability. His passionate assertion seems quaint at best as he eventually finds himself stuck in the desert. In this scene, he faces the first of two crisis moments wherein his commitment to the overall quest risks annihilation. During a talk with his son in an exchange of masculine solidarity, he reveals his haunting anxieties, telling Rusty (Anthony Michael Hall) that he remembers well the family vacations of his youth and the sad fact that in eighteen years they "never had fun." In what would seem to be a logical liminal moment in which he could learn a valuable lesson and thus acknowledge a fault in his dream-quest, Griswold demurs. Sitting on a rock in the middle of a desert, his family in varying stages of distress and his car crashed and immobile, he reasserts the goal: "We're gonna' have fun." A liminal moment is wasted. There is no awakening here.

As episode after episode demonstrates, Griswold is a failure, but he is not a quitter. Moments after his "good talk" with Rusty, he sets out to find a way out of the desert so that his family can continue on. His quest survives this crisis only to find yet another collision that brings the family to the abyss. After leaving the corpse of Aunt Edna (Imogene Coca) behind, the family confronts Griswold, demanding an end to the madness. "It's been a real drag, Dad," says Rusty. Griswold stops the car and responds, standing firm in his devotion to what he calls a "quest for fun" and "a pilgrimage to see a moose." Sounding more like Ahab than a pilgrim, he preaches again in faithful support of the vacation ritual. Though this seems to be a renewed claim of liminality, it actually thwarts any potential change. He remains steadfast to his faulty original quest. The journey continues, and the Griswolds make it to

Wally World. The parody road narrative concludes with a comic climax of absurdity and amusement park fun, complete with a SWAT team and the goodwill of Roy Wally. In the end, the stability of the family has been affirmed, and Griswold pays no further price beyond a few minutes in handcuffs for his errand into the vacation wilderness.

Griswold achieves his quest. His lack of growth in the process, however, smacks of failure. We should note that, as the photographs included in the closing credits make clear, the Griswolds fly home to Chicago. They do not stick to the road. Though he is capable of being temporarily sidetracked by subversive dreams, Griswold remains committed to being the head of a mainstream household. He is an amalgam of Willy Loman and David Mann, men with limited skills behind the wheel who resent the confinements of domesticity but who are wholly devoted to completing their jobs nonetheless. Clark Griswold takes to the road in support of a stable ideal, and despite his overall incompetence, he survives without learning anything at all.

SMOKE SIGNALS

Smoke Signals begins with fire. After a brief interlude featuring scenes of daily life on the Coeur d'Alene reservation, the haunting image that serves as the framing for the film's title sequence is a house on fire. The blaze expands to fill the screen. There are two conflagrations implied by this opening imagery. The primary road narrative that follows is initiated by the home burning because it forever links the two protagonists, Victor (Adam Beach) and Thomas (Evan Adams). Arnold Joseph (Gary Farmer), Victor's father, unwittingly caused the fire that results in the death of Thomas's parents. The broader scope inferred in the image, however, is the genocidal tragedy endured by the native peoples of America. *Smokes Signals* is a tier 1 road film arising from a holocaust to reclaim a sense of selfhood and a sense of place. It is also a road film catalyzed by the desperate efforts of a young man to define himself in reference to his father. The narrative progresses on lines of mobility compromised by generations of confinement and destruction. Yet screenplay author Sherman Alexie and director Chris Eyre create one of the most powerful expressions of the American road narrative tradition.[13]

A seminal road narrative, *Smoke Signals* earned a formidable viewing audience on its release and continues to gain scholarly attention. Critics have demonstrated how it embraces the ideals of American road mythology while also subverting conventions and reclaiming the open road.[14] As discussed in the opening chapter, Frederick Jackson Turner claimed in 1893 that the idea of the frontier had defined the American character more so than any other facet of culture. The road mythology resulting from these ideals is matched by no other national cultural behavior, yet its history is by no means universal.

Turner's thesis and the cultural imperatives related to it in the nineteenth and twentieth centuries are derived from Euro-American consciousness. The narrative celebrates, in its most positive connotation, the building of a nation, but at the same time, in its most horrific sense, the grand frontier vision ignores genocide. How should American Indians respond to American road mythology?

The screenplay was based on Alexie's collection of short stories titled *The Lone Ranger and Tonto Fistfight in Heaven*, and he drew from material in several of the stories but took its core plot from "This Is What It Means to Say Phoenix, Arizona."[15] In transforming his short story collection into a screenplay, Alexie puts the well-established traditions of the road film to effective use. In explaining his choice, Alexie notes that "the road movie was a very time-honored structure," and he also points out the affordability of its implicit structure because it was "easy to film."[16] Underestimating the challenges of making any film, he nonetheless followed an insightful idea to exploit the genre more aggressively than his original fiction had considered, and the results proved fruitful. Although Alexie avers that the choice was practical, the resulting narrative reveals the substantive strength of the idea.

Fully aware of the "mythic structures" of road narratives, Alexie was keen to subvert them as well. He points out that the "revolutionary or groundbreaking" content comes from the simple fact that "the characters in it are Indians, and they're fully realized human beings."[17] *Smoke Signals* claims the American open road, taking a form reflecting Euro-American privilege and making it subservient to the equally mythic narrative of Indian heritage. In this way, Alexie refashions its tropes to assert a confident and competent selfhood in defiance of erasure on the American landscape. When Victor and Thomas take to the road, they begin an essential journey of discovery that symbolically makes a simple claim: their right to exist. Thomas defines this context in one of his stories about Arnold Joseph, noting that he was arrested and charged with "being Indian in the twentieth century."[18] The satirical point is clear. By being alive, Arnold had committed the "sin" that most frustrated mainstream America. The historical backing for the narrative is also given strength by exploring the devastation wrought on American Indians via the loss of family stability. More specifically, the narrative is driven by the tumultuous struggles of fathers and sons. The underlying narrative of loss and discovery becomes a full-force heroic quest dependent on the road for its expression. Victor has a job to do. He must make his existence cohere with the twentieth century, he must unify his heritage, and he must bring his father home.

Smoke Signals is a circular journey arising from the need to reestablish and redeem the homeplace. The motivation pushing mobility is therefore in the stable mode, in spite of the subversion foisted on Victor and Thomas because of their racial heritage. The film moves through five stages of significant expressions of mobility, each creating liminal moments along the road. In the process of awakening, Victor encounters collisions, physically and emotionally, each directly tied to expressions of masculinity. His crossing of multiple thresholds makes possible the fulfillment of the quest.

In the first stage of mobility, viewers are immersed into a world of compromised mobility on the Coeur d'Alene reservation. The movement within the confines of the reservation reflects a modern American car culture that has been adopted but without the accompanying economic power. The irony of automobility is best illustrated comically by KREZ radio, "voice of the Coeur d'Alene reservation," and its regular morning traffic reports, a mainstay feature of any metropolitan area in the United States. The towns of the reservation are far from having the population that would require a traffic report, but KREZ features them as a performance of modernity. It is a significant representation of participation in a mobile culture, but the facts betray a more captive reality. The traffic report is provided by Lester Fallsapart (Chief Leonard George) as he sits on top of a van "broken down at the crossroads"—a phrase that encapsulates the plight facing American Indians, immobile on reservation lands minuscule when compared with the expanses their ancestors called home. The phrase implies liminality (crossroads) while also suggesting the impossibility of any transition whatsoever. The van, which, according to DJ Randy Peone (John Trudell), has been parked in that spot since 1972, sits beside a dirt road that goes directly toward the distant horizon, an image that matches road iconography suggestive of the future, an optimism that is decidedly absent in the shot. The reports, though offering some potentially interesting gossip, define a core fact of life on the reservation: "Ain't no traffic, really" (fig. 8.11).

In the second stage of mobility, Victor and Thomas leave home and begin moving through "a whole different country," the phrase used humorously to claim that the United States is "as foreign as it gets."[19] The comments, though jovial, are astute and set up the transition for the two young men as they prepare to board a bus headed for Phoenix. In a liminal moment, they stand just outside the bus and question each other's preparedness to move: "Are you sure about this?"; "I'm sure. Are you sure?"[20] The scene emphasizes the key threshold moment, and their anxiety-driven hesitation betrays a lack of confidence in the face of a formalized world of mobility. They are racial outsiders entering a world that is unwelcoming. In this phase, the bus serves as a microcosm for American culture; Victor and Thomas are mobile but lack agency, maneuvering in an unfamiliar and unfriendly space.

Fig. 8.11. *Smoke Signals*, crossroads. DVD, Miramax/Buena Vista Home Entertainment, 1999. Author's screenshot.

The encounters during the bus segment carry significant weight as the two negotiate uncomfortable engagements with others on the bus, each conversation fraught with misunderstandings and always defined by underlying racism. The most significant collision occurs when, after stopping at a rest stop, the two return to their seats only to find that they have been taken over by "two white cowboys," as indicated in the screenplay. The loss of their seats directly parallels the loss of land to Euro-American expansion.[21] The two are forced to move to the back of the bus, a conscious allusion to the historical fact of American Indian displacement. Victor and Thomas regain some power by singing a song mocking John Wayne, the most popular "white cowboy" of all time. They thereby assert their presence on the bus, something with which other riders must contend. They may not be able to retain their seats, but they refuse to be ignored. Given the significant limitations to autonomy on the bus and in the United States, the vocalization of their anger subverts the power dynamics qualifying their mobility.

It is the preceding scene, however, that demonstrates best the contentiousness of the bus journey, especially as linked to masculinity. Victor confidently gives Thomas a lesson regarding the "warrior" persona. In perhaps the most often referenced line in the film, Victor admonishes Thomas's lack of toughness, telling him to "get stoic." Victor's concerns are valid as the two move through a place that defines them almost exclusively based on superficial representations in popular culture. Victor seems to be unaware, though, that he is also mouthing such assumptions, telling Thomas that he must "look mean or people won't respect you. White people will run all over you if you don't look mean. You got to look like a warrior."[22] Thomas's point that their ancestors were fishermen has no impact on Victor.

The agitation dominating Victor derives directly from his introspective memory of running after his father. In a compelling use of the side-window roadview, the scene opens with young Victor running down the road as his father drives away. This is the key moment for the road narrative and the evolving sense of self for Victor. He mouths basic assumptions of what a male American Indian should be, accepting the prolific stereotypical characteristics foisted on him by American popular culture. His confusion is complicated by his father's abandonment of the family. In a side-window roadview memory sequence, we see several moments in the aftermath of Arnold's departure. As Victor looks out the front window of their home, his mother, Arlene, makes a poignant comment: "He sawed us into pieces, didn't he? I feel like my head is in the kitchen, my belly's in the bathroom, and my feet are in the bedroom." Victor agrees.[23] This inference that the home, implied by references to body parts scattered around the household, has been torn asunder is especially powerful as it depicts the direct damage done to the family. Immediately following Arlene's observation, young Victor faces Thomas who asks, "Does he hate you?" In a rage, Victor begins punching Thomas, only stopping when Arlene intervenes. He then runs away. The shot fades into Victor running on the open road, chasing his father. As the child moves out of frame to the right, the flashback ends, and the focus returns to the adult Victor looking out of the bus window (fig. 8.12). He turns toward Thomas, who once again asks about Arnold. Victor attacks him again, this time verbally. With aggression and malice, he questions Thomas's authenticity both as an Indian and as a man, a "warrior." The sequence arises from pain and hopelessness defined by a lack of power. Victor, in both his young and adult selves, is chasing a father he cannot catch, a horizon he cannot reach.

This frustration, as expanded on during the bus segment, leads to the third stage of mobility in the narrative, Arnold's stasis. After the difficult bus trip and a lengthy walk along a dirt roadway, the men arrive at Arnold's Phoenix home, a small trailer in a sunken arid landscape. The scene mirrors images of the Coeur d'Alene reservation, with familiar suggestions of failed mobility. As the screenshot reveals, Arnold, despite his successful separation from his family, has only found another way to be trapped. His home is a trailer on a piece of land that also has a mobile home. Several junk cars litter the landscape as well. Though these figures are suggestive of mobility, they are all thoroughly static. Only the pick-up truck has any reasonable chance to exit the bowl (fig. 8.13). Although Arnold had often implied that he could vanish ("poof"), for the first time Victor witnesses the abject failure of the so-called magical disappearance. Arnold abandoned his family and moved to nowhere.

Fig. 8.12. *Smoke Signals*, bus window. DVD, Miramax/Buena Vista Home Entertainment, 1999. Author's screenshot.

Fig. 8.13. *Smoke Signals*, Phoenix. DVD, Miramax/Buena Vista Home Entertainment, 1999. Author's screenshot.

Arnold remains static for ten years in Phoenix. The only hint of mobility is the yellow truck, the vehicle that powered his original departure. As Suzy Song (Irene Bedard), Arnold's neighbor, reminisces about the friendship she had with him, we learn that the truck often failed to start. She mentions that Arnold would often give her rides, but Song's story emphasizes that he struggled to get the engine cranked: "He was always working on that truck." If Arnold desired to make a return journey, he never managed to act on it. He dies in his sleep. It is only in this failed homestead on the outskirts of Phoenix that the complexity of Victor's quest becomes more apparent. He must not simply retrieve Arnold's ashes; he must also bring the truck home. He must complete Arnold's road quest and make it his own.

In the fourth stage of mobility, Victor takes control of the truck. For the first time in the film, he has some autonomous mobility, but the power that he assumes is an illusion. He and Thomas begin the drive home, but there is a major collision, a crisis that takes form not simply as symbol but as physical fact. In Thomas's voice-over narrative of the drive homeward, it becomes clear that Victor is disengaged from the road experience, and the movement reflects no expansion of his consciousness. Thomas confirms this indeterminant state by noting that "after Victor butchered his hair, he thought the ceremony was over" and that they were traveling with "illusions."[24] Victor's assumed control as driver is a mirage made possible by his assumption that his emotional journey has been completed by retrieving the ashes. He remains isolated and thus incomplete.

The car crash is presaged by the most substantive argument between the two protagonists, the first one wherein Thomas is aggressively confrontational. As Victor focuses on the failures of the father, Thomas insists that "your dad was more than that." They both become more animated and focus more directly on Victor's life choices. Thomas implies that for the last ten years Victor has been trapped in his continual refusal to acknowledge that Arnold was "more" than the abandonment. As the two men argue, the truck moves down a dark highway. The collision—physical and symbolic—occurs as they come upon a stalled Cadillac in the roadway. Victor swerves and the truck comes to rest in a ditch. Everything stops. The road is a dangerous place, but it can also be the setting for awakening. The crash makes possible Victor's escape from the stifling legacy of his father, not because of the brute force reality of the wreck but because of Victor's willful choice to move. In a scene of chaos, Victor acts and provides the only hope for a positive outcome from this collision. He sacrifices himself, offering some hope for those at the roadside: "I'll go for help." He runs to seek assistance but gains deliverance (fig. 8.14).

After Victor's torturous overnight run and the successful closing of the wreck crisis, the fifth stage of mobility begins, and Victor returns to the road with redemptive power, a man gripping the wheel for the first time with an eye on the horizon. Having made the selfless overnight run, he can now move without illusions and as his own man. The awakening is verified once he gets back into the truck and, unlike his father, begins the trip home. This moment is the only pure and free moment of joy on the road for Victor and Thomas as they rejoice when the engine engages (fig. 8.15). Victor and Thomas begin the true trip home.

Fig. 8.14. *Smoke Signals*, Victor's run. DVD, Miramax/Buena Vista Home Entertainment, 1999. Author's screenshot.

Fig. 8.15. *Smoke Signals*, starting truck. DVD, Miramax/Buena Vista Home Entertainment, 1999. Author's screenshot.

Smoke Signals begins with fire and ends with water. The conclusion shifts the focus to the future. In a road context, the change implies a looking-out roadview and thus suggests the horizon. Victor has healed the home by returning with Arnold's ashes. Victor's release of those ashes into the ever-flowing water further emphasizes the connection of his quest to the broader community, both in the surrounding landscape and through the generations. A son who has gained a future by embracing a challenging past completes his quest. Victor symbolically acknowledges the completion of his stable road journey from the liminal bridge, the river's power energizing him from below, the sun's glare sanctifying him from above. He is not free of pain, and in the last image audiences see of him, Victor is still experiencing the convulsions of the emotional release, but he is no longer a static figure. He owns a truck and is not stymied by his father's departure or his ancestral pain. Any road ahead will be Victor's. He is alive in America in the late twentieth century—without apology (fig. 8.16).

Fig. 8.16. *Smoke Signals*, bridge. DVD, Miramax/Buena Vista Home Entertainment, 1999. Author's screenshot.

* * *

Asserting power behind the wheel is perpetually alluring. Its promise of control amid the chaos of life speaks to everyone. Finding contentment while asserting such power, however, often proves elusive. Traditional cultural norms have granted men the privilege of driving the open road, and popular culture is rife with men holding steering wheels with seeming ease and bravado. However, as road narratives reveal, they do so with varying expectations, desires, and capacities. Their control is always tenuous and at times illusory. With every turn, at every crossroads, they fight for control of their horizons. They move often with a strong sense of obligation as they try to interpret and apply the deeply flawed notions of masculine performance. In response, men drive along the open road—succeeding and failing—all the while paradoxically dreaming of release.

Conclusion

The Road Ahead

I STILL HAVE the *Rand McNally Atlas of the United States* that I used to plan and record my first cross-country drive in 1985. I have my movements highlighted—the drive westward, then eastward, the full stop in Oklahoma City and the bus ride home, the return flight a month later to pick up the car and drive home again to South Carolina. Each segment is noted with stars for the major stops and different colors for car, bus, and air travel. Like any road trip, the overall journey was often enjoyable, but I found myself often jolted as if on a very long stretch of rough pavement, to say the least.

Two years after I completed that odyssey, my Mustang convertible presented another challenge that seems worth mentioning. As I drove at interstate speed on I-20 near Aiken, South Carolina, the rear driver's side wheel came off. I caught a glimpse of it bounding into the interstate median as I swerved to regain control and pull into the emergency lane. The closest vehicle to me was at least a quarter of a mile behind, so the incident did not cause an accident, and the driver of that car pulled over to offer help. Roads are like that more often than we would prefer to think. And life too. We often move at the edge of disaster, but we also move within reach of helping hands. I wonder, though, what coming generations will think about the open road. Will they dream about it?

There is no doubt that things are changing and that the centrality of car culture is going through a significant transition in the twenty-first century. Such fluctuations have the potential to remake the American notion of automobility. Few of us use paper maps these days. We no longer plan our routes at a kitchen table with the map spread out before us (never to be folded properly again), giving us an image of an unknown but knowable world. We depend on screens for framing and on global positioning systems (GPS) and

Google Maps on our smartphones to track every passing mile. Even if we spurn the idea of a carefully planned trip, we do so not to assert that we prefer spontaneity. Not at all. We have access to so much in-time data supporting our every move that such planning is unnecessary beyond a few clicks on our phones. We own the technological support to seemingly know so much about the road ahead that we need not worry about it. If we need gas or are hungry, our phones inform us of resources nearby. "Would you like directions?"

The technology shifts to the automotive landscape do not just show up on our mobile phones. The cars are changing as well in ways that alter the driving experience dramatically. I learned to drive using a manual transmission with a temperamental clutch (aren't they all?). The road was loud beneath my seat, and to cool off I rolled down the window with a crank. In the late 1970s, that basic driving experience was standard and very close to the same technological context that had created expectations for most drivers since World War II. My children, on the other hand, have had a very different set of assumptions for their driving. They have never driven a car without air conditioning, or air bags, or electric windows, or computer chips to provide steady diagnostic information. Yet even their experiences are remarkably close overall to mine as a young man and, for that matter, to those of drivers throughout the twentieth century. The incremental shifts in the driving experience have certainly provided substantially more safety and comfort, if not style, for anyone behind the wheel, but the basics of interior design have remained the same—a steering wheel, foot pedals, front seats and back seats. That is about to change.

We are told that self-driving cars are the wave of the near future. In 2022 the National Highway Traffic Safety Administration (NHTSA) updated its safety regulations for "autonomous" vehicles to allow for the removal of steering wheels and foot pedals. In other words, driverless cars will no longer be required to include any features heretofore necessary for direct manual control of the vehicle's movement. Prototype vehicles, so far, have kept such accoutrements, perhaps simply in obeisance to tradition or in acknowledgment of the psychological reassurance such things offer all of us (how do I stop this thing!?). The way has been cleared for vehicles of the future to have no steering wheels or pedals for acceleration or braking, details that General Motors calls "human-centered features."[1]

Can there be a vibrant open-road mythology when drivers can travel at highway speeds safely without accepting any responsibility for the active movement of the vehicle? What is lost when we no longer have a direct physical capacity to speed up, to slow down—to *drive*? Even as I type this, though, I feel reactionary and rather old. I remind myself of this inescapable fact: in such cars, humans will still be moving. And, most importantly, they will still have desires. All automotive imaginaries—car, road, landscape—will remain involved in the overall experience. Americans will still dream of horizons.

The road abides. The way Americans move in automobiles will remain often invigorating, often stressful, and, of course, always liminal. The road narratives that arise from the upheaval created by advancing technology will most certainly reflect the change. Nonetheless, Americans will still go and will still be curious about the road ahead. They will move with excitement, apprehension, and hope. What will the open road mean to subsequent generations of Americans? That is a complex question. We all have such concerns and even some answers mulling around our heads and hearts.

In the end and from the beginning, that is all that matters. We *imagine* the open road, and that keeps it as an important component of who we are. Because we believe in it, because we insist on celebrating it, because it makes us happy, the American open road exists. It adapts, it evolves, and it expands. And we are the better for it. Although the open road as an idea has always struggled against sometimes overwhelming historical contexts that rendered it a lie for so many Americans, its core promise remains valuable and essential to the American experiment. Its aspirational framing provides a sense of purpose and direction. The balancing act we have always shared between stable and subversive roads holds firm in our dreams as well. There is no road without a sense of home; there is no home without a sense of the road. That we continue to desire that juxtaposition is important. The open-road idyll still serves Americans, and whenever we experience the best of what it offers, we find contentment that feels like a smooth stretch of highway. We share that pleasure and the challenge as well—to work toward making all roads as open as possible.

What's your road? That question implies answers that reflect individual desire and cultural imagination. Yes, our responses to the question have always varied and have been complicated by the tumultuous world around us, but we have always enjoyed the question itself and its implied horizons, every one filled with the precious promise of life to come.

Notes

Chapter 1

1. "Song of the Open Road," listed as "Poem of the Road," first appeared in the second edition of *Leaves of Grass* (Brooklyn, NY: Fowler and Wells, 1856), 223–39. The Walt Whitman Archive, accessed May 20, 2024.

2. For more information on this commercial, see Patrick Coffee, "Grey New York, Volvo and Walt Whitman Take to the Open Road," Agency Spy, accessed May 20, 2024.

3. Ronald Primeau, *Romance of the Road: Literature of the American Highway* (Bowling Green, OH: Bowling Green State University Press, 1996), 1.

4. Ann Brigham, *American Road Narrative: Reimagining Mobility in Literature and Film* (Charlottesville: University of Virginia Press, 2015), 3.

5. John Brinckerhoff Jackson, *A Sense of Place, A Sense of Time* (New Haven, CT: Yale University Press, 1994), 205. The passage is from an essay titled "Roads Belong in the Landscape."

6. Jack Kerouac, *On the Road* (New York: Penguin, 2003), 212.

7. Phil Patton, *Open Road: A Celebration of the American Highway* (New York: Simon and Shuster, 1986), 12.

8. Jackson, *Sense of Place*, 173. The passage is from an essay titled "Truck City."

9. Brigham, *American Road Narratives*, 4.

10. Frederick Jackson Turner, "The Significance of the Frontier in American History," American Historical Association, Chicago, Illinois, 1893.

11. Exact data is impossible to determine, but the number of settlers who traveled along the Oregon Trail, the main but by no means only route west for settlers, ranges from three hundred thousand to five hundred thousand between 1840 and 1866. See BLM.gov for more information. Turner's thesis and manifest destiny as related concepts have encouraged copious political and academic debates. For a few essential sources, see Anders Stephanson, *American Expansionism and the Empire of Right* (New York: Hill and Wang, 1995) and Steven E. Woodworth, *Manifest Destinies: America's Westward Expansion and the Road to the Civil War* (New York: Alfred A. Knopf, 2010).

12. For more information on the evolution of car culture, see Warren James Belasco, *Americans on the Road: From Autocamp to Motel, 1910-1945* (Baltimore, MD: Johns Hopkins University Press, 1979); James J. Fink, *The Car Culture* (Cambridge, MA: MIT Press, 1975); Mark S. Foster, *A Nation on Wheels: The Automobile Culture in America since 1945* (Belmont, CA: Thomson Wadsworth, 2003); John A. Heitmann, *The Automobile and American Life* (Jefferson, NC: McFarland, 2009); David L. Lewis and Laurence Goldstein, eds., *The Automobile and American Culture* (Ann Arbor: University of Michigan Press, 1980); and John B. Rae, *The Road and the Car in American Life* (Cambridge, MA: MIT Press, 1971).

13. Jeremy Packer, *Mobility without Mayhem: Safety, Cars, and Citizenship* (Durham, NC: Duke University Press, 2008), 2.

14. Packer, *Mobility without Mayhem*, 5.

15. Patton, *Open Road*, 1.

16. Patton, *Open Road*, 21.

17. Patton, *Open Road*, 9.

18. Richard O. Davies, *The Age of Asphalt: The Automobile, the Freeway, and the Condition of Metropolitan America* (Philadelphia: Lippincott, 1975), xii. For a source celebrating mobility, see Merrill Denison, *The Power to Go* (New York: Doubleday, 1956).

19. John Urry, *Sociology beyond Societies: Mobilities for the Twenty-First Century* (New York: Routledge, 2000).

20. "A Few Straws in a Big Wind," *Consumer Reports* (February 1956), 83.

21. *General Motors Builds Its First 50 Million Cars* (Detroit: Department of Public Relations, General Motors, 1954), 22. GM Heritage Center, Permanent Reference Collection, GM Historical Brochures, accessed May 24, 2024.

22. GM, *50 Million*, 22.

23. GM, *50 Million*, 23.

24. GM, *50 Million*, 23.

25. Primeau, *Romance of the Road*, 1. The use of "sacred" in such contexts is well established. For an especially valuable example, see John Sears, *Sacred Places: American Tourist Attractions in the Nineteenth Century* (New York: Oxford University Press, 1989).

26. Tim Cresswell, *On the Move: Mobility in the Modern Western World* (New York: Routledge, 2006), 2.

27. Adapted from Cresswell, *On the Move*, 3–4.

28. Cresswell, *On the Move*, 3.

29. The scene was filmed at Dead Horse State Park in Utah. "*Thelma & Louise*: 30 Years Later," Utah Film Commission, May 22, 2021, accessed May 10, 2024.

30. Jackson, *Sense of Place*, 151.

31. Tim Cresswell, "Introduction: Theorizing Place," in Ginette Verstraete and

Tim Cresswell, eds., *Mobilizing Place, Placing Mobility: The Politics of Representation in a Globalized World* (New York: Rodopi Press, 2002), 20.

32. Cresswell, "Introduction: Theorizing Place," 25.

33. For additional discussion of "place," see Edward Relph, *Place and Placelessness* (London: Pion Limited, 1976, 1983) and Cresswell, "Introduction: Theorizing Place."

34. For more discussion of framing road experiences, see Cresswell, *On the Move*, 1–27. He characterizes the dual perception of mobility with "two principal metaphysical ways of viewing the world: a *sedentarist metaphysics* and a *nomadic metaphysics*," 26 (italics in the original). He takes the phrase "sedentarist metaphysics" from Liisa Malkki, "National Geographic: The Rooting of Peoples and the Territorialization of National Identity among Scholars and Refugees," *Cultural Anthropology* 7, no. 1 (1992): 24–44. I am adapting and expanding those distinctions and prefer *stable* and *subversive*, with the former closely tied to sedentarist metaphysics and the latter to nomadic metaphysics. To my mind, stable and subversive are more straightforward in capturing the competing but interdependent discourses of the American road. Although Cresswell's framing is essential, the implication that mainstream mobility is "sedentary," and thus immobile, does not adequately capture the dynamics of the road narrative.

35. Cresswell, *On the Move*, 25–27. In discussing the two modes, or "metaphysics," Cresswell notes the importance of rootedness and belonging for sedentarists (similar to stable) and flow/flux for nomadics (similar to subversive).

36. Relph, *Place and Placelessness*, 50.

37. For a valuable overview of car culture in the United States, see John A. Jakle and Keith A. Sculle, *Motoring: The Highway Experience in America* (Athens: University of Georgia Press, 2009).

38. Relph, *Place and Placelessness*, 40.

39. Kerouac, *On the Road*, 5–6.

40. *The Andy Griffith Show*, season 1, episode 12, "Stranger in Town," directed by Don Weiss, aired December 26, 1960, on CBS.

41. Robert Frost, "The Road Not Taken," 1916, Poetry Foundation, accessed January 15, 2019.

Chapter 2

1. Jack Kerouac, *On the Road* (1957, New York: Penguin, 2003), 251. All references are to this Penguin 2003 edition.

2. Phil Patton, *Open Road: A Celebration of the American Highway* (New York: Simon and Shuster, 1986), 19.

3. Patton, *Open Road*, 41.

4. For more detailed information, see Richard O. Davies, *The Age of Asphalt* (Philadelphia: J. B. Lippincott, 1975); Bruce E. Seely, *Building the American*

Highway System: Engineers and Policy Makers (Philadelphia: Temple University Press, 1987); and Earl Swift, *The Big Roads* (Boston: Houghton Mifflin Harcourt, 2011).

5. Richard Thruelsen, "The Case of the Obsolete Highways," *Saturday Evening Post* (February 5, 1955), 28.

6. Davies, *Age of Asphalt*, 4.

7. *Let's Get Out of the Muddle*, General Motors (Detroit: General Motors, 1951), GM Heritage Center Historical Documents, accessed May 24, 2024.

8. *Let's Get Out of the Muddle.*

9. Italics in the original.

10. *Give Yourself the Green Light*, General Motors (A JAM Handy Production, 1954).

11. *Give Yourself the Green Light.*

12. William Laas, ed., *Freedom of the American Road* (Detroit: Ford Motor Company, 1956), in Ford Motor Company Public Relations, "Freedom of the American Road" campaign, 1956, box 8, Small Accessions Collection, Benson Ford Research Center, Dearborn, Michigan.

13. Bernard DeVoto, "Introduction: The American Road," *Freedom of the American Road* (Detroit: Ford Motor Company, 1956), in Ford Motor Company Public Relations, "Freedom of the American Road" campaign, 1956, box 8, Small Accessions Collection, Benson Ford Research Center, Dearborn, Michigan, 7.

14. DeVoto, "Introduction: The American Road," 8.

15. Richard Thruelsen, "Coast to Coast without a Stoplight," *Saturday Evening Post*, October 20, 1956, 23.

16. Thruelsen, "Coast to Coast," 54.

17. Thruelsen, "Coast to Coast," 64.

18. Thruelsen, "Coast to Coast," 64.

19. Thruelsen, "Coast to Coast," 69.

20. Patton, *Open Road*, 41.

21. "20 Years in Review, 1936-1956," *Consumer Reports*, May 1956, 254.

22. "Some Notes on the Auto Industry in 1955," *Consumer Reports*, May 1955, 243.

23. "Too Many Cars?" *Time*, July 4, 1955, 50.

24. "A Few Straws in a Big Wind," *Consumer Reports*, February 1956, 83.

25. "The Two-Car Family," *Consumer Reports*, November 1955, 520–22.

26. Image #DN706-56CH-612, Chevrolet advertising collection, General Motors Research Center, Sterling Heights, Michigan.

27. Image #THF135687, 1955 T-Z folder and Image #THF135693, 1956 T folder, box 32, accession 19, The Benson Ford Research Center, Dearborn, Michigan.

28. "Drive More," *Life*, May 7, 1956, 1.

29. Ellipsis in original.

30. For a helpful overview of the history of the motorcycle, *The Art of the Motorcycle* ([New York]: Guggenheim Museum, [1998]).

31. Numerous studies examine automobile culture in the United States, and many address motorcycles as well. For two especially useful sources, see James J. Fink, *The Car Culture* (Cambridge, MA: MIT Press, 1975) and David L. Lewis and Laurence Goldstein, eds., *The Automobile and American Culture* (Ann Arbor: University of Michigan Press, 1980).

32. D. Mark Austin, Patricia Gagne, and Angela Orend, "Commodification and Popular Imagery of the Biker in American Culture," *Journal of Popular Culture* 43, no. 5 (October 2010): 944–45. For more information, see Tom Reynolds, *Wild Ride: How Outlaw Motorcycle Myth Conquered America* (New York: TV Books, 2000); Art Simon, "Freedom or Death: Notes on the Motorcycle Film and Video," *The Art of the Motorcycle* ([New York]: Guggenheim Museum, [1998]); and John Wood, "Hell's Angels and the Illusion of the Counterculture," *Journal of Popular Culture* 37, no. 2 (2003): 336–51.

33. Austin, Gagne, and Orend, "Commodification and Popular Imagery," 946.

34. For more information, see Craig Campbell, *America's Cold War: The Politics of Insecurity* (Cambridge, MA: Belknap, 2009); John Lewis Gaddis, *The Cold War: A New History* (New York: Penguin, 2005); and Walter LaFeber, *America, Russia, and the Cold War, 1945–1971* (New York: Wiley, 1972).

35. "Cyclist's Holiday," *Life*, July 21, 1947, 31.

36. Quoted in Austin, Gagne, and Orend, "Commodification and Popular Imagery," 947.

37. *The Wild One*, directed by László Benedek, produced by Stanley Kramer (Columbia Pictures, 1953).

38. Ronald Primeau, *Romance of the Road: The Literature of the American Highway* (Bowling Green, OH: Bowling Green State University Press, 1996), 3. See also Ann Brigham, *American Road Narratives* (Charlottesville: University of Virginia Press, 2015), 157–58.

39. Relph, *Place and Placelessness*, 123.

40. Relph, *Place and Placelessness*, 1.

41. For a seminal discussion of Hudson River iconography, see Barbara Novak, *Nature and Culture: American Landscape and Painting, 1825–1875* (New York: Oxford University Press, 1980).

42. John F. Sears, *Sacred Places* (New York: Oxford University Press, 1999), 3. For an especially interesting and well-crafted exploration of the American picturesque in travel writing, see Beth L. Lueck, *American Writers and the Picturesque Tour: The Search for National Identity, 1790–1860* (New York: Garland, 1997).

43. Sears, *Sacred Places*, 51.

44. Image #DN706-55-CH13A, Chevrolet advertising database, General Motors Research Center, Sterling Heights, Michigan.

45. "New '56 Ford: the fine car at half the fine car price," 1956 J-N folder, box 60, accession 19, Benson Ford Research Center, Dearborn, Michigan.

Chapter 3

1. I have benefitted greatly from many substantive sources. I am especially indebted to several works among that number that merit special recognition as a canon for the field: Phil Patton, *Open Road: A Celebration of the American Highway* (New York: Simon and Schuster, 1986); Ronald Primeau, *Romance of the Road: The Literature of the American Highway* (Bowling Green, OH: Bowling Green State University Popular Press, 1996); Kris Lackey, *RoadFrames: The American Highway Narrative* (Lincoln: University of Nebraska Press, 1997); Rowland A. Sherrill, *Road-Book America: Contemporary Culture and the New Picaresque* (Urbana and Chicago: University of Illinois Press, 2000); David Laderman, *Driving Visions: Exploring the Road Movie* (Austin: University of Texas Press, 2002); Katie Mills, *The Road Story and the Rebel: Moving through Film, Fiction, and Television* (Carbondale: Southern Illinois University Press, 2006); Susan Sessions Rugh, *Are We There Yet? The Golden Age of American Family Vacations* (Lawrence: University Press of Kansas, 2008); and Ann Brigham, *American Road Narratives: Reimagining Mobility in Literature and Film* (Charlottesville: University of Virginia Press, 2015). See also David Laderman, "What a Trip: The Road Film and American Culture," *Journal of Film and Video* 48, no. 1/2 (Spring/Summer 1996): 41–57; Joseph Interrante, "The Road to Autopia: The Automobile and the Spatial Transformation of American Culture," in *The Automobile and American Culture*, eds. David L. Lewis and Laurence Goldstein (Ann Arbor: University of Michigan Press, 1980, 1986), 89–104; and Aaron Christopher Mitchell, *Liminality and* Communitas *in the Beat Generation* (New York: Peter Lang, 2017).

2. For more discussion of the conventions of American travel writing, see Jeffrey Melton, *Mark Twain, Travel Books, and Tourism* (Tuscaloosa: University of Alabama Press, 2002), chapter 2.

3. *Forrest Gump*, directed by Robert Zemeckis, written by Eric Roth (Paramount, 1994); Winston Groom, *Forrest Gump* (New York: Doubleday, 1986); *The War of the Worlds*, directed by Steven Spielberg, written by Josh Friedman and David Koepp (Paramount/Amblin, 2005) and adapted from the H. G. Wells 1897 classic of the same title; and Cormac McCarthy, *The Road* (New York: Alfred A. Knopf, 2006) and the film version of the same name, directed by John Hillcoat, written by Joe Penhall (New York: Dimension Films, 2009).

4. Many narratives exist in multiple mediums, especially novels that are adapted to movies. For close readings, I use the more popular version and thus the more representative text. For example, *Forrest Gump* is a fine novel, but the film version carries much more cultural weight. In addition, works of journalism, though often substantive, are beyond the scope of this study; therefore, *On the Road with*

Charles Kuralt, for example, is not considered. I hasten to add that anyone can make a case for any text to be regarded as a road narrative, and I hope that my tier designations encourage such discussion. Whereas I have tried to include a broad range of narratives, many additional worthy texts, which I have either chosen not to include or have unwittingly missed, do not appear. I must leave it to others to expand this discussion. All the texts regarded within these pages have passed muster for *my* expectations, and I can only hope others agree. Also, American popular music has a rich road tradition that merits attention, but songs are also beyond the scope of this book.

5. Arnold van Gennep, *The Rites of Passage* (originally published as *Les Rites de Passage* in Paris in 1909), translated by Monika B. Vizedom and Gabrielle L. Caffee (Chicago: University of Chicago Press, 1960). For an excellent extended discussion of liminality in reference to Jack Kerouac, see Mitchell, *Liminality*, especially 49–95.

6. Van Gennep, *Rites of Passage*, 21. See also Victor Turner, *The Ritual Process* (Chicago, IL: Aldine Publishing, 1969).

7. Van Gennep, *Rites of Passage*, 18.

8. Jack Kerouac, *On the Road* (1957; repr., New York: Penguin, 2003), 15. All subsequent references are to Penguin's paperback edition.

9. William Least Heat-Moon, *Blue Highways* (Boston, MA: Little Brown, 1982, 1999), epigraph. All references are to the 1999 reprint.

10. I am using "roadview" as one word to emphasize the visual imperative of this discussion as well as the mobility essential to the visual framing of experience throughout.

11. *Vanishing Point*, directed by Richard Sarafian, written by Guillermo Cabrera Infante (1971; Twentieth Century Fox Home Entertainment, 2003), DVD. All references are to the DVD version.

12. *Thelma & Louise*, directed by Ridley Scott, written by Callie Khouri (1991; MGM, 2003), DVD.

13. *National Lampoon's Vacation*, directed by Harold Ramis, written by John Hughes (1983; Warner Brothers, 2003), DVD. All screenshots are from author's personal DVD. For a more sustained discussion of *Vacation*, see chapter 8.

14. Heat-Moon, *Blue Highways*, 270.

15. *Psycho*, directed by Alfred Hitchcock (1963; Universal, 2014), Blu-Ray. All references are to the Blu-Ray version.

16. Heat-Moon, *Blue Highways*, 270.

17. Heat-Moon, *Blue Highways*, 343.

18. Kerouac, *On the Road*, 156.

19. *Duel*, directed by Steven Spielberg, screenplay by Richard Matheson (1971; Universal Studios, 2003), DVD. All references are to the DVD version. This tier 1 film is discussed at greater length in chapter 8.

20. *The Twilight Zone*, season 1, episode 16, "The Hitch-Hiker," directed by Alvin Ganzer, written by Rod Serling, aired January 22, 1960, on CBS.

21. Heat-Moon, *Blue Highways*, 219.

22. *American Graffiti*, directed by George Lucas (1973; Universal Pictures Home Entertainment, 2005), DVD. All references are to the DVD version.

23. *Dazed and Confused*, directed and written by Richard Linklater (1993; Universal Pictures Home Entertainment, 2011), DVD. All references are to the DVD version.

Chapter 4

1. Joseph Campbell, *The Hero with a Thousand Faces* (New York: Pantheon, 1949, 2008). All references are to the 2008 text.

2. For more information on Campbell's work, see Robert A. Segal, *Joseph Campbell: An Introduction* (New York: Penguin, 1990).

3. Joseph Campbell, "The Call to Adventure," *Hero with a Thousand Faces*, 45–54.

4. For more on travel writing conventions, see Jeffrey Alan Melton, *Mark Twain, Travel Books, and Tourism* (Tuscaloosa: University of Alabama Press, 2002), chapter 2.

5. Jack Kerouac, *On the Road* (1957; repr., New York: Penguin, 2003), 10. All references are to this edition.

6. Kerouac, *On the Road*, 9.

7. John Steinbeck, *Travels with Charley* (1962; repr., New York: Bantam, 1963), 3. All references are to this edition.

8. Mark Twain, *Adventures of Huckleberry Finn* (1885; repr., New York: Oxford University Press, 1996), 19.

9. Steinbeck, *Travels with Charley*, 5.

10. Steinbeck, *Travels with Charley*, 23.

11. *Rain Man*, directed by Barry Levinson, written by Barry Morrow and Ronald Bass (United Artists, 1988); *Smoke Signals*, directed by Chris Eyre, written by Sherman Alexie (Miramax, 1998); *War of the Worlds*, directed by Steven Spielberg, written by Josh Friedman and David Koepp (Paramount/DreamWorks/Amblin, 2005).

12. Campbell, *Hero with a Thousand Faces*, 89.

13. William Least Heat-Moon, *Blue Highways* (Boston, MA: Little Brown, 1982, 1999). All references are to the 1999 edition.

14. Heat-Moon, *Blue Highways*, 38.

15. Heat-Moon, *Blue Highways*, 38.

16. Heat-Moon, *Blue Highways*, 180.

17. Heat-Moon, *Blue Highways*, 180–81.

18. Heat-Moon, *Blue Highways*, 185. *Blue Highways* receives a more focused discussion in chapter 5.

19. *Thelma & Louise*, directed by Ridley Scott, written by Callie Khouri (1991; MGM, 2003), DVD. All references are to the DVD version.

20. *The Graduate*, directed by Mike Nichols, written by Buck Henry and Calder Willingham (Los Angeles: Embassy Pictures, 1967).

21. Kris Lackey, *RoadFrames* (Lincoln: University of Nebraska Press, 1997), 16.

22. Lackey, *RoadFrames*, 4–5.

23. John Brinckerhoff Jackson, "Auto Territoriality," *Landscape* 17, no. 3 (Spring 1968): 1–2. Reprinted in *Landscape in Sight*, revised edition (New Haven, CT: Yale University Press, 2000), 353.

24. Kerouac, *On the Road*, 212.

25. Kerouac, *On the Road*, 212.

26. Kerouac, *On the Road*, 231.

27. Kerouac, *On the Road*, 127.

28. Kerouac, *On the Road*, 138–39.

29. *Ferris Bueller's Day Off*, directed by Kenny Ortega, Bennie Dobbins, and John Hughes; written by John Hughes (1986; Paramount, 1999), DVD. All references are to the DVD version.

30. Mona Simpson, *Anywhere but Here* (1986; repr., New York: Vintage Contemporaries, 1992), 102.

31. *Twin Peaks*, directed by David Lynch, written by Mark Frost and David Lynch (ABC, 1990–1991); *Twin Peaks: The Return*, directed by David Lynch, written by Mark Frost and David Lynch (Showtime, 2017).

Chapter 5

1. Lars Erik Larson, "Free Ways and Straight Roads: The Interstates of Sal Paradise and 1950s America," *What's Your Road, Man?: Critical Essays on Jack Kerouac's* On the Road (Carbondale: Southern Illinois University Press, 2009), 35–59.

2. Larson, "Free Ways and Straight Roads," 35.

3. Larson, "Free Ways and Straight Roads," 35–38.

4. Jack Kerouac, *On the Road* (1957; repr., New York: Penguin, 2003), 5–6. All references are to Penguin's paperback edition.

5. Clinton Twiss, *The Long, Long Trailer* (New York: Thomas Y. Crowell, 1951; facsimile ed., Franklin Classics, 2018). All references to the book are to the facsimile reprint. *The Long, Long Trailer*, directed by Vincente Minnelli, written by Albert Hackett and Frances Goodrich (1954; MGM, 2006), DVD. All references to film are to the DVD.

6. Scant information is available on the sales figures. Yet the trailer for the film refers to the book as a "best seller," and there were at least eight printings by 1954.

7. The trailer is available in the DVD version released by Warner Bros, Archive Collection, 2018.

8. Twiss, *The Long, Long Trailer*, 50.

9. Kerouac, *On the Road*, 8.

10. Kerouac, *On the Road*, 1.

11. Kerouac, *On the Road*, 21.

12. Kerouac, *On the Road*, 25.

13. Kerouac, *On the Road*, 78–79.

14. Kerouac, *On the Road*, 107.

15. Kerouac, *On the Road*, part 4, chapter 5. I am thinking particularly of the experiences described at a house of prostitution; the sequence is deplorable.

16. Kerouac, *On the Road*, 301.

17. Kerouac, *On the Road*, 306.

18. Kerouac, *On the Road*, 306–7.

19. Kerouac, *On the Road*, 307.

20. Kerouac, *On the Road*, 307.

21. John Steinbeck, *The Grapes of Wrath* (New York: Viking Press, 1939) and *The Grapes of Wrath*, directed by John Ford, written by Nunnally Johnson (Twentieth Century-Fox, 1940).

22. A contentious debate has arisen regarding the factual legitimacy of *Travels with Charley*. For more information, see Bill Steigerwald, *Dogging Steinbeck: Discovering America and Exposing the Truth about* Travels with Charley (Seattle, WA, and Pittsburgh, PA: Fifty Fifty Books, 2013). In defense of Steinbeck, see William Groneman III, "Travels Unraveled," *Steinbeck Review* 9, no. 2 (Fall 2012): 78–88.

23. For more discussion of travel writing conventions, see Jeffrey Melton, *Mark Twain, Travel Books, and Tourism* (Tuscaloosa: University of Alabama Press, 2002).

24. Rocinante is Don Quixote's horse in Miguel de Cervantes's *Don Quixote*, published in two parts, 1605 and 1615.

25. John Steinbeck, *Travels with Charley* (New York: Viking Press, 1962), 56. All references are to this text.

26. Steinbeck, *Travels with Charley*, 71.

27. Steinbeck, *Travels with Charley*, 71.

28. Steinbeck, *Travels with Charley*, 77.

29. Steinbeck, *Travels with Charley*, 207.

30. Steinbeck, *Travels with Charley*, 207.

31. Steinbeck, *Travels with Charley*, 208.

32. Steinbeck, *Travels with Charley*, 208.

33. Steinbeck, *Travels with Charley*, 274.

34. William Least Heat-Moon, *Blue Highways* (Boston, MA: Little, Brown, 1982); *Prairyerth* (Boston, MA: Houghton Mifflin, 1991); *River-Horse* (Boston, MA: Houghton Mifflin, 1999); and *Roads to Quoz* (Boston, MA: Houghton Mifflin, 2008).

35. Heat-Moon took his trip in 1978; Kerouac's trips were 1947–1949.

36. Heat-Moon, *Blue Highways* (1982; repr., Boston, MA: Little, Brown, 1999), 3. All references are to the 1999 reprint.

37. Heat-Moon, *Blue Highways*, 3.

38. Heat-Moon, *Blue Highways*, 9.

39. Heat-Moon, *Blue Highways*, 115.

40. Heat-Moon, *Blue Highways*, 116.

41. Heat-Moon, *Blue Highways*, 160.

42. Robert Frost, "Mending Wall," *North of Boston* (Boston, MA: David Nutt, 1914) and "Desert Places," *A Further Range* (New York: Henry Holt, 1936).

43. Heat-Moon, *Blue Highways*, 162.

44. Heat-Moon, *Blue Highways*, 163.

45. Heat-Moon, *Blue Highways*, 165.

46. Heat-Moon, *Blue Highways*, 411.

47. Heat-Moon, *Blue Highways*, 411.

48. Parts of this chapter appeared in significantly different form in my essay "'Immediate Consciousness' and the American Open Road: Robert Pirsig's *Zen and the Art of Motorcycle Maintenance*," *Studies in Travel Writing* 17, no. 4 (November 2013): 398–410.

49. See relative content on this background in chapter 2. For an extended discussion of this issue, see Tom Reynolds, *Wild Ride: How Outlaw Motorcycle Myth Conquered America* (USA: TV Books, 2001).

50. *Easy Rider*, directed by Dennis Hopper (1969; Columbia/Tri-Star Home Video, 1999), DVD. All references are to the DVD version.

51. For especially insightful essays not mentioned in subsequent notes, see Richard H. Rodino, "Irony and Earnestness in Robert Pirsig's *Zen and the Art of Motorcycle Maintenance*," *Critique* 22, no. 1 (July 1980): 21–31; and Geoffrey Galt Harpham, "Rhetoric and the Madness of Philosophy in Plato and Pirsig," *Contemporary Literature* 29, no. 1 (Spring 1988): 64–81.

52. Robert Pirsig, *Zen and the Art of Motorcycle Maintenance* (William Morrow, 1974; repr., Harper Perennial Modern Classics, 2005): xi (hereafter referred to as *ZAMM*). All references are to the 2005 edition. Pirsig quotes the *London Telegraph* and BBC radio for the phrase.

53. Beverly Gross, "'A Mind Divided Against Itself': Madness in *Zen and the Art of Motorcycle Maintenance*," *Journal of Narrative Technique* 14, no. 3 (Fall 1984): 201.

54. My use of the term *schizophrenia* refers only to generalized applications in popular culture and is in no way intended as a comment on the medical condition. Pirsig was diagnosed with paranoid schizophrenia, so the mental disorder is central to the narrative, but he also applies it symbolically in a literary context. I therefore depend on the term in a broad cultural context implied by Pirsig.

55. Pirsig, *ZAMM*, [vii].

56. Pirsig, *ZAMM*, 4.
57. Pirsig, *ZAMM*, 4.
58. Pirsig, *ZAMM*, 118.
59. Pirsig, *ZAMM*, 3.
60. Pirsig, *ZAMM*, 366.
61. Pirsig, *ZAMM*, 422.
62. Pirsig, *ZAMM*, 422.
63. Pirsig, *ZAMM*, 422.
64. Pirsig, *ZAMM*, 423.
65. Nancy Corson Carter, "1970 Images of the Machine and the Garden: Kosinski, Crews, and Pirsig," *Soundings* 61, no. 1 (Spring 1978): 119.
66. Carter, "1970 Images," 117.
67. It is crucial to note that these narratives arose from the eyes of privilege. Kerouac, Steinbeck, Pirsig, and Heat-Moon moved with a freedom that has been historically allowed to Euro-American males. The same applies to *The Long, Long Trailer* and *Easy Rider*. Desi Arnaz's racial background plays no role in the former film, and though the biker protagonists in the latter certainly face formidable challenges, their travels are not complicated by racial tensions. Only Heat-Moon has a more complex heritage, but his American Indian identity, though essential, is not evident to the vast majority of people he encounters. This statement does not undermine the legitimacy or value of these narratives in any way; this reality, however, certainly made their roads less complicated than the roads traveled by those without such racial status.

Chapter 6

1. Edward Relph, *Place and Placelessness* (London: Pion Limited, 1976, 1983), 45.
2. Kris Lackey, *RoadFrames* (Lincoln: University of Nebraska Press, 1997), 21.
3. Lackey, *RoadFrames*, 120.
4. Gretchen Sorin, *Driving While Black: African American Travel and the Road to Civil Rights* (New York: Liveright, 2020), xi. See also Candacy Taylor, *Overground Railroad: The Green Book and the Roots of Black Travel in America* (New York: Harry Abrams, 2020).
5. The publication has other titles, beginning with *Negro Motorist's Green Book*, and was often simply referred to as the *Green Book*, after its originator and publisher, Victor Green. In addition to Sorin, see also Evan Andrews, "The Green Book: The Black Travelers' Guide to Jim Crow America," History, February 6, 2017, revised March 13, 2018, accessed May 24, 2024.
6. Victor H. Green, *The Negro Travelers' Green Book* (New York: Victor H. Green & Co., 1957; facsimile edition, Camarillo, CA: About Comics, 2018), 2.
7. Martin Luther King Jr., *Why We Can't Wait* (New York: Mentor/Penguin, 1964): 76. All quotations are from this text. Written in segments as King composed it

using the limited paper available to him in jail, the letter was completed in April 1963. It was published in part in several newspapers. It was first fully published as "Letter from Birmingham Jail" in the June 1963 issue of *Liberation*; the June 12, 1963, edition of *The Christian Century*; and in the June 24, 1963, *The New Leader*.

8. King, "Letter from Birmingham Jail," 81.

9. John Howard Griffin, *Black Like Me* (1961; repr., New York: Signet, 2010). All references are to the 2010 edition.

10. Robert Bonazzi, "A Modern American Classic: The Fiftieth Anniversary of the *Black Like Me* Experiment," in *Black Like Me* by John Howard Griffin (New York: Signet, 2010), 195.

11. *Black Like Me*, directed by Carl Lerner (Continental, 1964).

12. Griffin, *Black Like Me*, 4.

13. Griffin, *Black Like Me*, 10.

14. Griffin, *Black Like Me*, 10.

15. Griffin, *Black Like Me*, 11.

16. Griffin, *Black Like Me*: see 52–61, 83–85.

17. Griffin, *Black Like Me*, 101.

18. Griffin, *Black Like Me*, 107.

19. Griffin, *Black Like Me*, 115.

20. Griffin, *Black Like Me*, 118-19.

21. Griffin, *Black Like Me*, beginning on 122.

22. Griffin, *Black Like Me*, 147.

23. John Steinbeck, *Travels with Charley* (1962; repr., New York: Bantam, 1963), 207. All references are to this edition.

24. Ann Brigham, *American Road Narratives: Reimagining Mobility in Literature and Film* (Charlottesville: University of Virginia Press, 2015), 95. Brigham provides an astute reading of *This Is My Country Too*; see 92–105.

25. John A. Williams, *This Is My Country Too* (1964; New York: Signet, 1966). All references are to the 1966 edition.

26. Williams, *This Is My Country Too*, 42.

27. Williams, *This Is My Country Too*, 43.

28. Williams, *This Is My Country Too*, 82.

29. Williams, *This Is My Country Too*, 86-87.

30. Williams, *This Is My Country Too*, 87.

31. Brigham, *American Road Narratives*, 101–2.

32. Williams, *This Is My Country Too*, 96.

33. Brigham, *American Road Narratives*, 99.

34. Williams, *This Is My Country Too*, 60.

35. Brigham, *American Road Narratives*, 102.

36. Williams, *This Is My Country Too*, 152.

37. Williams, *This Is My Country Too*, 153.

38. Eddy L. Harris, *Mississippi Solo* (New York: Nick Lyons Books, 1988) and *Native Stranger* (New York: Simon and Schuster, 1992).

39. Eddy L. Harris, *South of Haunted Dreams: A Ride through Slavery's Old Back Yard* (New York: Simon & Shuster, 1993), 13. All references are to this edition.

40. Harris, *South of Haunted Dreams*, 22.

41. Harris, *South of Haunted Dreams*, 23.

42. Harris, *South of Haunted Dreams*, 26.

43. Harris, *South of Haunted Dreams*, 31.

44. Harris, *South of Haunted Dreams*, 36.

45. Harris, *South of Haunted Dreams*, 43.

46. Harris, *South of Haunted Dreams*, 49.

47. Harris, *South of Haunted Dreams*, 51.

48. Harris, *South of Haunted Dreams*, 100.

49. Harris, *South of Haunted Dreams*, 102.

50. Harris, *South of Haunted Dreams*, 103–4.

51. Harris, *South of Haunted Dreams*, 230.

52. Harris, *South of Haunted Dreams*, 253.

53. Harris, *South of Haunted Dreams*, 253.

54. *The Twilight Zone*, written by Rod Serling (CBS, 1959–1964).

55. The reincarnations appeared in 1985–89, 2002–03, and 2019–20. The film version came out in 1983.

56. *The Twilight Zone*, season 1, episode 3, "Replay," written by Selwyn Seyfu Hinds, directed by Gerard McMurray, aired April 11, 2019, on CBS Always. *The Twilight Zone* (CBS Television/Paramount, 2020), Blu-Ray. All quotations are drawn from the Blu-Ray version.

Chapter 7

1. For especially useful discussions of women on the road, see Ann Brigham, *American Road Narratives: Reimagining Mobility in Literature and Film*. (Charlottesville: University of Virginia Press, 2015); Deborah Clarke, *Driving Women: Fiction and Automobile Culture in 20th Century America* (Baltimore: Johns Hopkins University Press, 2007); Alexandra Ganser, *Roads of Her Own: Gendered Space and Mobility in American Women's Road Narratives* (Amsterdam: Rodopi, 2009); and Sidonie Smith, *Moving Lives: Twentieth Century Women's Travel Writing* (Minneapolis: University of Minnesota Press, 2001).

2. For more information, see Lizabeth Cohen, *A Consumer's Republic: The Politics of Mass Consumption in Postwar America* (New York: Vintage Books, 2004).

3. "Ford's Out Front From a Woman's Angle," J. Walter Thompson, 1947, accession 19, box 28, The Benson Ford Research Center, Dearborn, Michigan.

4. Joan Didion, *Play It as It Lays* (New York: Farrar, Straus and Giroux, 1970, 2005). All references are to the 2005 reprint.

5. Didion, *Play It as It Lays*, 15.

6. Didion, *Play It as It Lays*, 15–16.

7. Mark Twain, *Life on the Mississippi* (Boston, MA: James. R. Osgood, 1883). See especially the segment often referred to as "Two Ways of Seeing a River," chapter 9.

8. Didion, *Play It as It Lays*, 17.

9. Didion, *Play It as It Lays*, 18.

10. Didion, *Play It as It Lays*, 195–96.

11. Didion, *Play It as It Lays*, 197.

12. Didion, *Play It as It Lays*, 198.

13. Didion, *Play It as It Lays*, 199.

14. *In Country*, directed by Norm Jewison (Warner Brothers, 1989).

15. Bobbie Ann Mason, *In Country* (1985; repr., New York: Harper Perennial, 2005), 3. All references are to the 2005 edition.

16. Mason, *In Country*, 6.

17. Mason, *In Country*, 58.

18. Mason, *In Country*, 75.

19. Mason, *In Country*, 75.

20. Mason, *In Country*, 162.

21. Mason, *In Country*, 176.

22. Mason, *In Country*, 178.

23. Mason, *In Country*, 231.

24. Mona Simpson, *Anywhere but Here* (1986; repr., New York: Vintage Contemporaries, 1992). All references are to the 1992 edition.

25. Ralph Waldo Emerson, "Considerations by the Way," *The Works of Ralph Waldo Emerson Vol. 6* (Boston: n.p., 1909), 252. The epigraph for the novel is a quote from Ralph Waldo Emerson that includes this statement: "There are three wants which never can be satisfied: that of the rich, who wants more, that of the sick, who wants something different, and that of the traveler, who says, 'Anywhere but here.'"

26. Simpson, *Anywhere but Here*, 3.

27. Simpson, *Anywhere but Here*, 3.

28. Simpson, *Anywhere but Here*, 61.

29. Simpson, *Anywhere but Here*, 61.

30. Simpson, *Anywhere but Here*, 65.

31. Simpson, *Anywhere but Here*, 245–46.

32. Barbara Kingsolver, *The Bean Trees* (New York: Harper Perennial, 1988, 2009). All references are to the 2009 edition.

33. Kingsolver, *The Bean Trees*, 11.

34. Kingsolver, *The Bean Trees*, 11.

35. Kingsolver, *The Bean Trees*, 12.

36. Kingsolver, *The Bean Trees,* 12.
37. Kingsolver, *The Bean Trees,* 13.
38. Kingsolver, *The Bean Trees,* 36.
39. Kingsolver, *The Bean Trees,* 205.
40. Kingsolver, *The Bean Trees,* 213.
41. Kingsolver, *The Bean Trees,* 214.
42. Kingsolver, *The Bean Trees,* 220.
43. Kingsolver, *The Bean Trees,* 245.
44. *Thelma & Louise,* Box Office Mojo by IMDbPro, accessed January 12, 2021.
45. *Thelma & Louise,* directed by Ridley Scott, written by Callie Khouri (1991; MGM Home Entertainment, 2004), DVD. All references are to the DVD version. For an especially useful anthology of essays in addition to the sources on women on the road listed earlier, see Bernie Cook, ed., *Thelma & Louise Live! The Cultural Afterlife of an American Film* (Austin: University of Texas Press, 2001).
46. Brigham, *American Road Narratives,* 139–40.

Chapter 8

1. Ann Brigham, *American Road Narratives: Reimagining Mobility in Literature and Film* (Charlottesville: University of Virginia Press, 2015), 58.
2. Gerald Weales, ed., *Arthur Miller:* Death of a Salesman, *Text and Criticism* (New York: Penguin, 1981), 80. All references are to this text.
3. John Lahr, "Arthur Miller and the Making of Willy Loman," *New Yorker* online (January 17, 1999), accessed October 17, 2018.
4. Lahr, "Making of Willy Loman," 2.
5. Lahr, "Making of Willy Loman," 16.
6. *Vanishing Point,* directed by Richard Sarafian, written by Guillermo Cabrera Infante (1971; Twentieth Century Fox Home Entertainment, 2003), DVD. The screenplay was written by Guillermo Cabrera Infante but credited as Guillermo Cain.
7. *Vanishing Point,* directed by Richard Sarafian. All references are to the DVD version.
8. Richard Sarafian, "Director Comments," *Vanishing Point* (Twentieth Century Fox Home Entertainment, 2003). DVD.
9. *Duel,* directed by Steven Spielberg, screenplay by Richard Matheson (1971; Universal Studios, 2003), DVD. All references refer to the full version presented in the DVD. *Duel* first appeared on television as an ABC Movie of the Week on November 13, 1971. It was expanded and released for theaters in Europe and Australia, with some theaters showing it in the United States.
10. Richard Matheson, "On the Writing of *Duel,*" *Duel,* DVD (Universal Studios Home Entertainment, 2005), DVD.
11. *National Lampoon's Vacation,* IMDb, accessed January 22, 2021.
12. *National Lampoon's Vacation,* directed by Harold Ramis, written by John

Hughes (1983; Warner Brothers, 2003), DVD. All quotations refer to the DVD version.

13. *Smoke Signals*, directed by Chris Eyre, written by Sherman Alexie (Miramax, 1998), DVD. All quotations refer to the DVD version.

14. For useful related discussions, see Brigham, *American Road Narratives*, 151–86; James Cox, "Muting White Noise: The Subversion of Popular Culture narratives of Conquest in Sherman Alexie's Fiction," *Studies in American Indian Literatures* 9, no. 4 (Summer 1997): 52–70; Jhon Warren Gilroy, "Another Fine Example of the Oral Tradition? Identification and Subversion in Sherman Alexie's *Smoke Signals*," *Studies in American Indian Literatures* 13, no. 1 (Spring 2001): 23–42; and Gordon Slethaug, "Hurricanes and Fires: Chaotics in Sherman Alexie's *Smoke Signals* and *The Lone Ranger and Tonto Fistfight in Heaven*," *Literature/Film Quarterly* 31, no. 2 (Spring 2003): 130–40.

15. Sherman Alexie, *The Lone Ranger and Tonto Fistfight in Heaven* (New York: Atlantic Monthly Press, 1993).

16. Dennis West and Joan M. West, "Sending Cinematic Smoke Signals: An Interview with Sherman Alexie," *Cineaste* 23, no. 4 (Fall 1998): 29.

17. West and West, "Cinematic Smoke Signals," 29.

18. Sherman Alexie, *Smoke Signals: A Screenplay* (New York: Hyperion, 1998), 38–39. I cite the screenplay when the text of the film matches it. If a scene is significantly different from the screenplay text, I cite the film.

19. Alexie, *Smoke Signals: A Screenplay*, 40–41.

20. Alexie, *Smoke Signals: A Screenplay*, 42.

21. For an especially useful discussion of this scene, see Leo Zonn and Dick Winchell, "*Smoke Signals*: Locating Sherman Alexie's Narratives of American Indian Identity," in *Engaging Film: Geographies of Mobility and Identity*, eds. Tim Cresswell and Deborah Dixon (Lanham, MD: Rowman & Littlefield, 2002): 140–58.

22. Alexie, *Smoke Signals: A Screenplay*, 61–62.

23. Alexie, *Smoke Signals: A Screenplay*, 57.

24. Alexie, *Smoke Signals: A Screenplay*, 165. The film does not follow the screenplay, which depicts a "goodbye" scene as Victor and Thomas leave Phoenix. In the film, the two leave without saying goodbye to Suzy. As Alexie reports in the "Scene Notes" (151–68) appended to the published screenplay, he wrote Thomas's voice-over, which includes the quoted phrases.

Conclusion

1. The phrase comes from GM's petition to the NHTSA asking permission to remove steering wheels, etc. from its Cruise Origin vehicle as the company prepares it for commercial service. See Joseph Guzman, "Regulator No Longer Requiring Autonomous Cars to Have Steering Wheel, Pedals," The Hill, March 11, 2022, accessed March 25, 2022.

Selected Bibliography

Alexie, Sherman. *The Lone Ranger and Tonto Fistfight in Heaven*. New York: Atlantic Monthly Press, 1993.

———. *Smoke Signals: A Screenplay*. New York: Hyperion, 1998.

Andrews, Evan. "The Green Book: The Black Travelers' Guide to Jim Crow America." History. Accessed May 24, 2024.

Austin, D. Mark, Patricia Gagne, and Angela Orend. "Commodification and Popular Imagery of the Biker in American Culture." *Journal of Popular Culture* 43, no. 5 (October 2010): 942–62.

Belasco, Warren James. *Americans on the Road: From Autocamp to Motel, 1910–1945*. Baltimore: Johns Hopkins University Press, 1979.

Benedek, László, dir. *The Wild One*. Columbia Pictures, 1953.

Bonazzi, Robert. "A Modern American Classic: The Fiftieth Anniversary of the *Black Like Me* Experiment." In *Black Like Me* by John Howard Griffin, 195–200. New York: Signet, 2010.

Brigham, Ann. *American Road Narratives: Reimagining Mobility in Literature and Film*. Charlottesville: University of Virginia Press, 2015.

Campbell, Joseph. *The Hero with a Thousand Faces*. 1949. Reprint, New York: Pantheon, 2008.

Carter, Nancy Corson. "1970 Images of the Machine and the Garden: Kosinski, Crews, and Pirsig." *Soundings* 61, no. 1 (Spring 1978): 105–22.

Clarke, Deborah. *Driving Women: Fiction and Automobile Culture in 20th Century America*. Baltimore: Johns Hopkins University Press, 2007.

Coffee, Patrick. "Grey New York, Volvo and Walt Whitman Take to the Open Road." Agency Spy. Accessed May 21, 2024.

Cohen, Lizabeth. *A Consumer's Republic: The Politics of Mass Consumption in Postwar America*. New York: Vintage Books, 2004.

Cook, Bernie, ed. *Thelma & Louise Live! The Cultural Afterlife of an American Film*. Austin: University of Texas Press, 2001.

Cox, James. "Muting White Noise: The Subversion of Popular Culture Narratives of Conquest in Sherman Alexie's Fiction." *Studies in American Indian Literatures* 9, no. 4 (Summer 1997): 52–70.

Cresswell, Tim. "Introduction: Theorizing Place." In *Mobilizing Place, Placing Mobility: The Politics of Representation in a Globalized World*, edited by Ginette Verstraete and Tim Cresswell, 11–31. New York: Rodopi Press, 2002.

———. *On the Move*. New York: Routledge, 2006.

Davies, Richard O. *The Age of Asphalt: The Automobile, the Freeway, and the Condition of Metropolitan America*. Philadelphia: Lippincott, 1975.

Denison, Merrill. *The Power to Go*. New York: Doubleday, 1956.

Didion, Joan. *Play It as It Lays*. 1970. Reprint, New York: Farrar, Straus and Giroux, 2005.

Eyre, Chris, dir. *Smoke Signals*. Written by Sherman Alexie. Miramax, 1998.

Fink, James J. *The Car Culture*. Cambridge, MA: MIT Press, 1975.

Foster, Mark S. *A Nation on Wheels: The Automobile Culture in American since 1945*. Belmont, CA: Thomson Wadsworth, 2003.

Frost, Robert. "The Road Not Taken." *Mountain Interval*. New York: Henry Holt, 1916.

Ganser, Alexandra. *Roads of Her Own: Gendered Space and Mobility in American Women's Road Narratives*. Amsterdam: Rodopi, 2009.

Ganser, Alvin, dir. *The Twilight Zone*. Season 1, episode 16, "The Hitch-Hiker." Written by Rod Serling. Aired January 22, 1960, on CBS.

Gilroy, Jhon Warren. "Another Fine Example of the Oral Tradition? Identification and Subversion in Sherman Alexie's *Smoke Signals*." *Studies in American Indian Literatures* 13, no. 1 (Spring 2001): 23–42.

Green, Victor H. *The Negro Travelers' Green Book*. New York: Victor H. Green & Co., 1957.

Griffin, John Howard. *Black Like Me*. Houghton Mifflin, 1961. Reprint, Signet, 2010.

Groneman, William III. "Travels Unraveled," *The Steinbeck Review* 9, no. 2 (Fall 2012): 78–88.

Gross, Beverly. "'A Mind Divided against Itself': Madness in *Zen and the Art of Motorcycle Maintenance*." *Journal of Narrative Technique* 14, no. 3 (Fall 1984): 201–13.

Harpham, Geoffrey Galt. "Rhetoric and the Madness of Philosophy in Plato and Pirsig." *Contemporary Literature* 29, no. 1 (Spring 1988): 64–81.

Harris, Eddy L. *South of Haunted Dreams: A Ride through Slavery's Old Back Yard*. New York: Simon & Shuster, 1993.

Heat-Moon, William Least. *Blue Highways*. Boston: Little Brown, 1983.

Heitmann, John A. *The Automobile and American Life*. Jefferson, NC: McFarland, 2009.

Hitchcock, Alfred, dir. *Psycho*. Universal, 1960.

Hopper, Dennis, dir. *Easy Rider*. Columbia Pictures, 1969.

Interrante, Joseph. "The Road to Autopia: The Automobile and the Spatial Transformation of American Culture." In *The Automobile and American Culture*, edited by David L. Lewis and Laurence Goldstein, 89–104. Ann Arbor: University of Michigan Press, 1980.

Jackson, John Brinckerhoff. *A Sense of Place, A Sense of Time*. New Haven: Yale University Press, 1994.

Jakle, John A., and Keith A. Sculle. *Motoring: The Highway Experience in America*. Athens: University of Georgia Press, 2009.

Kerouac, Jack. *On the Road*. Viking Press, 1957. Reprint, Penguin, 2003.

King, Martin Luther Jr. *Why We Can't Wait*. New York: Mentor/Penguin, 1964.

Kingsolver, Barbara. *The Bean Trees*. New York: Harper Perennial, 1988.

Laas, William, ed. *Freedom of the American Road*. Detroit: Ford Motor Company, 1956.

Lackey, Kris. *RoadFrames: The American Highway Narrative*. Lincoln: University of Nebraska Press, 1997.

Laderman, David. "What a Trip: The Road Film and American Culture." *Journal of Film and Video* 48, no. 1/2 (Spring/Summer 1996): 41–57.

———. *Driving Visions: Exploring the Road Movie*. Austin: University of Texas Press, 2002.

Lars, Erik Larson, "Free Ways and Straight Roads: The Interstates of Sal Paradise and 1950s America." In *What's Your Road, Man?: Critical Essays on Jack Kerouac's* On the Road, edited by Hillary Holladay and Robert Holton, 35–59. Carbondale: Southern Illinois University Press, 2009.

Let's Get Out of the Muddle, General Motors Department of Public Relations. Detroit: General Motors, 1951.

Lewis, David L., and Laurence Goldstein, editors, *The Automobile and American Culture*. Ann Arbor: University of Michigan Press, 1980.

Linklater, Richard, dir. and writer. *Dazed and Confused*. Universal, 1993.

Lucas, George, dir. *American Graffiti*. Universal, 1973.

Lueck, Beth L. *American Writers and the Picturesque Tour: The Search for National Identity, 1790–1860*. New York: Garland, 1997.

Mason, Bobbie Ann. *In Country*. Harper and Row, 1985. Reprint, Harper Perennial, 2005.

McCarthy, Cormac. *The Road*. New York: Alfred A. Knopf, 2006.

McMurray, Gerard, dir. *The Twilight Zone*. Season 1, episode 3, "Replay." Written by Selwyn Seyfu Hinds. Aired April 11, 2019, on CBS Always.

Melton, Jeffrey. *Mark Twain, Travel Books, and Tourism*. Tuscaloosa: University of Alabama Press, 2002.

———. "'Immediate Consciousness' and the American Open Road: Robert

Pirsig's *Zen and the Art of Motorcycle Maintenance*." *Studies in Travel Writing* 17, no. 4 (November 2013): 398–410.

Miller, Arthur. *Death of a Salesman*. New York: Viking Press, 1949.

Mills, Katie. *The Road Story and the Rebel: Moving through Film, Fiction, and Television*. Carbondale: Southern Illinois University Press, 2006.

Minnelli, Vincente, dir. *The Long, Long Trailer*. MGM, 1954.

Mitchell, Aaron Christopher. *Liminality and* Communitas *in the Beat Generation*. New York: Peter Lang, 2017.

Nichols, Mike, dir. *The Graduate*. Written by Buck Henry and Calder Willingham. Embassy Pictures, 1967.

Ortega, Kenny, Bennie Dobbins, and John Hughes, dir. *Ferris Bueller's Day Off*. Written by John Hughes. Paramount, 1986.

Packer, Jeremy. *Mobility without Mayhem: Safety, Cars, and Citizenship*. Durham: Duke University Press, 2008.

Patton, Phil. *Open Road: A Celebration of the American Highway*. New York: Simon and Schuster, 1986.

Pirsig, Robert. *Zen and the Art of Motorcycle Maintenance*. William Morrow, 1974. Reprint, Harper Perennial Modern Classics, 2005.

Primeau, Ronald. *Romance of the Road: The Literature of the American Highway*. Bowling Green: Bowling Green State University Popular Press, 1996.

Rae, John B. *The Road and the Car in American Life*. Cambridge, MA: MIT Press, 1971.

Ramis, Harold, dir. *National Lampoon's Vacation*. Written by John Hughes. Burbank, CA: Warner Brothers, 1983.

Relph, Edward. *Place and Placelessness*. London: Pion Limited, 1976.

Reynolds, Tom. *Wild Ride: How Outlaw Motorcycle Myth Conquered America*. New York: TV Books, 2000.

Rodino, Richard H. "Irony and Earnestness in Robert Pirsig's *Zen and the Art of Motorcycle Maintenance*." *Critique* 22, no. 1 (July 1980): 21–31.

Rugh, Susan Sessions. *Are We There Yet? The Golden Age of American Family Vacations*. Lawrence: University Press of Kansas, 2008.

Sarafian, Richard, dir. *Vanishing Point*. Written by Guillermo Cabrera Infante. Twentieth Century Fox, 1971.

Scott, Ridley, dir. *Thelma & Louise*. Written by Callie Khouri. MGM, 1991.

Sears, John F. *Sacred Places*. New York: Oxford University Press, 1999.

Seely, Bruce E. *Building the American Highway System: Engineers and Policy Makers*. Philadelphia, PA: Temple University Press, 1987.

Sherrill, Rowland A. *Road-Book America: Contemporary Culture and the New Picaresque*. Urbana: University of Illinois Press, 2000.

Simon, Art. "Freedom or Death: Notes on the Motorcycle Film and Video,"

The Art of the Motorcycle. [New York]: Guggenheim Museum, [1998].
Simpson, Mona. *Anywhere but Here*. Alfred A. Knopf, 1986. Reprint, Vintage Books, 1992.
Slethaug, Gordon. "Hurricanes and Fires: Chaotics in Sherman Alexie's *Smoke Signals* and *The Lone Ranger and Tonto Fistfight in Heaven*." *Literature/Film Quarterly* 31, no. 2 (Spring 2003): 130–40.
Smith, Sidonie. *Moving Lives: Twentieth Century Women's Travel Writing*. Minneapolis: University of Minnesota Press, 2001.
Sorin, Gretchen. *Driving While Black: African American Travel and the Road to Civil Rights*. New York: Liveright, 2020.
Spielberg, Steven, dir. *Duel*. Written by Richard Matheson. Universal, 1971.
———. *War of the Worlds*. Written by Josh Friedman and David Koepp. Paramount/Amblin, 2005.
Steigerwald, Bill. *Dogging Steinbeck: Discovering America and Exposing the Truth about* Travels with Charley. Seattle, WA: Fifty Fifty Books, 2013.
Steinbeck, John. *Travels with Charley*. New York: Viking Press, 1962.
Stephanson, Anders. *American Expansionism and the Empire of Right*. New York: Hill and Wang, 1995.
Swift, Earl. *The Big Roads*. Boston: Houghton Mifflin Harcourt, 2011.
Taylor, Candacy. *Overground Railroad: The Green Book and the Roots of Black Travel in America*. New York: Harry Abrams, 2020.
Thompson, George F., ed. *Landscape in America*. Austin: University of Texas Press, 1995.
Thruelsen, Richard. "The Case of the Obsolete Highways," *Saturday Evening Post*, February 5, 1955.
———. "Coast to Coast without a Stoplight." *Saturday Evening Post*, October 20, 1956.
Twiss, Clinton. *The Long, Long Trailer*. Thomas Y. Crowell, 1951. Facsimile reprint by Franklin Classics, 2018.
Urry, John. *Sociology beyond Societies: Mobilities for the Twenty-First Century*. New York: Routledge, 2000.
Van Gennep, Arnold. *The Rites of Passage*. Translated by Monika B. Vizedom and Gabrielle L. Caffee. Chicago: University of Chicago Press, 1960.
Weales, Gerald, ed. *Arthur Miller:* Death of a Salesman, *Text and Criticism*. New York: Penguin, 1981.
Whitman, Walt. *Leaves of Grass*. The Walt Whitman Archive. Accessed May 21, 2024.
Williams, John A. *This Is My Country Too*. Signet, 1965. Reprint, 1966 paperback edition.
Wood, John. "Hell's Angels and the Illusion of the Counterculture." *Journal of Popular Culture* 37, no. 2 (2003): 336–51.

Zemeckis, Robert, dir. *Forrest Gump*. Written by Eric Roth. Paramount, 1994.
Zonn, Leo and Dick Winchell. "*Smoke Signals*: Locating Sherman Alexie's Narratives of American Indian Identity." In *Engaging Film: Geographies of Mobility and Identity*, edited by Tim Cresswell and Deborah Dixon, 140–58. Lanham, MD: Rowman & Littlefield, 2002.

Index